PHILOSOPHY BITES AGAIN

PHILOSOPHY BITES AGAIN

DAVID EDMONDS &
NIGEL WARBURTON

OXFORD
UNIVERSITY PRESS

OXFORD
UNIVERSITY PRESS

Great Clarendon Street, Oxford, OX2 6DP,
United Kingdom

Oxford University Press is a department of the University of Oxford.
It furthers the University's objective of excellence in research, scholarship,
and education by publishing worldwide. Oxford is a registered trade mark of
Oxford University Press in the UK and in certain other countries

Published in the United States of America by Oxford University Press
198 Madison Avenue, New York, NY 10016, United States of America

British Library Cataloguing in Publication Data

Data available

Library of Congress Control Number: 2014936064

ISBN 978–0–19–870269–6

Printed in Great Britain by
Clays Ltd, St Ives plc

PREFACE

*P*hilosophy Bites Again is the third volume of interviews based on our popular audio podcast 'Philosophy Bites'. We are still amazed and delighted by the number of enthusiastic listeners this series has worldwide.

As with the earlier books, *Philosophy Bites* and *Philosophy Bites Back*, these are not verbatim transcripts of audio: in collaboration with the interviewees, we've adapted the interviews so that they work on the page. For some interviews, this has resulted in only minor tweaks; for others, the interviewees have suggested significant changes.

Philosophy Bites Back focused on the ideas of great dead philosophers, from Socrates to Derrida. This book returns to the format of the first, with topic-based interviews grouped under various themes.

We've opened with a compilation of responses to the question, 'Who is the most impressive philosopher you've met?' We sprang this question on our unsuspecting interviewees while making the series: these answers too have been edited for the book.

We launched Philosophy Bites in 2007, and since then we've made five spin-off series:

- *Ethics Bites* <http://www.open.edu/openlearn/whats-on/ethics-bites>;
- *Bioethics Bites* <http://www.neuroethics.ox.ac.uk/bio-ethics_bites>;

- *Multiculturalism Bites* <http://www.open.edu/openlearn/history-the-arts/multiculturalism-bites>;
- *Free Speech Bites* <http://www.freespeechbites.com>; and
- *Social Science Bites* <http://www.socialsciencebites.com>.

We would like to thank the Open University for permission to use the Nancy Fraser and Sue Mendus interviews, which first appeared in the *Multiculturalism Bites* series. The Jeff McMahan interview is from *Bioethics Bites*, for which we received a grant from the Wellcome Trust.

But *Philosophy Bites* is parent to them all. At the time of going to press, we have conducted around 260 interviews and have had 21 million downloads. That success is largely down to the high quality of our contributors. For us, at least, the series continues to be both hugely enjoyable and educational. It's been a privilege to meet so many of the world's leading philosophers, and to receive what amounts to private individual tuition on such a broad range of topics. Most of the people we have interviewed have been inspirational not just in the content of what they say, but in their contagious enthusiasm for thinking and ideas.

We have conducted many of our interviews at The Institute of Philosophy, part of London University—thanks to Shahrar Ali and Barry Smith for arranging that. For a few of our interviews we have used office space at Oxford's Uehiro Centre for Practical Ethics, and would like to thank Rachel Gaminiratne, Nailya Nikitenko, Deborah Sheehan, and Miriam Wood, and the Director, Julian Savulescu. We would also like to thank Charles Styles, Hannah Warburton, Mollie Williamson, and Katrina Woolley for transcribing the interviews, and Hannah Edmonds for performing her traditional proofreading role. At the time of writing, *Philosophy Bites* the podcast series is self-funded; we are extremely grateful for donations that have come in via our website at <http://www.philosophybites.com>, which have allowed us to keep on releasing episodes on a fortnightly basis.

Thanks to our partners Anna Motz and Liz Edmonds for putting up with our obsession with *Philosophy Bites*. The last time we dedicated a book in this series it was to three children. Another one has appeared on the scene. So this book is for Hannah, Joshua, Saul, and Isaac.

David Edmonds and Nigel Warburton
<http://www.philosophybites.com>
<http://www.twitter.com/philosophybites>

CONTENTS

THE MOST IMPRESSIVE PHILOSOPHER I'VE MET . . .

Tim Bayne: The philosopher who's had the greatest impact on my development is my PhD supervisor *David Chalmers*. He has a wonderful ability to come into a debate and see the conceptual structure of it, and present it extremely clearly. One has the sense immediately on reading his work of what's going on. Very impressive.

John Campbell: *Michael Dummett*: the sense of depth and seriousness and intellectual power that he brought to the subject was unparalleled.

Noël Carroll: the late *Arthur Danto*: a man of exceeding rigour, but also incredibly imaginative, as anybody who has ever read any of his wonderful thought experiments, like the exactly nine red paintings in his book *The Transfiguration of the Commonplace*, will immediately recognize.

Tim Crane: *Bernard Williams* is probably the most impressive philosopher I've met in terms of his brilliance, his breadth of knowledge, and his ability to say interesting things about so many different topics in philosophy.

Roger Crisp: I am fortunate, being in Oxford, to have met a lot of impressive philosophers. None of them was more impressive than *Derek Parfit*. Arguing with him can be a rather disturbing experience because it's quite clear that once the argument starts he's about three steps ahead of everybody else.

Fiery Cushman: The two philosophers that I've learnt the most from are both named Josh: *Josh Greene* and *Josh Knobe*. Each in his own way has been a huge source of insight.

Jonathan Dancy: *Gareth Evans* was terrifying. He was so quick, and his thought seemed to be so rich. Other people are less immediately impressive, but still at the same level. *John McDowell* I think of as like that. Gareth was all up there in your face. John is very gentle.

Daniel Dennett: I suppose it would be my mentor and friend *Willard Van Orman Quine*. I think he got more things right. He was dedicated to getting everything clear and straightforward, he hated jargon, and he had very deep philosophical insights that are still not properly appreciated.

Ronald Dworkin: Very hard question. I'll tell you two: *John Rawls* and *Thomas Nagel*. No, I take it back, I have to add *Bernard Williams* and *Tim Scanlon*. Now if you insisted on one, I would plead the 5th Amendment. Of John Rawls, everyone knows about the importance of his great work on the theory of justice: he's one of those very few philosophers whose saintliness infected the philosophical diction. Reading him has the enormous advantage that knowing him makes what he says sound true. He's an example of what he says. Now there's another philosopher about whom I'd say exactly the same thing. And that's Tim Scanlon. Tim Scanlon has a house on Martha's Vineyard where I spend a large part of each summer, so I spend a lot of time with him. And again when he writes about what is *reasonable*, what you can *reasonably* reject, a lot of critics say, 'Well, that's an empty word, what do you mean by "reasonable"?' But if you know Tim Scanlon, then you have a very good sense of what a reasonable person is; it's a person who would act like him. Bernard Williams, well, it's very hard to try and capture the combination of brilliance and irony that made him such a distinctive person. We taught a seminar together for many years, and many times what he said left you uncertain whether to gasp at the brilliance or roar at the humour, because they were both there. Tom Nagel is my brother, in a way. We've given a colloquium together in New York every Fall term for close to 30 years. And I would say about Tom that the enormously impressive thing is his unwillingness to stop diving before we all get the bends: a passion for depth that sometimes leaves you uncertain...he often says 'this, this is too deep a question for us'. But you know that he's identified a deeper level of the question than you had before he explained it.

Gary L. Francione: *Tony Woozley*, who was my supervisor, had a profound impact on me, and I hope taught me how to think clearly. I should also say that I spent an entire evening in New York city some years ago on a table with one other person and *Jacques Derrida*, talking about animals. It was one of the most interesting experiences that I've ever had, but it convinced me that post-modernism, post-structuralism, is not commensurate with the animal issue.

John Gardner: I still find the most impressive philosopher I've ever met to be the late *Jerry Cohen*, who died too young. He was a man of extraordinary wit and charm, but what was wonderful was that he could integrate this wit and charm into argument of the most extraordinary elaborateness and the greatest depth. I also thought he was incredibly likeable. I thought it was a remarkable thing that so much intellectual brilliance could be combined with so much humanity in a single person.

Simon Glendinning: *Jacques Derrida*. I met him a number of times, and he was always impressive. There was one particular occasion when he was speaking at a conference in Reading that I'd organized in 1999 when there was a difficult panel, partly composed of analytic philosophers, and he was having to improvise. His responses were both incredibly generous and had an extraordinary cutting edge of critical force—an originality that saw problems and questions where no one else had seen them. He was a kind of electric light that both illuminated everything in a new way, and cut through other peoples' criticisms of him.

Alison Gopnik: Well, one of my favourite philosophers was *Fred Dretske*. Fred Dretske was a philosopher of mind and he had a clarity about both the way he wrote and the way he talked. He was just a completely straightforward philosophical guy—there were no frills and furbelows. It's a bit like a Madame Grès dress, where it's just a plain Grecian column, and it looks like it's completely simple, and then you realize that to get it to be that simple you have to do a great deal of work.

Leslie Green: Well, this is going to come as a surprise to my colleagues, who know my views about this, but one of the most impressive philosophers I've met is someone we've recently lost—*Ronnie Dworkin*. His views, I think, were misguided on almost all the issues that I'm interested in, but he was polymathic, he was absolutely committed to his subject, he had a magnetic power to draw students into the subject, and really he pushed lines of arguments just as far as they would go, and sometimes further. I admired him for that, and I miss him.

Rom Harré: *John Austin*. He was my supervisor for my BPhil. Most people regarded him as formidable, but I had a scientific education and was a mathematical teacher before I came to do my graduate work, and somehow we hit it off. He was ruthless in the demands he made on himself and on other people. You weren't allowed to get away with any kind of sloppy, careless way of expressing yourself. You had to go on. I remember when he looked at the contents list of my BPhil dissertation he had a narrow smile, and he said, 'I'm not sure I would put it that way.' And I thought, 'Oh my God, I'll have to do it again!'

Dale Jamieson: There are several philosophers. *Derek Parfit* is extremely impressive simply for his genius. *Peter Singer* is extremely impressive because of his moral integrity with respect to his principles. And *Jonathan Glover* is one of the most impressive philosophers that I've ever met for his kindness, his intellectual openness, his openheartedness, and his focus on what really matters.

Nicola Lacey: Well, in terms of mesmerizing speed and articulacy combined with a certain kind of moral force, it was pretty amazing watching *Ronald Dworkin* in his prime.

Rae Langton: People will tease me, but I'm going to mention two philosophers who are impressive in completely different ways, *David Lewis* and *Sally Haslanger*. David Lewis thought with incredible imagination about almost every topic. He had mind-boggling theories about the world which almost nobody believes, but nobody can say quite why they don't believe them. He was a wonderful person and an inspiration. Now, Sally Haslanger, she more than any other person has helped me how to think philosophically about topics that really matter politically.

Fiona Macpherson: Oh my goodness! A philosopher I admire very much is *E. J. Lowe*, who is professor of philosophy at the University of Durham. And I like his work because he argues for traditional views that are very out of fashion, but he argues for them in very innovative ways.

Noel Malcolm: Well, when I was an undergraduate I met *Elizabeth Anscombe*. I even slightly by mistake had an argument with her about whether one of the Ten Commandments was Thou Shalt Not Kill, or Thou Shalt Not Commit Murder. And although I found her pretty terrifying, I also found her quite wonderful. I went to her lectures, though I'm not sure how much of them I understood. She is the one who sticks in my mind as someone who was completely unblinking in what she did, and in her focus on what she was thinking about, although I still think I got the better of our tiny argument about the Ten Commandments.

Mike Martin: You can't put me on the spot that way! *Michael Dummett* was brilliant to see in person. Michael Dummett is an absolute pain to read on the page if you've never heard him speak: because you don't get his prosody if you don't hear him speak. And since he spoke in the long paragraphs that he wrote, it makes sense of that. But just to see somebody who even in his late 60s was still a five-year-old and treated every philosophical problem as if it were a game of conkers, a new pleasure to start anew, was, I always thought, incredibly inspiring.

Colin McGinn: That's a very difficult question. They're impressive in different ways. *Jerry Fodor, Peter Strawson, Thomas Nagel*, are probably the three that have impressed me the most. I wouldn't want to rank them one against the other. But I would also add *Noam Chomsky*—though Chomsky is normally thought of as a linguist. Jerry Fodor reintroduced a strongly mentalist position into philosophy of mind and psychology because of the language of thought. Peter Strawson reintroduced metaphysics after the age of positivism. Thomas Nagel faced up to the mind–body problem more than anybody had before and emphasized the problem of consciousness, and I think that had a large influence on many people, including me.

Jeff McMahan: There are really three philosophers I have known who were all extraordinarily impressive: *Noam Chomsky, Bernard Williams*, and *Derek Parfit*. Of those three the most impressive is Parfit. Both Parfit and Williams were supervisors of my dissertation work at Oxford and Cambridge. Williams was wittier and in a way more dazzling than Parfit. He could talk amusingly and interestingly on any subject. But for depth, originality, rigour, and imagination, nobody I know comes close to Parfit. Let me give you a sense of what it was like to have a supervision with Derek. I would go to his rooms at All Souls, and he was always extraordinarily kind and generous. He would have read some paper of mine, and he would say,

'This is excellent work; I think it can go right into the thesis with very little modification; you've made tremendous progress with this and I have only a few very minor comments to make.' And then he would proceed to refute every single thing I'd said in the dissertation in the most kindly possible manner, after which he would very constructively help rebuild my argument. His ability to work with the ideas so far surpassed my own that I remain completely intimidated by him today, even though we've been friends for a very long time. I feel like a shy, inept school boy in his presence.

John Mikhail: That's an easy question. The most impressive philosopher I've ever met is *Noam Chomsky*. Some commentators do not consider him to be a philosopher because he was primarily trained as a linguist. But Chomsky is far more philosophical than most linguists, and after having read him for many years, and having become acquainted with him fairly well on a personal level as his graduate student, dissertation advisee, and teaching assistant, I am inclined to think that he is one of the truly outstanding philosophers of our time. Particularly in the areas of the philosophy of language and philosophy of mind, as well as the history and philosophy of science, Chomsky's ideas and arguments are extremely powerful. Future reputations are hard to predict, of course, but it certainly seems likely that, even centuries from now, philosophers will still be reading him and coming to grips with his fundamental insights.

Jessica Moss: Well, I was probably most impressed by *Ruth Marcus*, who recently passed away. She was my first philosophy professor and taught a Great Books class—which she was probably sick of teaching—and she had to teach us Plato. We read the *Phaedo* on the first day of class. There's an interesting apparent contradiction in the first few pages where Plato first says that pleasure and pain come together and then that you can't have them at the same time. Ruth Marcus said Plato is being lazy and he's contradicting himself. I was very excited on the first day of class and I put up my hand and said—

something I still think is true—maybe he's not being lazy, and these contradictions are just superficial and he's asking us to look deeper into the text and to think for ourselves. She gave me this weary look, and said, 'That's the kind of paranoid thinking that reminds me of the followers of Leo Strauss. Philosophy is about truth!' And I made it all the way to the bathroom before I cried! But she ended up being a great mentor and supporter.

Philip Pettit: Oh dear God! I found *David Lewis* extraordinary. He would take his time in answering a question. He took so long that sometimes you didn't know if he had heard you. And then he would produce this paragraph in perfect form. And what I found remarkable was not so much his clarity and the imagination of his own views but his capacity to capture the views of others and situate them in relation to his own; most of us are hard put just to get our own views clear. There's someone else who just gobsmacked me for his sheer quickness: *Bernard Williams*. He was wonderfully entertaining company and I liked him, as did everybody else, though I wasn't deeply influenced by him. When I first heard Bernard speak in Cambridge, I was a research fellow and had just arrived, and I remember saying to a visiting American, my God, this guy can just do everything! So those two stand out. But you haven't given me much time to think. I may regret these answers.

Huw Price: I think it would have to be *W. V. O. Quine*. I met Quine once when I was a graduate student at Cambridge in the late 1970s. I came to Cambridge with a rather limited undergraduate background in philosophy, but Quine was one of the people that I had read: classics like 'Two Dogmas of Empiricism'. I liked the way in which in places like that he challenged views that had been taken for granted by philosophers for centuries.

Adina Roskies: I'd have to say *David Lewis*. He was just amazing in terms of his breadth and creativity and the depth at which he understood problems.

Mark Rowlands: A great opportunity to offend lots of people! *John Searle* is very impressive: the combination of sheer ability combined with clarity. I think he said once that if you can't say it clearly, then you don't really understand it, and I think that's absolutely right. I think *Galen Strawson* is a very good philosopher. I like his work not only because it's very good, but also because it's so eclectic. He seems to know everything about everything. And I've always been an admirer of *Andy Clark*'s work, and he's a thoroughly nice guy as well.

Alan Ryan: The answer to that has to be threefold. In terms of the ability to bring ideas to life, it really has to be *Isaiah Berlin*; in terms of patient determination to be absolutely clear about what one thinks, then the person who is my intellectual conscience is *Herbert Hart*; and in terms of someone who united sheer goodness and sweetness of character with meticulousness and determination in thinking his way through the puzzles in front of him, then I would go for *John Rawls*: he's the nearest thing to a secular saint that I have ever encountered.

Jenny Saul: *Chris Hookway*, because he manages to be incisive and yet generous and broadminded at the same time.

Tim Scanlon: I think *Saul Kripke*. He has a property of intensity—intensity of focus on questions that are deeply puzzling—combined with the patience and thoroughness to work out the answers and not be satisfied with any answer that has any loose end hanging or the slightest question hidden underneath it. Other people I know have this. *Derek Parfit* and *Frances Kamm* are two other people who have this enviable kind of philosophical intensity and that's something I admire very much.

Samuel Scheffler: I've had the good fortune to know a large number of extremely impressive philosophers, so singling out two for special mention is bound to be somewhat arbitrary. Having said that, and setting aside philosophers who are still living, let me first mention

John Rawls. He wasn't immediately impressive in personal discussion or conversation, but it was simply the cumulative power of his work that made him so impressive, and I found it very rewarding to be able to talk to him about philosophy. The other person I'll mention is my former colleague and friend at Berkeley, *Thompson Clarke*, who never published very much, but has a bit of an underground reputation and is much admired by some people. I admired greatly his sheer intellectual intensity and single-minded and unwavering focus on philosophical questions. There was a kind of purity and depth to his interest in philosophy that impressed me enormously, and I've never known anybody else who exhibited quite that intensity of philosophical passion.

Eric Schwitzgebel: I need a minute to think about this! I have to say *Shaun Nichols*. I was inspired by him because I was very impressed by the diversity of methods that he uses to get at the questions that interest him. He finds a big philosophical question or a big psychological question, and if that means he has to read centuries-old manuals of etiquette and code them, if that means he's going to do survey polls, if that means he's going to look at anthropology or developmental psychology, he just goes for it. I'm very interested to read all of his stuff because there's a freshness to it, and there's a willingness to go wherever the questions take him.

Barry Smith: Two. First, *Crispin Wright*. He's a man who speaks with enormous intensity, he gets to the depth of a philosophical problem. He doesn't always provide answers, but certainly makes you feel the urgency of philosophy in the raw. And he says things in perfect syllables. The words come out in perfect order. You think this is a composition on the page, but it's actually coming out in his thought as he mulls things over. Second, *Donald Davidson*. He was one of the most consistent and systematic philosophers I ever met. To discuss with him you had to demonstrate that you knew your way around his system, but once that was established, the conversation could begin. It was always acute, subtle, and kept you on your mettle. No gap was left open, no chink of light. It was always possible to feel the force of that powerful philosophical mind at work.

Tom Sorell: *Tom Nagel.* It's not meeting him in person that makes him inspirational, but his writings are outstandingly good. He has a way of looking at a range of problems in ethics, in philosophy of mind, and more broadly in metaphysics that is extremely systematic, using this quite familiar and usually tatty, but in his hands really sophisticated, distinction between the subjective and the objective. A quite outstandingly good philosopher.

Galen Strawson: I think my favourite philosopher is *Tom Nagel.* When I bought and read his book *The View From Nowhere* in 1986, I was very moved because I was feeling beleaguered in Oxford. Almost everybody seemed to be a Wittgensteinian or a Davidsonian or an anti-realist of one sort or another, and in general I felt that there was nobody else who thought in the way that I did. And then I read *The View From Nowhere*, and I thought it was wonderful to find a kindred spirit. In fact, it restored my belief in other minds!

Robert Talisse: It would have to be *Ronald Dworkin.* I met him in 2003 when at Vanderbilt we had organized a small series of lectures on the legacy of John Rawls, who had recently passed away. What was so impressive about Ronald Dworkin was that he spoke extemporaneously about Rawls' legacy and Rawls' contributions to political theory. It seemed as if he were speaking totally off the cuff; cataloguing six things that Rawls had achieved. It was as if he were reading from a book that had been copy-edited by the best copy-editor in the world. When presenting his own views, he was philosophically so fluid, well argued; he addressed the questions beautifully and fairly; there was nothing that one could say to him that he hadn't already thought through very, very deeply. It was incredibly impressive.

John Tasioulas: Invidious question, but the most impressive philosopher I've met is *Herbert Hart*. He seemed to me to exhibit a kind of continuity between the sorts of views that he was famous for and his actual personality. So you felt there was a kind of integrity between his philosophy and who he was as a person, and I subsequently came to realize that this is not something to be taken for granted. Another aspect which I found deeply impressive about him was that he was incredibly modest. His great success as a philosopher seemed to co-exist with having a very modest and moderate attitude to his own achievements, and willingness to listen and to talk to all sorts of different people.

John Tomasi: Easily *Bernard Williams*. Williams was my supervisor when I was doing my doctorate at Oxford. When I would go and speak with Bernard, I always felt there was some shelf of books somewhere in some library that I had never read, and nobody I knew had ever read: he seemed to have a way of taking this oblique approach to philosophical questions that I thought I knew the literature about. Every time he would surprise me with the way he would go at them.

Michael Tye: Only two philosophers that I've ever met have intimidated me: *David Lewis* and *Saul Kripke*. Kripke intimidated me because, well, he was Kripke. Lewis intimidated me, before I got to know him, because he not only seemed bizarre, he seemed from another planet, and he also struck me as exceedingly brilliant.

Kendall Walton: That's a hard question. One person who comes to mind is *David Lewis*. There are two things that are remarkable about him. One is that his writing is wonderfully clear and straightforward; he gets things right, he uses the smallest number of words he can. But, more importantly, he's a philosopher who is willing and eager to say some crazy-sounding things, some imaginative things, to put forward theses that are surprising, and surprisingly often turn out to be plausible, and are a lot more interesting than if he had just stated what seems to be obvious.

Liane Young: I'm going to have to say my undergraduate advisor, *Frances Kamm*. I started as a philosophy major in part because of Peter Singer. I didn't share a lot of his intuitions, at least when he takes them to their logical extreme, and I really wanted to develop the smarts to be able to argue for my intuitions in this sort of post hoc rational way, and I found myself trying to figure out my intuitions and moral principles and being optimistic about Frances' project and the project of deontological moral philosophy. Frances is just a genius at developing her intuitions to these cases, developing the cases, developing the principles and the theories that make the full set of intuitions and cases coherent. I don't know if she or anyone has the answer yet. But if somebody is going to find it, I'll put my money on Frances.

JOY AND PAIN

I

THOMAS HURKA ON
Pleasure

David Edmonds: *Pleasure is unquestionably one of the good things in life. But how do we contrast pleasure with other human goods, like knowledge or accomplishment? How do we compare different types of pleasure? And what is the link between pleasure and happiness? The American philosopher Robert Nozick imagined an Experience Machine that could give us whatever pleasurable feelings we might want and, once plugged in, we wouldn't know whether or not these experiences were real. We might believe we were eating a chocolate éclair, though the delicious sensation was actually caused by wires attached to our brain. The question Nozick asks is this:* Would you choose the machine over real life? *He thinks you wouldn't, and that this shows that pleasure is not as important as thinkers like the late-eighteenth-century British utilitarian Jeremy Bentham believed it to be. Our guide around the concept of pleasure is Thomas Hurka—Professor of Philosophy at the University of Toronto.*

Nigel Warburton: *The topic we're going to discuss is pleasure. Pleasure's a good thing isn't it? That's fairly obvious.*

Thomas Hurka: I hope so. A lot of us are wasting our time if it's not a good thing. But I take it there's a strong intuitive sense that pleasure—by which I mean all kinds of good feeling, any sensation, any internal feeling that feels good or has a positive buzz—is a good thing. People use different words for different types of good feeling: 'pleasure', 'contentment', 'enjoyment', 'happiness'. I include all of that, and I think, yes, feeling good is good.

NW: *But feeling good comes in different varieties. It's not all the same kind of thing, surely?*

TH: That's what I want to talk about. I think the classical utilitarians like Jeremy Bentham thought that pleasure was just one thing—there were these 'pleasure pellets', as it were. But I think there are different types of good feeling. When I say that pleasure is good, I don't think it's the only good thing. So, the best life is not necessarily the most pleasant life. Achievement is a human value; knowledge is a human value; being a morally good person is a human value; but pleasure is also a human value, and I don't think we could imagine a good life without pleasure. It's an essential element. But, as you suggested, there are different types. The first distinction is between pleasures that are simple feelings and aren't about anything, on the one side; and pleasures that are about something—that are 'pleasures *that*'—on the other. So, let's say you're eating a chocolate. You close your eyes and you concentrate on the feeling. You're getting the pleasure—it's the wonderful pleasant sensation of rich

2

creamy chocolate—but you're not pleased *about* anything. You're not pleased *that* something is the case. It's just a sensation that feels good.

NW: *So what you're saying is that these simple pleasures are really just sensations—good sensations.*

TH: Each one of them will be a complex sensation with a dimension of pleasantness, but also other elements that make one pleasant sensation different from another. So, the eating chocolate pleasure will be a combination of pleasantness and chocolate taste and rich, creamy feel. And the lying-in-the sun tanning pleasure will be the dimension of pleasantness and the hot sand underneath one's body, warm-glow-on-the-skin sensation. So each of them will be a total package that's different, but each will have this dimension of pleasantness. You can never experience pleasantness on its own: it's always got to be with something else.

NW: *So what's the other case? The case of pleasure* that *something.*

TH: Well, that's when you're pleased *that* something is the case. You have a thought that something has happened in the world—or will happen—and you're pleased that that will happen. So, you can be pleased *that* Liverpool just scored five minutes ago. You can be pleased *that* your child has just started to walk. You can be pleased *that* people seemed to like the lecture you just gave, and they asked smart questions at the end of it. So, you're pleased *that* something is the case. That's more complex than a simple, physical sensation, because you can't be pleased *that* Liverpool scored five minutes ago unless you have the *thought* that Liverpool scored five minutes ago. We might

3

think that animals, for example, can have simple physical pleasures: they can eat meat and get the pleasure of eating meat. But they can't have the pleasure *that* Liverpool scored unless they have the thought that Liverpool scored, and most animals can't do that.

NW: *So, we've got the distinction between simple pleasures, like eating chocolate, and pleasures like the pleasure* that *Liverpool just scored. Is that the whole range of pleasures we have available to us?*

TH: No. I think there's another distinction, independent of that and cross-cutting against it, between what you can call *specific* pleasures and more general—or extended—pleasures. So let me take that first on the side of the simple pleasures which are not 'pleasures *that*'. If you take a physical pleasure, like eating chocolate or sun-tanning, it's often localized in part of your body. So, you feel the pleasure of sun-tanning-on-your-back, or the pleasure of eating chocolate in your taste organs. And similarly, pains are often localized: you have a pain in your right elbow, or an ache in your left thigh. So those are localized and they're also discrete elements in consciousness. You can have several of them at the same time: you can have the ache in your right elbow and the pleasure of sun-tanning while eating chocolate and having soreness in your left thigh, all at once. They're discrete elements in consciousness. The more extended simple pleasures are the ones of being in a good mood. You just feel generally up; you feel generally elated. Now, that's not localized. You don't feel in a good mood in your left elbow or in your right thigh. It's not physically localized and it's not just a discrete element of consciousness, alongside others, either. It permeates consciousness. Your whole mental state is permeated with this feeling of being up. Again, there can be differences of intensity: you can be in a slightly good mood, or you can be elated, which is in an intensely good mood. Moods are different from physical pleasures in that they spread through consciousness—they pervade it, they're the background to all the other mental states, like a blue wash on a painting that colours everything slightly blue. And, of course, the opposite is a bad mood or depression, where a negative feeling permeates your consciousness.

NW: *So moods are very general and not about anything, in contrast with emotions which are about things.*

TH: That's right. So, when we talk about a good mood, that's more general—more extended—than a physical pleasure, but we're still on the simple sensation side, rather than on the 'pleasures *that*' side. There's also a more general or more extended kind of good feeling that you can have on the 'pleasures *that*' side. What I've mostly described are pleasures *that* very specific things have happened. So I'm pleased *that* Liverpool just scored, or I'm pleased *that* my child just learned to walk, or *that* people appreciated the lecture I just gave. But I could take 'pleasures *that*' in much bigger objects, and a very important one is being pleased, or feeling satisfied, with my life as a whole. I look at my life as a whole from its earliest stages to now and projecting into the future, and I'm not looking at just one aspect of my life, I'm looking at my personal life, my career, my hobbies and activities, my friendships—all those things. Taking the whole package and looking at my life as a whole, I feel good about it. I'm pleased *that* my life has gone the way it has. That's a pleasure *that*; I'm pleased *that* something is—or has been—the case. But it's not just Liverpool scoring, it's something much bigger: it's my life as a whole. So we have, if I can just outline the four-part distinction: (a) simple and localized pleasures—those are physical pleasures; (b) simple and extended pleasures—that's an overall good mood. Then we've got: (c) the 'pleasure *that*' and particular—pleasure *that* Liverpool has just scored; and (d) the 'pleasure *that*' and more extended—I feel satisfied with how my life as a whole has gone and will go. Those are all ways of feeling good, but they're different.

NW: *So, we've got the taxonomy now. But how do we compare these different pleasures?*

TH: I'm going to be a little bit Benthamite again because I think that they involve good feeling. They all involve a positive buzz, and that buzz can be more or less intense. My thought is: all that matters is how much buzz you get. Now, that's not what everybody has thought. If you just think about the words we use in English, 'pleasure' sounds a little tawdry: 'He devoted his life to pleasure'—well, that's not what you'd say by way of praising somebody. But 'happiness' has much more positive connotations: 'I want to be happy'—that sounds better. People have often used the word 'happiness' for the more extended of those four types of good feeling. So, I think you'd be more likely to call somebody happy if he's in an overall good mood; if he's just overall feeling good, you'd be inclined to call him happy. Whereas, if he's just getting a specific pleasure from eating chocolate, you'd say, 'Well, that's pleasure—but it's not happiness.' Likewise, if someone is pleased *that* Liverpool has just scored a goal or that his daughter has learned to walk, you wouldn't say that *that* makes him happy. But if someone has got a good feeling about his life as a whole, I think we would be inclined to say that he or she is happy. A lot of philosophers have defined happiness as satisfaction or a good feeling with one's life as a whole. So, if you use the word with positive connotations for the more extended forms of good feeling, I think that's trying to get us to believe that those are better. But I'm not persuaded by that. Think of the song, 'Any love is good love'—well, any good feeling is good feeling! What matters is just its intensity.

NW: *So you're saying that pleasure's good however you get it. It seems to follow from that, that somebody who engages in the very simple, basic pleasures and has lots of intense experiences is living as pleasurable and happy a life as someone who engages in much more cerebral, intellectual pursuits.*

TH: I'm not going to say that the first person is leading as good a life, because pleasure is not the only good. But if you ask how much pleasure—how much good feeling—is there in a life, the answer might be: it's just as good as the more cerebral life that you describe. Let me give you a pair of contrasts. On one side, there's a sensualist—a Don Giovanni—who spends his life eating glorious meals and having wonderful erotic adventures, but he's not convinced that he's leading the best life. He has pangs of guilt about what he's doing and therefore he doesn't feel much life satisfaction; he doesn't feel good about his life as a whole. Nonetheless, he has all these intense particular pleasures. And on the other side, we have an ascetic monk. He eats bread and water, he gets very few physical pleasures; but, on the other hand, he has a persistent feeling of contentment—not intense contentment, but an overall persistent, good mood permeating his consciousness. He is doing what he thinks is right; he's serving his God and he feels life satisfaction. He's not jumping up and down, but he feels a quiet sense of satisfaction with how he's living his life. These people have pleasures of very different kinds but it's possible that, if you ask whose life has the most pleasure, there's no answer. They're equal, or roughly equal; you can't say that one has a more enjoyable life or a more pleasant life, or a life with more good feeling than the other. The sensualist—the Don Giovanni—has all these intense physical pleasures, not much pleasure of a good mood, not much extended 'pleasure *that*'. The ascetic does have a persistent good mood and life satisfaction, but he doesn't have many physical pleasures. What one gets in one form of pleasure, the other gets in the other. It may be that, at the end of the day, they've led equally pleasant, enjoyable lives in their very different ways.

NW: *We've just been talking about pleasure regardless of how it's caused, but in real life it matters how pleasure is caused. If I get my pleasure from torturing animals, that's not a good thing.*

TH: I couldn't agree more. We've been talking about pleasure as one good thing in life, and I've said that I don't believe it's the only good thing. There are other elements of a good life, such as achievement, knowledge and understanding, certain kinds of personal relationships, and also being a morally good person. So, to take Bentham's famous remark that 'quantity of pleasure being equal, pushpin is as good as poetry' (pushpin was an eighteenth-century game like tiddlywinks), it might be true that, as far as the pleasures involved, the two are equally good; but poetry involves the exercise of intellectual capacities, understanding, sympathetic feeling, that are additional to the pleasure and give the activity of reading poetry much more value than an equally pleasurable playing of pushpin. It goes even further. You were talking about someone getting pleasure from torturing animals. Well, I said that being a morally good person is another good thing and, of course, being a morally bad person—being vicious—is a bad thing. If you take pleasure in some other being's pain—sadistic pleasure, let's say, in an animal's or another person's pain—that might have some positive value in so far as it's pleasant. But it also has negative value: it's evil in so far as it's malicious and involves a positive attitude of wanting and taking pleasure in something evil, namely someone else's pain. So, it's good in so far as it's pleasant, and bad in so far as it's vicious. First, that makes it worse than equally intense pleasures that don't have an evil object; and also, if the pain that one takes pleasure in is a great pain, then the sadistic pleasure is, on balance, evil: its badness in so far as it's vicious is greater than its goodness in so far as it's pleasure.

NW: *It's very clear from what you've said that, although you're very interested in pleasure and see pleasure as one of the good things in life, you're not a utilitarian. You reject the idea that the only good thing possible, for a human being, is pleasure.*

TH: Yes, I'm not a utilitarian and I'm not—more specifically—a hedonist about value. Two major objections to hedonism traditionally are first about mindless pleasures and second about morally vicious pleasures. So, mindless pleasures are the pleasures of pushpin as against poetry, the pleasures of the Deltas and Epsilons in *Brave New World*, or the pleasures of people in Robert Nozick's Experience Machine. If all that's valuable is pleasure, then pushpin is as good as poetry. The Deltas and Epsilons who say, 'We're all happy here', actually have the best lives, and we should all go on the Experience Machine. But most of us don't think that. We think that a life that is less pleasant but involves real activity and real accomplishment, real knowledge and understanding of your place in the world—rather than delusion—is a better life than one that is more pleasant, but lacks those additional goods. So, I reject hedonism or utilitarianism, first of all because it values mindless pleasures at the same level as activities that involve challenge and the exercise of skill and so on. The second objection concerns morally vicious pleasures because a strict hedonist thinks that a torturer's pleasure in his victim's pain only makes the situation better. If the torturer's pleased by his victim's pain, we should applaud—that's better than if he was indifferent to the victim's pain, or worst of all if he was pained by it. Hedonism also thinks that there are no good pains. But if you've suffered some tragedy, and I feel compassionate pain at your suffering or your loss, isn't that a good thing? I would say it's a good thing, because compassionate pain at your tragedy is a morally fitting or appropriate response to something evil that's happened to you, and on that basis it's good. But hedonism says: 'No. It's best not to feel pain at other people's tragedies. That's just wasted pain. You should, if anything, forget about it or, if possible, feel pleased by it.' But that's hard to believe—or at least I can't believe it.

NW: *But pleasure is good. How do we weigh it against these other goods in life?*

TH: You're ending on a killer difficult question. There is no simple answer to that because we're talking about completely distinct objects of value: pleasure on the one side, knowledge and achievement on the other. I think pleasure is good, but I think that other things tend to matter more. And one of these things is the form of virtue that involves being pleased by good things. So, if you lead a life that has all the other values in it—you have understanding of the world around you, you seek difficult goals and achieve them, and you're morally virtuous—then one aspect of your moral virtue will be that you'll be pleased to have knowledge and understanding of the world around you, you'll be pleased at all your achievements, and your life will contain pleasure. This pleasure will be valuable partly because it's pleasure. But I think it will be more valuable because it's appropriate pleasure in something else that's good, namely your understanding and your achievement. So, you've asked me a difficult question, and some philosophers might come in here and say, 'Well, you know, knowledge and achievement, those are good, but what really matters is feeling good so long as it's not horribly vicious, and so long as it's not completely mindless.' I'm more at the other end. If we have Nozick's Experience Machine—we've all got it at home—some philosophers would say, 'The minute you get home from work, your life will be best if you spend lots of the evening on there.' Well, I would say, ration it the way you ration your kids' TV and Internet time. It's of some value, but if it's interfering with achievements and personal relationships to any significant degree, it's taking away from other things that are more valuable.

2

MICHAEL TYE ON
Pain

David Edmonds: *There are several intriguing philosophical puzzles about pain. Where, for example, do we experience it? If I cut my finger, is the pain in my finger, or in my brain? What does pain reveal about consciousness? It was a pleasure to discuss these questions with Michael Tye of the University of Texas.*

Nigel Warburton: *We're going to focus on pain. Obviously that's an important topic in most people's lives from an experiential point of view, but what's the philosophical view here?*

Michael Tye: I doubt that there's one philosophical problem of pain, but I'm interested in pain as a conscious state, and in understanding how to locate the characteristic conscious feel of pains within a world which I think as a whole is purely material.

NW: *So, somebody steps on my toe, I feel the pain. I'm a conscious pain-suffering individual. I don't understand what the philosophical problem is there?*

MT: Well, if someone steps on your toe, then you feel pain and you feel it in a particular location in your toe, and there's a characteristic phenomenal aspect, or subjective aspect to your experience, one that distinguishes it from feeling an itch in your toe, or a tickle, or whatever. One question is, 'How do we understand what it is for the pain to be in your toe?', and the other is, 'How do we understand the awful painful aspect of pains?' The first of these may seem to be easy to answer, but on reflection it's not because you can feel a pain in a toe even if you lack a toe: there's the well-known phenomenon of phantom-limb pain. You can't have a coin in a pocket unless you have a pocket, so how can you have a pain in a toe if you don't have a toe? The answer to that is that pains are, in this respect, like perceptual experiences: you can have a visual experience of a dagger even if there is no dagger, as Macbeth did, and that's because Macbeth's visual experience represented to him that a dagger was before him when in reality there wasn't, so it was a case of misrepresentation. Analogously, we should think of pains as experiences that, in part, represent bodily parts, for example toes, and in some cases can misrepresent, so that you can have 'a pain in your toe', even if there is no toe there.

NW: *There's a difference between the hallucination in the case of Macbeth, where the dagger doesn't actually exist in front of him, and the case where I'm mislocating the causes of my pain. I've still got a genuine pain because of that intrinsically subjective-felt experience of pain. That's what pain is.*

MT: I agree that there is that disanalogy. There are two things that need to be distinguished here: there's the disturbance in the body, which in normal cases will exist—there'll be some damage to a bodily tissue, but it needn't exist in every case. In the case of phantom-limb pain, there may be no disturbance in the limb, because, after all, the limb doesn't occur there at all, and there may be no disturbance in any other part of the body.

You can imagine a neurosurgeon directly stimulating the brain and producing the experience of pain in the limb. But you're right, the pain itself in all of these cases definitely exists, and in that way the pain itself is not like Macbeth's dagger, say, which, after all, doesn't exist. So, what are we to say about the pain itself? I think that if you have a pain, then you have to *feel* a pain, and if you feel a pain, then you have to have a pain. It's not like the case of heat, say. You can have heat around you without feeling heat, or you can feel heat without having any heat around. Heat and the feeling of heat are distinct; but pain and the feeling of pain are not distinct. Why is this? The answer is because pain is a feeling: pain is nothing more than a feeling. As such, as a feeling, it's a certain kind of experience, and a pain in a leg is, if you like, a leg-pain feeling or experience. A pain in an arm is an arm-pain experience, and those two experiences obviously have something in common: they're both painful. They also differ. The disturbance that you take to be present is in one bodily limb, and in the other case, your experience locates it in the other bodily limb.

NW: *You've said the pain is a feeling, but obviously not all feelings are painful, so what is it that allows us to characterize a particular feeling as a painful one?*

MT: Part of what pains do, as experiences, is to represent or inform us of certain kinds of disturbances that occur in our bodies. The difference in that respect between a pain and an itch, or a tickle, is that the relevant experience is tracking or informing us of a different kind of disturbance in each case. With a tickle, for example, it's a certain kind of surface disturbance to which the experience is responding; with a pain, it may be an internal disturbance of a certain sort, and there'll be various physiological differences between the relevant disturbances. Nonetheless, this still doesn't really come to grips with the painful aspect of pains. The painful aspect has, in part, to do with the kind of disturbance that is tracked; but it also has, in part, to do with the fact that pains feel bad, and in that way they contrast, for example, with orgasms. Sex is so popular because orgasms feel good. So why do pains feel bad? The answer is because pains not only inform us, or represent to us that there are certain kinds of disturbances in our bodies, but they're trying to tell us that these disturbances are bad for us, and in that respect, they're the exact opposite of orgasms, because orgasm experiences are trying to tell us that the relevant disturbances are good for us. So in my view, there's a *valuational* aspect to pain experience, one that groups it with things like orgasms, tasting ripe strawberries, and so on.

NW: *When people talk about the pain of loss, or of bereavement, that's a genuine feeling of pain, but is it a metaphorical use of the word 'pain', or does it have a close connection with the bodily damage type of pain?*

MT: That's a case of emotional pain, and while there will be connections, because there is some phenomenology of 'badness', as it were, that kind of pain is more easily grouped with cases, say, of anger or fear, or whatever. It's interesting that the ancient Greeks grouped pains generally with the appetites and emotions, and they didn't think of pains as going along with bodily sensations. By contrast, modern neuroscience has focused almost exclusively on the sensory aspect of pains. That now is changing somewhat: it's now widely admitted that pain experience is tied not only to activity in the somato-sensory cortex, which is the usual locus of bodily sensation, but also to activity in the anterior cingulate cortex, and that seems to be what's responsible for the unpleasant aspect of pain. Subjects who have certain kinds of brain damage and who don't get the relevant activity in the anterior cingulate cortex nonetheless feel pains, but they report that the pains don't feel bad to them, that they don't mind the pains, that they're not bothersome in the same way. So it looks as if the usual experience of pain is constituted by these two different aspects: one responding to what's going on in the body, and the other then telling us that it's bad for us. Pains in some ways are like warning lights in cars. You're driving along and the warning light flashing red tells you the oil level is low, and it flashes red because it wants you to take immediate action to cure the problem. Likewise, pain is the way it is because you can think of it like a kind of warning light for the organism: it's telling us that there's something wrong in the body, something that we ought to fix as fast as we can.

NW: *But isn't there an analogy there with psychological pain: there's something bad in my life that's causing me angst and agony, and I ought to do something about that?*

MT: To that extent there is this connection between emotional pain, and what we might call pain as a bodily sensation—that's the unpleasant aspect in both cases. What's lacking in the emotional pain case is the bodily sensory component: you're not going to get the same activity, for example, in the somato-sensory cortex.

NW: *What's pain's relation to pleasure? There are people who claim to take pleasure in pain; there are people who say that pleasure and pain aren't even on the same dimension. Is pain a thing unto itself, or is it on a continuum with pleasure?*

MT: I was talking recently to someone who is a masochist, and what he told me was that in normal contexts, walking down the street or whatever, if he steps on a pin or bumps into something, then he responds to pain in the normal way; but there are certain contexts in which when he experiences pain, he doesn't have that kind of response to it at all. I'm inclined to think what's going on there is that there's a difference in cognitive reaction to the pain, brought about by the relevant context. The usual desire that pain go away, a desire that we who are not masochists have pretty much in all cases, is brought about simply because the pain feels bad. We want pain to go away a lot because pain feels very bad to us. But in the case of this particular man, when he's in certain contexts he doesn't want the pain to go away. Now, I asked him, does it still feel bad to you in those contexts? He said, 'Yes, it sort of does. But I don't want it to go away in the way in which I want it to go away when I bang myself walking down the street.' There's the unpleasant aspect to pain itself, and then there are the cognitive reactions to the pain, and the desire that it go away.

NW: *You've described your theory of consciousness as representationalist. How can the mind represent pain?*

MT: The basic model I have is an instrument model. If you think about simple instruments—compasses, speedometers, or whatever—they're built in such a way that certain states of the instrument are causally coordinated with certain external states, and simply via that causal co-ordination, or causal co-variation, or tracking rotation, states of the instrument manage to represent external states. In the case of a speedometer, when the pointer points to 60, it represents that the car is going at 60 miles an hour, not because the driver is interpreting the speedometer, but because the speedometer is built in such a way that the pointer's position, when it's at 60, is causally co-ordinated with the car going at 60 miles under design conditions. You can get misrepresentation if the speedometer is not functioning as it was meant to, or in poor conditions, and, analogously, Mother Nature has built part of our brain so that it gets active under certain conditions when there's a certain kind of bodily disturbance that's bad for us, and thereby it manages to represent that disturbance.

NW: *Can you be mistaken about your own pain?*

MT: I think that you can be mistaken about your pain, at least in the sense that you can think that you're in pain, or that you're feeling pain, when in reality you aren't. So, take the case of the man who's being tortured: a red hot poker has been put on his back ten times in a row, say. He's felt intense pain ten times, on the eleventh time, he sees his torturer go around the back with the red hot poker, something touches his back, he cries out, for a moment he thinks he's feeling intense pain, and then a little bit later he thinks to himself, 'Wait a minute, that didn't feel quite the same way as the ones before', and the torturer comes out the front and shows him an ice cube. I think what's going on there is that, for a moment, the man believes that he is in intense pain, when in reality he isn't. So, in that way, I think you can be mistaken about your pain. Nonetheless, I do think that if you're genuinely feeling pain, then you are in pain. It's just that sometimes you can think that you're feeling pain without feeling pain.

3

NOËL CARROLL ON
Humour

David Edmonds: *A man and his friend are out for their weekly game of golf when a funeral procession crosses the road next to the course. The man stops in mid-swing, takes off his golf cap, and bows down to pray. 'Wow', says his friend, 'that's thoughtful. How touching!' 'Well', says the man, 'we were married for thirty-five years.' That, according to one survey, is what Americans think is the world's funniest joke. But what makes something humorous? Do all jokes share one or more characteristics? And can a joke be so sick that it ceases to be funny? Nigel Warburton plays straight man to Noël Carroll of the City University, New York.*

Nigel Warburton: *The topic we're going to focus on today is humour. What is humour?*

Noël Caroll: Humour is what causes us to be comically amused. For example, let me tell you a joke. An Irishman named Pat goes into a bar in New York City. He goes in and he orders three shots of Jameson. 'Set them up, right away, three of them!' The bartender sets them up. Pat orders three more. Three more. Three more. Finally, the bartender says 'Why do you always order your drinks in groups of three?' He says, 'Well, I have two brothers: one's in Sydney, one's in Dublin, and I like to make believe we're all drinking together.' Well, Pat becomes a regular. As soon as he comes through the door, the bartender sets up three shots. One day, Pat comes up to the bar and says, 'No. Today, just two.' The bartender looks and says, 'Oh, I'm sorry to hear of your loss.' Pat says, 'What loss?' He says, 'Well, you're only ordering two drinks, did one of your brothers pass away?' He says, 'No, it's me. Don't you know I'm on the wagon?'

NW: *(Laughs) That's an example of comic amusement; I'm amused by that.*

NC: That's exactly right. Now we can go on from that to talk about what it is.

NW: *So what is it?*

NC: Well, philosophers have been interested in it for quite a long time. One view, apparently the most ancient, is called the superiority view, first advanced by people like Plato and Aristotle. It's the view that when we laugh, we laugh at someone who is inferior to us. Plato might have said, we laugh at people who don't respect the Delphic adage of knowing thyself—the people who think they're smart or handsome or stronger or better athletes than they actually are. Hobbes, of course, was the most famous proponent of this. He said laughter is the sudden glory we feel when another in comparison to us seems less than us, when we seem better than they are. So the first view of comic amusement is that it's a form of contempt. That view held a great deal of sway until about the eighteenth century, when the Scottish philosopher Francis Hutcheson and then someone he influenced, another Scot, James Beattie, in the

Scottish Enlightenment, argued against it. They said, 'Look, it couldn't possibly be that superiority is the source of comic amusement. For example, consider this: oysters are inferior but we never laugh at them.' So, what philosophers and psychologists, including myself, now think is a better bet is what we call an incongruity theory. The source of comic amusement is the perception of something that seems incongruous. For example, if you're walking down the street and you see a Morris Minor parked next to a stretch Hummer, you might think that that's really humorous. And, of course, jokes like the one I just told about Pat involve an incongruity, namely, that Pat thinks that being on the wagon is consistent with having only two drinks, as long as he's not drinking for himself.

NW: *So, laughing at somebody according to the superiority view involves the opinion that somehow I'm better than that. It seems to me that that does occur. It's not that it never occurs. We do laugh at people who are inferior to us: it may sound nasty, but we do.*

NC: It's not the case that one wants to dismiss the superiority theory across the board. But very often these superiority genres really depend more on incongruity: that's what's doing the work. So, there are British jokes against the Irish; French jokes about the Belgians; Belgian jokes against the French; Indian jokes about Sikhs; American jokes about Poles, and so on. These jokes take a very definite pattern, and they almost all involve incongruity. Really, they're all 'moron' jokes. How can you tell an Irishman has been using your personal computer? There's white-out on the screen. I could also tell that as a Polish joke. I originally heard it as a 'Newfie' joke. Newfie jokes are jokes about people from Newfoundland in Canada. Now, if there's some particular group that you'd like to put down, you can use the moron structure to do it, mocking a character who commits logical and other errors of stupendous sorts.

NW: *Now it seems obvious to me that not all incongruity is funny. There must be plenty of examples of things that are incongruous but that aren't funny at all.*

NC: That's a terrific point. Alexander Bain raised it in the nineteenth century. Even if incongruity, or *perceived* incongruity, is necessary for humour, it's not *sufficient* because, as you say, there are all of these kinds of incongruities that are anything but amusing. So, when you try to revise an incongruity theory for the present, what you've got to do is put in some qualifications. The first one is that the incongruity shouldn't involve the production of any sort of anxiety. For example, psychologists have noted that, with infants, a caregiver—a mother, or an uncle, or someone with whom the infant is acquainted—can make a strange face and the baby will giggle; but if a stranger does the same thing, the baby will wail. The point is that there has to be a certain safety. Aristotle even talked about this: he said there can't be real destruction involved in comedy.

NW: *Does that mean that you can't have 'edgy' humour, the kind where a comedian deliberately goes a little bit too far and puts the audience under a kind of pressure?*

NC: There are several devices that really are going to permit you to introduce a certain degree of what may appear anxiety producing, but this is buffered in very important ways. Take the clown figure: clowns are really not like us. They're not really quite human: they're either too fat or too skinny.

But they're also able to do things like be hit on the head with a brick and then, in a matter of seconds, be standing up and able to behave normally. So one thing you do is to reassure the audience that the figures are not really being hurt, as in slapstick comedy. Then, of course, the other feature that is very important here is that we have all kinds of conventions to signal that we're going to enter a zone in which people shouldn't be worried or anxious about what's going to happen. Either I say to you, 'Did you hear the one about...?', or maybe I change my intonation, or maybe I just wink at you. All of those features allow the humour to absorb a certain amount of the anxiety that you might otherwise feel. You need those buffers.

NW: *There are some people who find violence funny. That's the sad truth. Are they just inappropriate?*

NC: That raises the whole question of black humour. My own view of black humour, though, is that the reason that we're amused by, for example, dead baby jokes like, 'What is brown and gurgles?' 'A baby casserole', is that in jokes like that it's not the baby that we're laughing at: we're laughing at the people we think will become apoplectic upon hearing it. Remember that black humour was inaugurated by André Breton, who thought of black humour as the enemy of sentimentality. He thought of it as another way of outraging the bourgeoisie. So, black humour—to a certain extent—is about directing us to think about how our puritanical and sanctimonious neighbours will respond. A friend of mine likes to say: black humour is doing something that would drive your mother crazy.

NW: *So we've talked about one aspect of humour, according to the incongruity theory, namely that the relevant events aren't anxiety producing. Are there any other aspects of incongruity that are important in understanding humour?*

NC: Well, another qualification we need on the relevant kind of incongruity is that the incongruity not be the sort that provokes, what we might call, a genuine problem-solving attitude. So, there are lots of incongruities that take the form of puzzles and that motivate us to solve the puzzle: crossword puzzles, chess problems, mathematical theorems, for example. These, though, are very different from what we encounter with the incongruity relevant to humour. Here's a typical two-stage joke: Aaron calls his friend Moshe on his cell phone; Moshe is driving and Aaron says, 'Be careful. The radio says there's a nut who's driving the wrong way on the highway.' And Moshe says, 'You're telling me! There are hundreds of them!' Now, as in most jokes, the punch line is a kind of puzzle that calls for a solution. The solution to this is that Moshe is the 'nut' who's driving the wrong way on the highway. But, of course, there's something very strange about these interpretations we use to solve the puzzles in jokes: that is, they're as absurd as the punchlines themselves. It's absurd to think that someone could be on a crowded highway and not know that he was driving in the wrong direction. Now, that contrasts with what I call genuine problem solving, where you expect to be correct; you're genuinely trying to solve a puzzle.

NW: *Several of the examples you've used could be considered quite offensive, particularly the 'moron' jokes, which deliberately demean a particular group of people. Do you think there is anything about an immoral joke that stops it being funny?*

NC: There are two dimensions here. One is morality: there's no question that a joke could be immoral or that it could be told for immoral reasons. Someone might tell an anti-Semitic joke in order to stoke anti-Semitism. On the other hand, comic structures have a kind of formal interest. Not every anti-Semitic joke need be told for anti-Semitic reasons. Most of the kinds of jokes that outsiders tell about Jewish people are exactly the same as the jokes that insiders tell. That is also the case with African-Americans. The jokes that are told with invective against them are the same types that insiders tell. There *are* jokes that are told with harmful intent; there it may, in fact, be the case that the joke is both immoral *and* funny. To face your question head-on: are there cases where some jokes are so immoral that they become unfunny? I think it's a possibility. Some theorists like Ted Cohen think, 'No, you just have to accept as a fact of the sadness of human life that sometimes very very horrid examples of humour are simultaneously funny.' I would—to a certain extent—agree with that, but I wouldn't go as far as he does, which is to say that the funniness of a joke could never be upended, so to speak, by its immorality.

NW: *So, in a sense, the logical structure of incongruity that you've talked about isn't the only factor that makes something funny. There's a sense in which some content would just put a shutter down and that's it. Despite having the correct form, it's not going to be funny.*

NC: That's the direction I lean in, yes.

NW: *Something behind this which has been intriguing me is why we have a sense of humour at all? Why have human beings developed with a sense of humour?*

25

NC: One thing that humour depends on is that we think in terms of certain heuristics, certain norms. Those heuristics work pretty well, but they also—because they're very fast ways of scoping out situations—have a lot of imperfections. Here's an example; it's a Chinese story. A man sees another man walking along the road in front of his horse. And he goes up to the man who's walking in front of his horse and he says, 'Why are you walking in front of the horse? Why don't you get on? The horse would get to Beijing much faster!' The man says, 'Ah, yes. But six legs are faster than four.' So, that heuristic works most of the time, probably, but not this time. Or, to come to our own culture: a somewhat heavy man goes into a pizza parlour and orders a pie. The man behind the counter says, 'Do you want it cut into eight slices or four?' He thinks for a second and says, 'Well, four. I'm on a diet.' So in those cases, we see how the heuristics that we usually use can go wrong in certain situations. A lot of humour is about showing us how our heuristics can go wrong, reminding us how the many heuristics we have have holes in them. We've been rewarded by evolution to take pleasure in discovering these bugs in our cognitive functioning, and it serves the vital purpose of our cognitive wellbeing. It's not, as the superiority theorists thought, a way of celebrating our superiority; it's not about arrogance. Humour is about humility: realizing what cognitively frail beings we are.

MORALITY

4

JEFF McMAHAN ON
Moral Status

David Edmonds: *A stone on the beach, we assume, has no moral status. We can kick or hammer the stone, and we've done the stone no harm. Typical adult human beings do have moral status. We shouldn't, without a good reason, kick people. Often, contentious moral issues, such as embryo research, or abortion, or whether to turn off a life support machine, turn on disagreement about the moral status of the embryo, foetus, or individual—so the key questions are who or what has moral status, and why? Jeff McMahan takes on these tricky questions.*

Nigel Warburton: *The topic we're going to focus on today is humans and moral status. Let's start at the beginning—what is moral status?*

Jeff McMahan: To have moral status is to have certain moral claims against others for one's own sake. Moral status is based on intrinsic properties possessed by an individual that ground moral reasons for treating that individual in certain ways—reasons that may differ from those deriving solely from the individual's interests.

NW: *What do you mean by an* intrinsic *property? Could you give an example?*

JM: Sure, the possession of the capacity for self-consciousness, or minimal rationality, or a moral sense. Usually, the foundations of moral status are thought of by most people as psychological capacities of some sort; but some people of a religious inclination think that it might be something like the possession of a soul.

NW: *Does that mean that moral status is all-or-nothing; that you either have it, or you don't?*

JM: There are different ways in which the term is used. Some people use it in that way. I prefer to think of moral status as a matter of degree, and that some individuals have a higher moral status than others. You might think that there are some individuals who have a minimal kind of moral status—that is, they might have sentience, or bare consciousness—and this provides a basis for their having interests, and many philosophers think that our treatment of those beings should be governed solely by a concern for their interests. But their being sentient gives them a moral status that plants lack, though some philosophers claim that plants also have interests.

NW: *So, what you're saying is that there is both a range of statuses that could be occupied by human beings, and that there's a hierarchy. Not all human beings have equal moral status?*

JM: That would be my view. A more common view is that all human beings have the same moral status.

NW: *One finds the idea that people all have the same moral status in Christianity, in Immanuel Kant, and elsewhere: there are lots of philosophers who think that that kind of equality is a starting point for ethics. How do you reach the position that some individuals can have a higher moral status than others?*

JM: One way to do it is to compare human beings with non-human animals. If you look at the candidate properties that people have suggested as the foundation or ground of human moral status, you will find that, in general, there are some human beings who seem to lack those properties, and there are some animals who seem to have them.

NW: *Could you give me an example of two human beings who have radically different moral status?*

JM: Yes. An adult human being with normal psychological capacities, in my view, has a higher moral status than a human foetus that hasn't yet acquired the capacity for consciousness. I think that an adult human being with normal psychological capacities also has a higher moral status than a late-term foetus that does have the capacity for consciousness. I also think that a normal adult human being has a higher moral status than a newborn infant.

NW: *That makes everything much more complicated because if you've got a 'one size fits all' approach to moral status, you could say 'every human being has the same kind of rights, we're all equal'; so when someone has something bad done to them, you know automatically that that is something that shouldn't have happened. It seems to be a consequence of your view that we have to know quite a lot about the victim of an abuse of rights before we can determine how bad the action is.*

JM: Yes, and I think that's quite plausible, and consistent with most people's intuitions. Most of us believe, for example, that the killing of a 10-year-old child is a tragedy; but if we hear about an abortion that kills a foetus a month after conception, most of us won't think that the month-old foetus was the victim of grave wrongdoing, or of a terrible misfortune.

NW: *We're talking in particular about humans and their moral status. When does a human start to exist as a human? Some religious people argue that sperm are sacred, but most people don't believe that. What about a fertilized egg? Is that a human? Don't we face a kind of Sorites problem when we try to identify the point when it becomes a human being? At what point does it start to have any rights at all?*

JM: Most people believe that people like you and me began to exist at conception, when a new living entity came into existence as a result of the fusion of a sperm and an egg cell. It's really quite implausible, metaphysically, to suppose that I ever existed as a sperm or as an egg. However, there are also good arguments against the idea that we began to exist at conception. My view is quite radical. I don't think that we are human organisms at all. I think that we begin to exist when a conscious subject begins to exist in association with the human organism, which occurs about five months into pregnancy. My view is that, before that time, there is a living human organism; but that living human organism, in my case, wasn't me, but was the vehicle through which I came into existence. So I take the same metaphysical and moral view about early human embryos that many people take of a sperm and egg pair prior to conception. I think that an early human embryo is just the physical material out of which someone like you or me may develop.

NW: *That's interesting. That's not unlike what John Locke says about the difference between being a person and being a man, as he put it—by which he meant man or woman. The man is the animal, what you call the organism, which may or may not go together with consciousness. But it's the consciousness that makes us a person, and the consciousness which makes us morally significant to each other.*

JM: That's right. I see my view as being in the Lockean tradition. The view that I hold implies that there are actually two distinct entities sitting in the chair that I'm sitting in at the moment. There's a living human organism and there's me, and if you want to ask, 'Well, what am I?', I'm not a soul or an immaterial substance, or something like that. I am actually a part of my organism. I am the part of my organism that generates consciousness and mental activity. I am, in effect, those parts of my brain in their active, or potentially functional, state which are capable of generating consciousness and mental activity. It's on the basis of that metaphysical view that I believe that we come into existence a little after the middle of pregnancy.

NW: *Well, we come into existence then as conscious beings, but we have the potential to do so before consciousness emerges—and lots of people think that it's the potential that's important. So they may accept your metaphysical account of what it is to be fully human, but still believe that the organism that is the precursor to the conscious being has rights just because it has the potential to become this full human being.*

JM: Well, the organism becomes me only in a rather peculiar sense. It doesn't ever become me in the sense of ever being identical with me; it becomes me in the sense of co-existing with me. The form of potential that is at issue here is what

I call 'non-identity potential', where the thing that has a certain potential actually never will be identical with the thing it has potential to give rise to. Think of the wooden chair that I'm sitting on. If we were to put it through a grinding machine and turn it into sawdust, we might say before that that the chair has the potential to become a pile of sawdust. But once it has fulfilled that potential, it has actually ceased to exist. What exists after we've run the chair through the grinder is a pile of sawdust, not a chair. Now, that doesn't happen in the case of the human organism and the person. The human organism continues to exist in association with the person. It gives rise causally to the existence of the person; but the person, or the conscious subject is, in my view, never actually identical with the organism. So the organism doesn't have the relevant kind of potential in its relation to the later person to have rights on that basis. The relevant kind of potential is what I call 'identity preserving'—it's the kind of potential that Prince Charles has to become the King of England. If Prince Charles becomes the King of England, the King of England will then be identical with Prince Charles in a way that this wooden chair would not be identical with the pile of sawdust that it has the potential to become.

NW: *What does your view entail about the moral status of an early embryo?*

JM: An early embryo, at least after about a fortnight after conception, is a human organism that is in a quite literal sense unoccupied: that is, it's an organism that is not host to a conscious subject or a person like you or me. It is devoid of any intrinsic moral status. It has the same moral status that an individual sperm or an individual egg has. So, if one were to destroy a human embryo, one would not be killing or destroying anybody like you or me; one would be preventing one of us from coming into existence. The destruction of a human embryo is morally indistinguishable, I think, from contraception.

NW: *Does that mean it would be morally acceptable to use, say, aborted embryos for experimentation—perhaps in preference to using sentient animals?*

JM: Yes, that is actually an implication of my view that most people would find morally repugnant—but I think it's actually correct. It is permissible to experiment on embryos, provided they're never going to develop into persons: that is, provided that their maturation is stopped before they ever give rise to the existence of an individual who would have moral status.

NW: *What of a parallel situation; what if somebody who has had the kind of sentience that you were talking about enters a persistent vegetative state? Does that mean that they then have the moral status of an embryo?*

JM: Not entirely. Let me say something first about the metaphysical status of individuals in a persistent vegetative state, and then say something about the moral status of individuals in a persistent vegetative state.

There are different types of vegetative state; in some cases, the physical basis for consciousness in the brain has been irreversibly destroyed. In these cases, in my view, the individual person has ceased to exist. There is a living human organism, but metaphysically it is quite like the embryo in that it is a living human organism that does not sustain the existence of a person. In that kind of case, though, the moral status of the human organism isn't exactly the same as that of an embryo, because the individual who once co-existed with that organism, and whose organism that was, may have had desires about what was to be done to that organism—and I think we have moral reason to honour those preferences, in just the same way that we have reason to honour people's wishes about other matters after they have ceased to exist. When a person ceases to exist, they don't cease to exert moral constraints on us, or moral pressures of certain sorts.

There's another kind of persistent vegetative state, however, in which the brain hasn't irreversibly lost the capacity to support consciousness. In that case, the individual continues to exist, and is still there as a proper subject of moral concern and, arguably, even if this individual has suffered certain sorts of brain damage, retains the same kind of status that he or she had prior to going into the persistent vegetative state. It follows that we should, to the best of our ability, do what's in this individual's interests and honour this individual's autonomous preferences, in so far as we can ascertain what they are.

NW: *Getting these questions right really matters, because it could be somebody's life depending on it. How do you justify your account, which rests so much on this notion of sentience? How do you know you're right?*

JM: You are right that these issues are extremely important. They are also extremely difficult, and a lot of people don't appreciate that. Most people have views about these issues. If you were to ask them to defend those views, they would give you a fairly simplistic response. It took me more than a 500-page book to give the arguments that support my conclusions here, so I'm not actually going to be able to give you the arguments. But that's what you should expect. If you ask me to explain to you the nature of physical reality according to quantum theory and the best contemporary physics, I wouldn't be able to do that simply in five minutes, either. A lot of it has to do with the metaphysics. We need to understand when it is we begin to exist, and when it is we cease to exist. We can't understand that, in my view, until we understand what kind of thing we essentially are. Are we essentially living biological organisms? If I were to pose that question, most people would say yes—but actually most of them don't really believe it, because they believe that they will survive the deaths of their physical organisms. They believe that their physical body will die and disintegrate, but that they will continue to exist.

The view at which I have arrived is that we begin to exist when there is *someone* there, rather than just *something*—someone who has the capacity for consciousness. One has to do some serious metaphysics to have defensible views about when we begin to exist and when we cease to exist. Until one has done that work, one really isn't entitled to strong moral views about the moral status of an embryo, or a human individual in a persistent vegetative state, or indeed a human individual who has been declared brain-dead, but whose vital functions are still being maintained by means of minimal external life support.

Once one has done the metaphysics, then one has to confront challenges to the consistency of one's moral beliefs about the remaining cases. I believe that late-term human foetuses are individuals like you and me, although our natures were very different when we were late-term foetuses or newborn infants. Then our psychological capacities were no higher than those of certain non-human animals. Most people believe that a late-term human foetus has a higher moral status than, say, an adult chimpanzee, even though the chimpanzee's psychological capacities are uniformly higher. They may claim, for example, that that is because the foetus has the potential to have higher capacities than those of the chimpanzee, as you suggested earlier. I don't think that mere potential confers moral status in that way. And, in any case, there are some human foetuses that lack that potential because their brains have failed to form in the necessary ways. But both the metaphysics and the morality are difficult, and I can't be sure I've got them right.

NW: So, what you're saying is that before you can make a judgement about moral status, you have to understand the metaphysics of what it is to be a person. And a consequence of that is that most people aren't actually equipped to make judgements about moral status.

JM: Unfortunately, I think that that's correct. These are issues about human beings (and other animals) whose nature is in some sense non-standard: embryos, foetuses, newborn infants, adults with certain cognitive impairments or radical deficits. These are individuals about whose moral status we should not have confident intuitions and confident moral views. Questions about abortion, the termination of life support, euthanasia, and so on, are really very difficult. We are right to be puzzled about these issues, and people who think that they know the answers and have very strong views about these matters without having addressed the difficult issues in metaphysics and moral theory are, I think, making a mistake. They should be much more sceptical about their own beliefs, and much more tentative about what they are willing to impose on other people through political institutions.

5

JOHN MIKHAIL ON
Universal Moral Grammar

Nigel Warburton: *Most parents know that young children are good at making moral judgements, particularly on issues of fairness. But how do they acquire this ability? Is it all a matter of imitation and instruction picked up in the home and kindergarten, or could there be some kind of innate or universal moral grammar, a human predisposition to structure moral judgements in particular ways? John Mikhail suspects that when it comes to issues of right and wrong, children aren't just blank slates.*

David Edmonds: *Today we're talking about the subject of 'universal moral grammar'. That's a bit of a mouthful. What is universal moral grammar?*

John Mikhail: It *is* a bit of a mouthful. The basic idea is that there might be an innate basis to our moral judgements. When we try to describe what that innate moral knowledge might be, we're describing a system of principles or rules that is perhaps analogous to what linguists who study the innate basis of language call 'universal grammar'.

DE: *So you're referring to the work of Noam Chomsky, a linguist based at the Massachusetts Institute of Technology. Chomsky argues that we all* *have an innate linguistic grammar, and that all languages have the same deep grammatical structure.*

JM: Yes, that's more or less right. Chomsky is probably best known for the work he did in the 1950s, 1960s, and 1970s in developing the idea that the way children learn language cannot be adequately explained by assuming that their knowledge of grammar is simply internalized from their surroundings—from the people whom they encounter, their parents, their friends, and so forth. And the main reason for this conclusion is that children appear to use grammatical rules and principles that are neither explicitly taught nor otherwise given to them by their environment.

DE: *And your contention is that morality parallels language in that way?*

JM: My contention is that morality *might* parallel language in that way. And I emphasize the word 'might' because this is meant to be an empirical hypothesis; it could be false. More broadly, my proposal is that we might be able to make progress in the study of moral judgement by drawing on ideas that have been useful in other domains like language.

DE: *So if the claim that morality has an innate basis is an empirical one, you must have some evidence, I assume. What's your evidence?*

JM: Yes. There's actually a lot of evidence that young children are what I would call 'intuitive lawyers'. They make moral judgements in ways that are surprisingly sophisticated, which seem to rely on the kinds of rules and principles that adults use in their everyday practice, and even on rules and principles that legal systems use. For example, three- and four-year-old children use *intent*—the actors' goal or purpose—to distinguish two acts with the same result. That's something that virtually every legal system does as well.

Likewise, four- and five-year-old children draw a distinction that's quite similar to the distinction that's drawn in law between what are called 'mistakes of fact' and 'mistakes of law'. Let me give you an example of this distinction. Suppose someone shoots and kills another person under the mistaken belief that the other person is a tree stump. Let's imagine that the agent is out on a hunting expedition and he turns and fires his gun, thinking he is shooting at, not a person, but some object. If his mistake was reasonable, that's what lawyers would call a reasonable 'mistake of fact'. Now consider a second case, in which someone shoots and kills another person in the mistaken belief that killing is not wrong. This is a different kind of mistaken belief. It is a mistake about the norm itself, or what lawyers would call a 'mistake of law'.

Ordinary adults would draw an intuitive distinction between these two cases. The first case could result in a kind of justification or excuse, or perhaps an acquittal on other grounds, because the agent lacks the intent necessary to form a criminal act. We certainly would not think of someone who makes such an error as a murderer. The second case strikes us as quite different. It's not a justification or excuse to say, 'I just don't think killing is wrong.'

Legal systems distinguish cases like these, of course, but what is interesting and noteworthy is that young children also apparently draw this distinction; moreover, they appear to do so in different cultural contexts. That's the kind of evidence to which I'm referring when I suggest that young children are intuitive lawyers, who possess tacit knowledge of an abstract system of moral rules, or what we are calling a moral grammar.

DE: *But how do you know that kids aren't picking those rules up from their parents, either explicitly or just by watching how their parents judge and behave?*

JM: That's a very good question. The first answer I would give is that they could be. In this sense, an empiricist theory of moral learning could turn out to be correct. These are tricky issues, and the only way to confront them is by studying child development in detail. Are children actually being taught these kinds of distinctions or does this behaviour go beyond their experience? If researchers can line up case after case after case in which children act like intuitive lawyers—that is, they display a sense of right and wrong that is sophisticated and seems to go beyond their experience—then this evidence can strengthen the argument that there is some kind of innate basis to their moral judgements.

DE: *What about cross-cultural evidence? Presumably, there's evidence that morality operates in pretty much the same way in cultures as varied as those in the United States, India, and China?*

JM: Here we have to draw a distinction, right off the bat, between behaviour and perception. There's no question that the anthropological record suggests a wide variety of practices in the domain of moral behaviour. On the other hand, the question that we're considering now is whether intuitive moral perceptions and judgements—which are only one component of why people act the way they do—have a shared basis across cultures. If one keeps this distinction in mind, then it will be more plausible to conclude that there may be cross-cultural evidence for a shared moral grammar.

One obvious point to consider in this context concerns the very notion of human rights. For some time now, people from different cultures around the world have been able to reach at least some agreement on basic norms of conduct, despite quite substantial differences in culture, language, and religious or philosophical backgrounds. This kind of phenomenon, universal human rights, has no counterpart in the case of language. What it suggests is that there may be more uniformity, universality, and built-in constraint in the moral domain than there is in the case of natural language.

DE: *And yet, some people might say, for example, 'Well, in Singapore, they are much less committed to free speech than they are in the United States. That's just a fact about their culture.'*

JM: Yes. That's a very important point. The best case for a shared moral grammar at the level of what is acquired by each individual is probably not going to involve norms about freedom of speech or other complicated norms that depend on institutions. Instead, it will concern the kind of pre-political normative principles that one typically finds in fields like criminal law, contract law, or tort law, basic norms that explain when it is wrong or permissible to harm one another, what kinds of harms might be justifiable, what are the obligations that derive from promises and mutual agreement, and other similar fact patterns.

DE: *So, you've got the evidence from children. You've got the evidence from shared cross-cultural moral values. Does that exhaust the empirical evidence for universal moral grammar?*

JM: I don't think so. Here, again, it's important to draw a distinction between the acquired moral grammar possessed by each individual and what we're calling universal moral grammar, which is the supposed innate basis for that acquired grammar. Let's just stick for a moment to the acquired moral grammar: the abstract system of moral rules and principles that each adult presumably carries around unconsciously in his or her mind. Well, there are many reasons to infer that each individual possesses such a system.

One argument to make in this context is what philosophers call an 'abductive' argument. The argument begins from the observation that ordinary individuals can make moral judgements about brand new situations, situations they've never encountered before. In the law, these are sometimes called 'cases of first impression'. The fact is that most people can do this: that is, they are capable of making moral judgements about these novel fact patterns. The argument for moral grammar holds that the best explanation of this behaviour must appeal to some kind of system of rules and principles. The moral judgements people make are too stable, too systematic, too widely shared, and too predictable for these judgements to be made on a case-by-case basis, without the support or guidance of rules or principles.

DE: *Can you explain that a bit more? You're suggesting that, although all of us have had different experiences in making moral choices in the past, when we're faced with a brand-new case, we reliably and predictably reach a particular conclusion.*

JM: Yes, that's right. It is often the case that people know the right thing to do in a given situation, even though they've never encountered that situation. The other point to emphasize here is that moral judgement is *intuitive*. For some time, philosophers may have operated under the mistaken impression that moral judgements are typically produced by the conscious application of rules and principles. But that doesn't seem to be accurate in many situations. We're frequently not aware that we're applying rules or principles when we make moral judgements. Nonetheless, the cognitive scientist can, after the fact, explain our moral judgements—or maybe even before the fact predict our moral judgements—by assuming that we're relying on rules or principles.

DE: *So give me an example of a new moral case where we are faced with a choice between various options and where we choose the option consistent with a rule that we might even be unaware of.*

JM: Sure. Some of the best examples concern the so-called 'trolley problems'. These are moral dilemmas, somewhat bizarre, and often highly artificial. Yet the surprising fact is that there appears to be widespread agreement, even around the world, on the permissible conduct in the given circumstances.

Let me give you two cases. The first case is sometimes called the 'bystander problem'. A train is rushing down the tracks and it's about to run over and kill five people. There's a bystander who is watching this happen, and he is standing next to a switch. The bystander can throw the switch, which will turn the train onto a sidetrack and save the five people from being killed. There's one person on the sidetrack, however, and if the train is turned, that one person will be run over and killed. The moral question is: is it permissible for the bystander to turn the train?

That's the kind of situation that most of us don't encounter in our daily life. Yet it turns out that the vast majority of people have a shared response. They respond in a more or less utilitarian fashion and say, 'Yes, it's permissible to turn the train.' In that kind of situation, if there are no better alternatives, then it's permissible to do something that would result in one death, rather than five. That's the better choice under the circumstances.

The second case might involve a surgeon who has five patients who are dying; each patient is in need of a different organ to survive. And the only way to save these five would be to cut up a healthy individual and distribute her organs to the five. Would it be permissible to do this, assuming the healthy individual did not consent? Very few people believe it would be.

Or imagine an even closer parallel to the first trolley problem. Suppose the train is rushing towards five people and the only way to save them would be to throw a heavy man off a footbridge in front of the train in order to stop it from crashing into the five. The heavy man would die, but the five people on the tracks would be saved. Would it be permissible to throw the man? Again, very few people believe that it would be, even though they may not be able to explain just why this case differs from the original bystander problem.

DE: *That's fascinating because in each of these train cases we are given the option of killing one to save five. But we think it's acceptable to kill one person on the side-track in the first scenario, but not the heavy individual in the second. We draw this distinction, and we may not know why we draw it.*

JM: That's correct. Beginning in the mid-1990s, my colleagues Elizabeth Spelke, Cristina Sorrentino, and I began studying these kinds of questions experimentally. And in addition to asking people for their intuitive moral judgements, we asked them to justify their judgements. We discovered that people are often incapable of giving an adequate explanation or justification of their judgements. They often say things like, 'I don't know why I decided differently in the second case.' Or they might say something self-deprecating like, 'I know what I said is not rational, but it's what I feel nonetheless.'

The critical point, however, is that these judgements *can* be explained with reference to principles or rules. For example, one way to explain the difference between these cases would be to appeal to the concept of battery. This simple norm, which one finds in legal systems throughout the world, prohibits intentionally causing harmful contact with another person without his or her consent. One key difference in all of the standard trolley problems, including the examples I just gave, is that in the permissible cases (such as the bystander problem) the actor commits battery only as a side-effect of achieving the good end of saving the five, whereas in the impermissible cases (such as the transplant or footbridge problems), the actor necessarily has to commit a battery as a means to achieve his good end. So, stepping back, one might say that the moral grammar, at least in part, consists of ethical rules that are sensitive to whether battery is being committed as a means to an end, or merely as a side-effect.

DE: *That appears to give us another parallel with language. We might be able to speak a language fluently, but if we were asked why we follow a particular rule, why we say the 'big, blue elephant' and not the 'blue, big elephant', for example, we might not be able to explain it, and yet linguists can tell us what rules we're following.*

JM: Yes, that's correct. In the case of language, the argument for universal grammar is basically a two-step argument. First, we have to appeal to unconscious rules to explain linguistic behaviour. Second, we might appeal to innate knowledge to explain how those rules are acquired. It's important not to conflate those two parts of the argument.

As to the first part, Chomsky's most famous example is a nice illustration of what you're talking about. Take a sentence like 'Colourless green ideas sleep furiously.' Well, that's a meaningless sentence. How can an idea be colourless and green at the same time? What does it mean for an idea to sleep furiously? The expression has an aspect of poetry to it, but it's semantically nonsensical. Nonetheless, Chomsky's point was that it's a well-formed sentence of English, at the level of syntax.

Contrast this case with another expression, in which the same five words are read backwards, 'Furiously sleep ideas green colourless.' That's not a well-formed sentence of English. Why not? Well, the explanation here might appeal to an unconscious rule that ordinary speakers of English possess, which says, in effect, 'If I encounter a construction that has the following grammar: adjective, adjective, noun, verb, adverb— that's going to seem acceptable to me. Whereas if I encounter a construction in which the same grammatical categories run in the opposite direction, that's not going to be a good sentence.' And we might think of the parallel to the moral case as drawing insight from this situation, in which there appear to be unconscious rules that explain our perceptual and cognitive behaviour. We don't have introspective access to these rules, but nonetheless, by appealing to these rules, we can successfully predict and explain people's moral judgements.

DE: *In the last decade or so neuroscience has flourished, and we now have access to quite sophisticated brain scanning. Does any of this cast light on whether or not we have universal moral grammar?*

JM: Yes, I think it does. All of these areas of research—child development, anthropology, philosophy of mind, neuroscience, and so forth—we can think of as supplying more pieces of the puzzle. No one piece proves the case, but collectively this body of evidence supports the plausibility of the thesis that human beings may possess an innate moral grammar.

In the past few years, quite exciting research has begun to identify the regions of the brain that appear responsible for various components of moral judgement. An obvious example to consider here would be—again, appealing to the law—the difference between what lawyers call *mens rea* and *actus reus*, or the guilty mind and the guilty act. In the criminal law, you typically need a concurrence of both the mental state component (the guilty mind) and the action component (the guilty act) in order to have a completed or fully fledged crime, which can warrant conviction. Brain scientists are now starting to find the regions of the brain that seem to be especially active in the way that we generate representations of *mens rea*: that is, of criminal intent or other mental states. If the moral grammar theory postulates that this is an important distinction, and this proposal leads scientists to examine how the brain processes mental state information and eventually to discover that there are specific regions of the brain that are primarily responsible for generating these representations, then that discovery would tend to support the moral grammar theory a bit more than if we didn't possess this evidence.

DE: *You say that the question of whether there's a universal grammar hasn't been fully determined yet. But I suspect that you think there is one. Now, if there is a universal moral grammar and if humans operate on a set of moral rules, perhaps very sophisticated rules, does that imply that we could train a computer to operate according to the same principles and come to the same moral judgements that a human being comes to?*

JM: That's a very interesting question. A couple of points to bear in mind here; first, the kinds of studies that moral psychologists have carried out thus far typically deal with very simple cases. So if you were to ask me, 'Could we design a computer that could handle many or most of the moral problems that we, as individuals or as a society, face in our daily lives?' I would answer: 'I'm sceptical.' However, if we consider a more specific question, then the answer might be different. Suppose you were to say, 'Here is a set of crimes. Can you design a computer to make judgements about the permissibility of the conduct in this small sub-set of cases?' Well, the answer there is probably 'yes'. In fact, we know that in liberal legal systems the answer almost certainly must be yes. Because the fact is that liberal legal systems are committed to codifying all of the criminal acts ahead of time. The principal of legality in the law says that there's no crime without law, no punishment without law, and no retroactive punishment. Liberal societies such as ours have already accepted the idea that at least some of our moral life can be codified. And if it can be codified, then, in principle, a computer could presumably carry out those operations.

DE: *Do you have kids?*

JM: I have two children.

DE: *What part are you playing in their moral upbringing?*

JM: (Laughter). I began working on these ideas before I had a family and children, and I think I've changed my mind a bit about the importance of instruction and explicit moral guidance. I used to think that the development of moral competence was more or less on auto-pilot, so that it was just going to happen, like growing an arm or a leg. After the experience of raising children, I don't think I would so casually affirm the same thesis anymore. But I still do believe that there is an innate basis to the sense of right and wrong, for the reasons I have indicated here and elaborated elsewhere in print. And the fact is that my kids and other kids are doing surprising things in the area of moral judgement all the time. In some respects, children often look like geniuses, making judgements on the basis of rules that they haven't been taught. So, I still do believe that the hypothesis of innate moral knowledge is plausible and worthy of serious consideration. And I'm excited and intrigued about the fact that many recent developments in cognitive science appear to be pointing in this general direction.

6

RAIMOND GAITA ON
Torture

David Edmonds: *There's a ticking bomb, and the only way the police can find out how to defuse it is to torture the terrorist who's planted it—thousands of lives are at stake. In such a scenario, is torture legitimate? Many philosophers enjoy debating such questions. But not Rai Gaita. Society, he says, is defined, in part, by what it refuses to debate. And he regrets that the question of whether torture is ever legitimate has even been raised.*

Nigel Warburton: *The topic we're focusing on is torture, specifically, the justification of state torture. Can you tell me how you got into thinking philosophically about torture?*

Rai Gaita: I began thinking about this when Alan Dershowitz, an academic lawyer at Harvard, published *Why Terrorism Works: Understanding the Threat, Responding to the Challenge*. He argued that citizens in democratic nations like the US, Britain, and so on, should consent to the torture of suspected terrorists, done openly, under law, when there is good reason to believe it would save many—perhaps thousands—of lives. I was shocked and incredulous. I had assumed that in western democracies there was no longer a case for torture that could be taken seriously, no more than there is, in those democracies, a 'case' for stoning women who have committed adultery.

Dershowitz on the other hand—and many people agreed with him—was incredulous that his opponents could be so irresponsibly intoxicated by an ideal of absolute value that they would refuse to take his case seriously. Generations of philosophers, after all, had discussed scenarios like that of 'the ticking bomb'. Now, however, no one could say these were merely fantastical examples.

I became interested in how best to characterize this dispute: to explore the complex relations between morality, law, and politics, to ask what place, if any, the idea that some things are undiscussable should play in a sober conception of public reason.

I also wondered what had changed since the Convention against Torture and other Cruel, Inhuman, and Degrading Treatment or Punishment came into force in 1987. 'Terrorism, stupid', someone might say. I don't think it is so simple.

Confronted in the twentieth century with politically motivated mass murder by the right and the left and by genocide in the heart of Europe, in Asia, in Africa, and in Central America (Guatemala), no one who was even moderately politically informed could have failed to realize how important it is for states to safeguard the lives of their citizens. Yet that, often bitter, realization prompted no one then seriously to propose publicly that torture should be one of the means with which to do it. To the contrary, that same blood-soaked century saw the development of international law, which included the prohibition of torture without exception. Could anyone seriously believe that those who drafted the Convention did not anticipate that compliance with it would almost certainly cause lives to be lost that would otherwise have been saved? To believe that would be to believe that they were moral and political dilettantes. And though governments have a defining obligation to protect the lives of their citizens, they also require their citizens to risk their lives in combat. For the most part, their citizens consent, not in order to create, or preserve political circumstances in which fewer lives would be lost in the future, but for the sake of Freedom and Dignity (capitals intended), values that often define their political identity. Like many others, I have pointed out that terrorists threaten only our lives: to save our lives, governments have threatened some of our deepest values. Some citizens consented to this. Others protested that in 'the war against terror' they are prepared to die for those values. They do not think of this as a constraint on the protection of the national interest: they think it is intrinsic to a richer conception of the national interest that citizens should be able to love their country without shame. They invited their fellow citizens to join them in a different kind of 'coalition of the willing'.

I have come to suspect, however, that there is an important difference—one that defines the nature of politics—between, on the one hand, being prepared to face death to protect political values like liberty, equality, the freedom to speak one's native tongue and to honour one's history without falsification, and on the other refusing to do evil 'though good may come of it'. Perhaps that explains the bitter political tone of *Gorgias*, Plato's dialogue in which Socrates professes, and, I think, introduced into western moral and political thought, the affirmation that it is better to suffer evil than to do it. His incredulous interlocutors scorned him for being so shameless as to refuse to do what was necessary to protect himself and, more importantly, those who were dependent on him if only evil means were available to him to do so. With M. M. McCabe I conducted a seminar on *Gorgias* at King's College London just after September 11. The atmosphere in that seminar was electric. Everyone knew what was at stake.

NW: *So, you seem to be suggesting that state torture is one of those things that is undiscussable in a civilized society? But, surely, you need an argument for that, not just an assertion.*

RG: Certainly, there should be discussion of whether some things are unthinkable. It is striking that there hasn't been such a discussion, even though, on the face of it, you can tell what kind of person someone is partly by what she finds morally unthinkable, and the character of a nation by noting what is undiscussable in it. However, it goes deep in our political culture and our intellectual tradition to believe that we should be open to being persuaded of any position for which a strong argument appears to have been mounted. But is it always a good thing to be open to persuasion? After all, it is not good to be open to persuasion that the earth is flat, or that one can read one's future in coffee grounds, or that Elvis is still alive and working for the CIA. To have an open mind on these matters shows that one is gullible, which is no virtue; it betrays a failure of judgement that undermines the capacity for radical critique that we hope will be achieved by always having an open mind. Some forms of open-mindedness are aptly caricatured in the joke that tells of a person whose mind was so open that his brain fell through.

Morally, too, there are things about which one should not have an open mind because one should fear to be the kind of person who believes them and takes them into her life. It is not

53

a moral or intellectual virtue to have an open mind about ethnic cleansing, genocide, castrating male paedophiles, or stoning women to death for adultery—to believe that a case might be made for such evils and that one should be open to being persuaded by it. But none of these have been shown to be false by something we could justifiably call moral knowledge. Nothing interesting in morality could be written up in text books or encyclopaedias of morality. If there could be textbooks of moral knowledge, then we could have Nobel laureates of morality and moral whiz kids.

If I'm right, it is not dogmatic to refuse to be open to persuasion about those matters. I'd go further, indeed, to argue that it is a criterion of moral seriousness not to be open to persuasion about some matters. It is a conceptual truth, a truth we can discern merely by reflecting on the concept of moral value, that a person must take seriously the moral values that she professes. To refuse to be open to some moral views is intrinsic to the kind of seriousness that defines morality and distinguishes it from other kinds of value.

NW: *Another way of formulating what you're saying is that those who want to justify torture see it as a means to an end. They're prepared to engage in a consequentialist analysis—to assess whether torture can be justified by its consequences. Whereas those who want to have an absolute prohibition on torture believe that it should not be tolerated, whether or not there are good consequences that might ensue from it—whether or not it saves thousands of lives.*

RG: Dershowitz is not a consequentialist, and I suspect that many people who think that their government should torture people when there is good reason to believe it would save many lives also think (if only implicitly) that consequentialism does not give a good account of political responsibility—the kind that Max Weber had in mind when he distinguished an 'ethics of absolute ends' from an 'ethics of responsibility'. Many of them, I am sure, believe that we must sometimes do evil to prevent a greater evil, even though the evil we are obliged to commit—the 'lesser' evil—is morally terrible. No consequentialist can believe that we can be obliged to do what is morally terrible.

NW: *In assessing the consequences of torture, there's one knock-down argument that people try to use against it—which is to say, 'torture just doesn't work'. And that's the reason why it's prudentially wrong to use it. Faced with the threat of pain or actual pain, most people, at some point, will say anything, true or false. So information from torture is unreliable.*

RG: That claim is more controversial than people who make it generally allow. The moral restrictions placed on torture by those who have defended it are high, so high, indeed, that people have justifiably ridiculed ticking bomb scenarios as belonging only to a political fairyland. But it is worth noting in this regard that Dershowitz was influenced by an Israeli commission of inquiry that successfully recommended that the use of 'moderate physical pressure' become lawful so that Israeli law could realistically allow the security services to protect the state, while at the same time controlling their excess. Yitzhak Rabin, who was then prime minster, complained that the security services could not operate effectively to prevent terrorist attacks if they were restricted to the forms of interrogation the commission allowed them. I assume he knew what he was talking about. Whether you regard torture as a useful means of getting information depends on what you are able and prepared to do to reduce the chances that people who are tortured will say anything to stop the torture. If you are prepared to torture their loved ones (which some nations are) and to accept a high level of 'collateral damage', then torture would probably be sufficiently effective to warrant its use alongside other methods.

NW: *Another kind of anti-torture argument concerns the intrinsic dignity or autonomy of individuals: this claim often has a Kantian underpinning. The eighteenth-century German philosopher, Immanuel Kant, said that you should not treat other people as means to an end.*

RG: Most, perhaps all, people who justify torture place moral constraints on when it is justified. They would therefore say that they have satisfied the imperative that one should never treat another human being *only* as a means to one's ends. It is also important to note that most Kantians did not argue that torture is never justified because it offends against the intrinsic or inalienable dignity of its victims. They argued that the concept of inalienable dignity reveals what kind of violation torture is; reveals why we should count torture as a violation whose character cannot fully be accounted for by the pain and psychological trauma it causes. Another way of putting it would be to say that they thought that to show torture to be a violation of the intrinsic dignity of its victim would be to show why it is morally terrible, even when we are obliged to do it.

The way we now speak about intrinsic dignity, inalienable dignity, or Dignity with a capital 'D', distinguishing it from the dignity that is so obviously lost when a person is tortured, owes more to Kant that to the Catholic natural law tradition, which also has a conception of the dignity of humanity. Such phrases occur in many of the preambles to instruments of international law and are presumably intended to indicate how we should elaborate what it means morally to commit acts proscribed by those instruments. They have great rhetorical power for us, but most people who respond to that power would have little idea of what to make of the claim that its moral force rests on the respect owed to rational agency. Imagine if a remorseful torturer were to say, 'My God! What have I done? I have violated the rational agency of this poor wretch.' Of course, that is a parody, and parodies can be unjust, but this one should alert us to something: an explanation is required as to why an account that is intended to make perspicuous to reason the distinctive seriousness of doing something morally terrible, looks like a parody.

NW: *So, you're saying that Kant is too cerebral—the argument that torture doesn't respect somebody's rationality doesn't encapsulate what's wrong with torture.*

RG: Yes and no. Kant is a magnificent example of a philosopher who believes that when we think about the great matters of morality and politics, the cognitive content of one's thought, the content that is strictly answerable to reason and truth, should always be, in principle, extractable from the form of its presentation. Much of my work has articulated reasons for believing that separation emaciates art (especially literature) and philosophy. My argument has not been only that the discursive thought characteristic of philosophy should be more respectful of art. It has been the more radical argument—that when we reflect on our critical responses to art and to life, when, for example, we reflect on whether we have been moved by something in art or in life only because we have succumbed to pathos or to sentimentality—then such reflection can yield a richer conception of discursive thought, one in which feeling and thought, form and content cannot be separated. Obviously, I can't elaborate on that here, but were I able to do so, I would explain why my parody of what remorse looks like when one moves from talk of inalienable dignity to its Kantian grounding in respect for rational agency is not unjust. It matters to have an ear for tone—for what, as Bernard Williams put it, 'rings true'. I would go further than Williams to say that the acknowledgment that discussions must 'ring true' should, in ethics, be part of a conception of what it is to try to see things as they are, rather than as they appear from any number of bad perspectives, of what it is be legitimately persuaded by considerations and, therefore, of what it is for truth and truthfulness to matter in this realm. That is why I hesitated to reply flatly, yes or no, to your question.

NW: *Torture involves a terrible combination of pain or threat of pain, helplessness, and degradation. What more can a philosopher do than emit a response of 'Yuck, that's a disgusting practice and one that we cannot tolerate?'*

RG: There is a lot philosophers can do to help us to see the many things at issue in contemporary disagreements about torture, the many perspectives on what is at issue, and how best to discuss them. To counter strong cultural and political forces that push us towards oversimplification, we need to draw many and fine distinctions.

Allow me to give another example, which I hope illustrates the complexity of the relations between morality, law, and politics. It will take us back to your opening remark—that we are thinking about torture committed by states in what they believe to be their national interest. That was assumed in most of the recent discussions, of course, but the focus on those discussions was almost exclusively on the lives of individuals. If that were all that was at issue, we could, as I suggested earlier, point out to our politicians that we are prepared to risk our lives, rather than to secure them at such moral cost.

Sometimes, however, if a political community suffers many and repeated terrorist attacks, as Israel did during the 1980s, those attacks threaten more than the lives of its citizens: they threaten the very conditions of civic life, of political communality indeed. In an article in the *Guardian*, the Israeli novelist David Grossman wrote that in such circumstances terror is 'a decomposition enzyme'. 'A country that fights terror', he said, 'fights not only for the physical security of its citizens. It also fights for their reason to live, for their humanity, for everything that makes them human and civilized.' In such circumstances, politicians will insist that it is 'necessary' to be prepared to do morally terrible things in order to protect the conditions of political communality, and they will ask their citizens to consent to such deeds, not as individual human beings, but as citizens mindful of the distinctive nature of political ethics. It might now be apparent that I think of the ethical, more or less as Bernard Williams suggested we do, as a realm in which we think about how we should live—about morality, of course, but also about law and politics, and other distinctive forms of value, in complex ways interconnected but not merely variants of one another: indeed, they may sometimes conflict.

In a fine paper in which he discusses the justification that people like Dershowitz and other American jurists offered, after September 11, for the legalization of torture in certain circumstances, the legal philosopher Jeremy Waldron says he was ashamed at the dishonour they had brought on American jurisprudence because they had proposed something which is entirely contrary to the spirit of 'our form of law', as he puts it. The prohibition against torture he says, is emblematic of the spirit of that law: 'Law', he writes, expressing not a statement of fact, but what he believes is the essence of 'our' law, 'is not brutal in its operation; law is not savage; law does not rule through abject fear and terror, or by breaking the will of those whom it confronts. If law is forceful or coercive, it gets its way by methods which respect rather than mutilate the dignity and agency of those who are its subjects.'

If I understand him, Waldron believes that breaking the will of a person by torture is always morally terrible, but he believes in addition that the jurists he criticized had dishonoured not only morality, but also the law as expressive of a value *sui generis*. For him, the law against torture has an ineliminable moral dimension, but it is not exhausted by that dimension, or by that dimension together with other practical concerns that could be characterized without reference to irreducibly legal concepts.

I hope that enables us to see how someone who believes that torture could be justified morally, might nonetheless oppose it becoming lawful, not because of the prudential reasons for which such a stand is often justified—the bad consequences that might ensure were it to become lawful—but because she believes, as Waldron does, that torture is an offence against the essential nature and dignity of law. And a politician might believe, without inconsistency, that torture can never be morally justified and that it is an offence against the sprit of law but that, nonetheless, in certain circumstances it must be done, not only to protect lives, but, as I said earlier, to protect the very conditions of political communality. Torn between incommensurable imperatives, one political the other moral, she might say that, if they are true to the responsibilities of their vocation, politicians must sometimes do what morally they must not do. To think that the conflicting imperatives must be moral imperatives if they are truly answerable to a serious conception of responsibility is, I think, to be in the grip of a moralistic conception of responsibility. It would also be a mistake to think that because the political imperative overrides the moral one for the politician, her elaboration of why it does so—an elaboration intended to reveal the distinctive responsibility her vocation has placed on her—must be intended as a justification for what she intends to do or has done. To insist that it must be offered as justification is to fail to understand the nature of tragedy. This is, I know, very controversial. I cannot defend it in this interview. I have mapped a conceptual terrain, hoping to reveal the difficulties in navigating it.

NW: *Would it be fair to encapsulate your view on this matter as this: we can salvage something from Kant. What we can salvage is some kind of respect for humanity, and this respect should be embodied in our civic institutions?*

RG: The idea that every human being possesses an inalienable dignity to which we owe an unconditional respect is, in certain contexts, a sublime one—when, for example, it requires us to respect unconditionally the human dignity of even radical evil doers—people who have committed the most foul deeds, who are entirely unrepentant of them, whose characters appear as foul as their deeds and in whom we can find nothing from which remorse might grow. But in some contexts the affirmation that there is a form of dignity that survives the most radical degradation, when alienable dignity is entirely lost, tries to express something wonderful but fails to do it.

An example might help to explain what I mean. It comes from Primo Levi's book, *If This is a Man*. Levi and a friend, Charles, were prisoners in Auschwitz. They could hear the Russian artillery and therefore had reason to believe that they might soon be liberated. In the barrack with them was a young man, Lakmaker, who had dysentery and who fell out of his bunk to lie on the floor in his faeces and vomit. Levi writes:

Charles climbed down from his bed and dressed in silence. While I held the lamp he cut all the dirty patches from the straw mattress and the blankets with a knife, he lifted Ladmaker from the ground with the tenderness of a mother, cleaned him as best as possible with straw taken from the mattress and lifted him into the remade bed in the only position in which the unfortunate fellow could lie. He scraped the floor with a scrap of tin plate, diluted a little chloramine and finally, spread disinfectant over everything including himself.[1]

Charles' behaviour is something to wonder at, but it can elicit two kinds of wonder. The first is directed towards him and his virtues: it is inspired by the fact he risked his life after years in Auschwitz, with freedom probably only weeks away, for the sake of someone who would almost certainly die, perhaps that same day. From the perspective of that kind of wonder, one

---

[1] Primo Levi, *If This is A Man* and *Truce*, trans. Stuart Wolf (London: Abacus, 2011), p. 173.

would rightly call Charles' behaviour supererogatory—'above and beyond the call of duty'. The second kind of wonder is quite different. It is inspired by the fact that Charles responded 'with the tenderness of a mother', which focuses our attention more on Lakmaker than on him. Supererogatory acts show us what people are capable of. They are, to exaggerate only a little, moral *feats* that leave us awestruck. Heroic deeds are their paradigm. Many people speak of saints and heroes in the same breath, but the works of saintly love do not leave us awestruck at the capacities of saints to do what they do. Instead, they illuminate the world for us, and in the case of deeds like Charles', they reveal to us, or remind us, that even people who are radically and incurably afflicted are infinitely precious. But if that is true, then to say that when Charles responded to Ladmaker 'with the tenderness of a mother', he responded to his inalienable dignity, visible even in such degrading affliction, is to speak in the wrong key—the heroic and noble key in which talk of inalienable dignity and so much else in Kant often moves us. For that reason, I suggest that we do what comes naturally and call the understanding shown in Charles' tenderness a form of love. Levi gives us no reason to believe that Charles was a religious man. Levi certainly was not. I am not. I hope though that you will understand why I call what Charles did a work of 'saintly love'.

Torture is the radical denial of what moves us in Levi's story. A torturer assaults that to which Charles responded in Ladmaker and which exists in every human being. It can reduce a person to the point where someone who responded to them as fully human, as though their humanity had not been radically diminished, would inspire the same kind of wonder in us as Charles does.

If I am right to say that the humanity of a radically degraded victim of torture is fully visible only to saintly love of the kind shown by Charles, then a torturer could not fully understand the evil he does, even when he does it believing it to be his duty. Yet, it is essential to the idea that torture is a lesser evil that we may be obliged to commit, that we could fully understand the evil we do to the person we torture. Only if the person's humanity remains fully visible to us is that possible. The paradoxical conclusion then is that only a saint could respond fully to the humanity of a degraded victim of torture. But a saint, we know, could not be a torturer or agree to torture.

NW: *So what are the implications for your arguments on how our civic organizations should be run?*

RG: Institutions of government and other civic institutions are often complicit in or actually encourage the dehumanization of some of their citizens and also the citizens of other nations when they denigrate them in jingoistic fervour. At first sight, dehumanizing people seems itself a gross offence against morality, but it is more basic than that. It creates the conditions under which their humanity is no longer fully visible to us because in those conditions we find it difficult to see that anything they can do or suffer could go deep in their lives, and therefore that they could be wronged as 'we' can be. Racism is an obvious example.

In *A Common Humanity: Thinking about Love and Truth and Justice*, I argued that a concern for justice is, in large part, a concern that our institutions encourage us to see, and to be fully responsive to, the full humanity of our fellow citizens, including those who threaten to kill us without mercy. More often than

64

not, our institutions fail in this, but it is not a demand we make only of saints. We make it—and it is essential to the institutions of civil society that we make it—of our fellow citizens. In our political and other public institutions—prisons, detention centres, mental hospitals, and homes for the aged, for example—no one should be so alienated from their ordinary, alienable dignity, that only a saint could respond to them with a compassion that was not spoilt by condescension or even an undertone of contempt.

My argument would be to the conclusion that, if we are to respond truthfully to affliction, it is imperative that we disengage our moral and political vocabulary from the illusion that even the most radically afflicted retain a dignity that their degradation cannot take from them—dignity that should be visible to us when our reason is not distorted by psychological and moral failings of one kind or another.

7

GARY L. FRANCIONE ON
Animal Abolitionism

David Edmonds: *Some philosophers change the world. Peter Singer's writings helped launch the animal welfare movement, sometimes called the Animal Rights Movement. Singer believed that we should take animal suffering seriously, that to dismiss animal pain, merely because it was animal and not human, was what he called 'speciesism'. Gary Francione of Rutgers University argues that Singer, and those like him who want to improve animal welfare, are utterly misguided, but not because they're too radical, quite the contrary.*

Nigel Warburton: *We're going to talk about animal abolitionism. Perhaps you could just begin by explaining what that is.*

Gary Francione: A little bit of history: for the past 200 years, our approach to animal ethics has been the animal welfare approach, the notion that it's alright to use animals as long as we treat them 'humanely'. This goes back to Jeremy Bentham. Bentham argued that animals can suffer, and that this suffering is morally relevant, but that animals aren't self-aware—they don't care *that* we use them, they only care about *how* we use them—and so we could continue to use animals as human resources as long as we treated them in a 'humane' manner.

We cannot inflict 'unnecessary' suffering. But we don't question use; we only discuss treatment. The modern animal movement is still stuck in that paradigm. If you look at the modern animal movement, which is dominated very much by the thinking of Peter Singer and these large animal charities that follow Singer's approach, no one is really challenging the use of animals. They're saying instead that we need to engage in compassionate consumption—'happy' meat, free-range eggs, things of that nature—and that really, the difference between the classical animal welfare view and the modern animal protection position, or whatever you want to call it, is that we've got to do a better job in providing 'humane' treatment, that we haven't done a very good job, we need to do it better. With the abolitionist approach that I've been developing, the primary component is that we really can't justify *any* animal use, and 'humane' treatment is a fantasy, on a par with Santa Claus, Easter Bunny rabbits, and things of that nature: silly. Humane treatment is impossible.

NW: *The welfare approach seems quite plausible to me. We know that animals have different kinds of capacities for suffering; they don't all have the same nervous systems. Higher mammals are presumably much more able to suffer in a way analogous to human beings than, say, an invertebrate. What's wrong with that approach?*

GF: Most of the animals we exploit are unquestionably sentient. I don't think we can say that the suffering of animals who are closer to us counts more than the suffering of other sentient beings, without begging the question about whether we can justify attaching greater moral weight to animals who are more 'like us', any more than we can attach greater weight to the interests of humans based on race or sex. And as far as our conventional wisdom on animal ethics is concerned, that sort of similarity shouldn't matter anyway. Most of us accept that we shouldn't inflict *unnecessary* suffering on animals. What do we mean by that? We could have an interesting discussion about what necessity means, but if the principle that we should not inflict unnecessary suffering means anything, surely it means that we shouldn't inflict suffering for reasons of pleasure, amusement, or convenience. Well, that rules out about 99.99999 per cent of our animal use, which is transparently frivolous. When you are deciding what to eat tonight, you won't be in any situation of compulsion or necessity, you'll be making decisions, life-and-death decisions, based on nothing more compelling than palate pleasure. When you choose clothes, your decision will be based on fashion sense, or things of that nature. As a matter of fact, the use of animals in experiments, which I object to completely, is the only use of animals that is not transparently frivolous. Everything else *is* transparently frivolous. So, therefore, if we take seriously the notion that we are not to inflict unnecessary suffering on animals, and we apply it to the issue of animal use, rather than beg the question and assume that wholly unnecessary uses are acceptable, the first thing we've all got to do is go vegan. We kill 56 billion land animals each year—that doesn't include aquatic animals. None of that is necessary. We're not in a situation where it is us or them. There's something peculiar about talking about the moral status of animals when we're killing and eating them and have no good reason whatsoever.

NW: *But isn't an amoeba much closer to a plant in terms of its capacity to feel pain than, say, a chimpanzee?*

GF: I don't think an amoeba is sentient. By sentience I mean subjective perceptual awareness. It may be difficult to draw the line. I recently have been having discussions with people about molluscs—these may be difficult cases. I don't eat any molluscs because I err in favour of assuming that they're sentient: there seems to be some evidence for that. When I walk, I try not to walk on grass so that I don't kill insects. I don't know whether insects are sentient, but I do know that fish and lobsters and pigs and cows and chickens, and all of the animals we routinely exploit, and all of the mice and rats that are used in laboratories, they are all sentient, perceptually aware, they value their lives, they have an interest in continuing to live: that is, they prefer, desire, or want to continue to live.

NW: *One of the common arguments in this area is that human beings have language and a capacity to reflect on their own experience, and that puts them into a special moral category. What you're suggesting is that we should lump all sentient beings together.*

GF: Yes and no. I'm not saying that cognitive characteristics don't matter morally under any circumstance; I'm saying that for purposes of use as a resource, they don't matter. Let's assume you have a normal human being and a human being who has transient global amnesia, with no sense of the past, no sense of the future, but a strong sense of the present right now. Or you can have someone who has Alzheimer's, who has no sense of the past, no sense of the future, but a strong sense of self in the present. Is that person self-aware? Yes. Does that person have an interest in continuing to live? Yes. Is that interest in continuing to live different from your interest and my interest? The answer is probably yes. Is it morally relevant? Maybe. Somebody who is mentally disabled, someone who has cognitive impairment of a particular degree may be someone you don't treat in the same way as someone who doesn't have an impairment. You may not want to give that person a driver's licence. If you're looking for a history lecturer, you might not want to appoint somebody who has got transient global amnesia, but if the question is not whom do we hire to be a lecturer but whom do we use as a forced organ donor, or as a non-consenting subject in a biomedical experiment, the answer is you don't use either of them. So cognitive characteristics matter: they can have moral significance. But for purposes of resource use, they don't. Not in my view. That's a foundational principle of the abolitionist approach.

NW: *So, that is very different from a thinker like Peter Singer, who presumably would allow that we could use animals in various ways, it's just that in the process, we should minimize the suffering we cause to them.*

GF: Yes. Peter's view is really no different from that of Bentham. Peter maintains that animals don't have an interest in continuing to live—he makes exceptions for the non-human great apes, and perhaps for dolphins or whatnot—but he thinks that, as a general matter, animals don't have an interest in continuing to live, and that they don't care that we use them. They only care about *how* we use them. He does not think killing them is harming them per se. It's that sort of thinking that leads to this 'happy' meat movement, the 'compassionate' consumption movement. (Although Singer more recently appears to think that more of the animals we routinely exploit *may* have some sense of the future, he has thus far failed to recognize that they have the kind of morally significant interest in continued existence that he accords to humans, non-human great apes, marine mammals, and elephants, and that would prevent him from supporting campaigns for 'happy' exploitation.)

As a matter of fact, right before I came in for the interview, I was having a cup of tea in the college cafeteria and they had all these 'happy' animal foods for sale: free-range this and free-range that, and I wanted to have a discussion with them and request that they take these items off the shelves. Portraying those foods as involving significantly greater protection for animal interests is wrong. The bottom line is, Britain treats animals more humanely than any other place in the world, but Britain still tortures and kills the animals it consumes for food. Think of the difference between water boarding somebody on a bare water board and water boarding somebody on a padded water board. If you think that that's really significant, I respectfully disagree.

NW: *Well, this is interesting because there's a pragmatic question here: an abolitionist is arguing that we should just get rid of using animals, and arguing for that case may not be the most effective way of bringing about a movement in that direction. So many people might say that it would be far more effective to do this in stages. We could look for more humane treatment of animals as a step towards a position in an ideal future where animals aren't used at all.*

GF: We would agree, I assume, that child molestation is a major problem. Nevertheless, nobody would suggest that we have a campaign for humane child molestation. We think it's wrong, and we think we ought to take a position of abolition with respect to it: a zero tolerance policy. The regulation of animal exploitation is fundamentally flawed. As a practical matter, putting aside the moral issues, it can't work. Animals are chattel property: they have no inherent or intrinsic value and have only extrinsic or external value. You might have a dog or a cat that you value, but that's simply because that's a piece of property that we allow you to value as you wish. Part of what property ownership means is that we allow you to value your property the way you want, so if you have an automobile and you want to take really exceptionally good care of it, we allow you to do that. If you don't want to take exceptionally good care of it, that's ok, as long as you take enough care of it so that it gets through its inspection. The same thing occurs with animals: they're economic commodities, it costs money to protect their interests, and we generally don't protect their interests unless we get some sort of benefit, generally economic, from doing so. Now, if that thesis is correct, then if you look at animal welfare reform, what you should expect to find is that in many, if not most cases, animal welfare reform actually makes animal use more economically efficient. Look at, for example, the movement away from the veal crate, that's very much an economic matter. If you take a veal calf out of the crate and put the veal calf into a small social unit, you actually decrease the veterinary costs. It really doesn't make a whole lot of difference in the grand scheme of things, and, frankly, in a really rational world, these reforms would occur anyway as a matter of economic rationality. In a sense, the modern animal movement involves animal groups working with industry to try to identify economically inefficient practices, but that has nothing to do with changing the status of animals as beings that have absolutely no intrinsic or inherent value. They're still economic commodities. The most humanely treated animals are subjected to treatment that would be torture if humans were involved.

NW: *Imagine a world where there was no factory farming and animals were living in this free-range way, but were still being slaughtered. Compare that with a world with lots of factory farming. Surely, the former would be better than the latter?*

GF: That's really no different from asking us to imagine a world in which children are molested, and a world in which children are molested and also beaten. A world in which they're just molested is better than a world in which they're molested and beaten. Well, that's a no-brainer. It's always better to cause less harm than more harm; but that doesn't answer the question about whether imposing *any* harm is morally justifiable. What you've just shown is how profound the impact has been of these large animal organizations, because what they're doing is making you think that that's the question, that what we need to be doing is moving away from factory farming and towards this idyllic world of happy animals lining up to be slaughtered. First of all, that's never going to happen as a practical matter. Second, it completely ignores the moral question. Is it better to torture less than to torture more? The answer is 'of course it is'. But that doesn't answer the question that matters.

NW: *Now, we've been mostly talking about harm to animals, but some kinds of uses of animals might not harm them in a way that causes suffering. I'm thinking particularly of the way some people humanely use pets. Do you object to that as well?*

GF: Domestication is a problem. My partner and I live with five rescued dogs. I absolutely love dogs: you won't find anyone on the planet who likes dogs, and enjoys being with them, more than I do. But if there were two left on the planet and it were up to me as to whether or not they reproduced so that we could continue to have pets, the answer is absolutely not. As much as I love our dogs and I hope they have a good life, the bottom line is it's a really troubling life in the sense that they're completely dependent on us for everything. They live in this netherworld of vulnerability; they're not really animals and they're not humans, and they're completely dependent on us. This strikes me as being, in certain ways, a sad existence, and I think we ought to take care of the ones that we have here right now, but I think that we ought to stop bringing domesticated animals into existence altogether.

NW: *There's a further problem with pets. If you have a pet, and the pet is a carnivore, and you're a vegan, does that mean you have to turn your pet into a vegan too?*

GF: Our dogs are all vegans, and have been for decades, and they do very well. The question I get asked as much as I get the 'What about plants?' question, is 'What do you do about vegan cats?' Many cats can be vegan, but I draw the distinction between justification and excuse. Domestication throws up a lot of ugly dilemmas for us. I don't think that feeding meat to cats is morally justifiable. It may be excusable in that it is morally problematic, but where the moral wrongness is mitigated. What else are you going to do? I'm often asked, 'Well, what if you're on a desert island, and there are no vegetables, and the only thing that you can do is eat a rabbit or die, do you eat the rabbit?' The answer is that if you, Nigel, and I are on the desert island, and there are no vegetables to eat and there are no rabbits to eat, then I might kill you and consume you. That doesn't mean it's morally justifiable, but we might say it's excusable, in the sense that it's the wrong thing I did, but we understand why I did it. If I had cats that needed meat, I would basically take the position, 'I'm not happy about doing this, I don't like doing this, but this is a situation in which I have to do something morally wrong in order to do the right thing.'

NW: *Earlier, you were talking about how some people, inconsistently in your view, eat free-range meat, and it somehow salves their consciences. Well, what about turning this round on you. Eating a vegan diet typically involves suffering to animals: you may not see it, but I've worked in a flour mill. To store grain involves killing rats, killing mice. There's no easy way around that, so it's not as if you don't have blood on your hands, either.*

GF: My friends in the Jain community would say that, basically, you can't live in the material world without engaging in conduct that is harmful to other beings. I agree with that: you can't. If I build a road, I know that there are going to be deaths on that road. There's still a difference between building a road where I know that people are going to get killed, and deliberately killing particular people. So if I say, 'Look, I don't want to engage in violence, I don't want to engage in killing, so I'm not going to eat animals, and I'm going to eat plants', obviously, I should endeavour to farm in ways in which there is as little harm as possible, but there will be unintended harm, that's inevitable.

NW: *If you came across a deer that had been killed in a road, would you be prepared to eat it? The deer is dead, it wasn't deliberately killed, it was an accident. If you don't eat it, the flesh and potential protein goes to waste. Is there anything wrong with eating it?*

GF: No, I wouldn't eat the deer any more than I would eat hamburgers that I found thrown away in a dumpster, or something like that. I want to get us away from the idea of animals as things to eat, just as if I went through a dumpster and found a nice warm human arm, I wouldn't eat that arm because humans are not things to eat.

NW: *Why do you think so few people actually believe what you believe? There are many people who are concerned about animals suffering, some of those stop eating red meat, some of them stop eating all meat and all fish, very few take the whole journey towards veganism. Why do you think that is?*

GF: There are several reasons for that. I think the most important reason is there is a whole movement out there, a huge, multi-billion dollar industry movement called the humane movement, or the animal movement, or the animal rights movement, whatever you want to call it, that is telling people they don't need to do that. It's very hard for them to take the position that we ought to support campaigns for free-range eggs, and then say people shouldn't eat free-range eggs, so they don't have a vegan message. What they're doing is promoting this 'compassionate consumption' notion. I must say that I hate that expression more than just about any expression on the globe, 'compassionate consumption'. They've got the father of the animal rights movement, Peter Singer, saying that if we are conscientious about eating 'happy' meat and other animal foods, that's morally defensible. Well, if the father of the animal rights movement says that, then why should you think about veganism? But I'm here to tell you, if you care about animals—and I really believe this—you can't eat them, wear them, or use them. You go vegan.

MIND, SELF, AND IMAGINATION

8

NED BLOCK ON
Consciousness

David Edmonds: *Ned Block is Professor at New York University of not just one subject but three: Philosophy, Psychology, and Neuroscience. His seminal work on consciousness combines all three elements. The problem of what constitutes consciousness is as vexing as any in philosophy. Block believes one can be conscious of something without realizing it. Sounds counterintuitive? Let him explain.*

Nigel Warburton: *The topic we're going to focus on is the problem of consciousness. What is the problem of consciousness?*

Ned Block: I don't think there's *one* problem of consciousness. In fact, one of the interesting things about the neuroscience of consciousness is that it's come up with some problems that we didn't quite know we had. One of the most interesting such problems is the problem of whether conscious perception is rich or sparse. The reason we have this issue is because it's been discovered in psychology that people can, surprisingly, miss obvious items in the space right in front of their eyes if they are attending elsewhere. One interesting example that you can find versions of on YouTube is of people asked to count the passes between the white-shirted members of a basketball team and ignore the black-shirted members. That's a highly attention-demanding task: lots of passes, it's hard to count. While they're doing this, someone in a gorilla suit walks across the stage right in front of their eyes, and a very large percentage of the people report not seeing the gorilla. People are very surprised when you then replay the video and then they say, 'Oh my god, I didn't see *that*! It's right in front of me!' Versions of this have been run with pilot simulators in which pilots who are distracted don't see oncoming planes right in front of their eyes.

NW: *What does that reveal about consciousness? It's interesting, but what does it show us?*

NB: Not surprisingly, people disagree about what it shows us. One theory is that we can be conscious of only a very small number of things at once—the things we attend to. Another view is that we have a rich visual field, but that only some of the things in that visual field are accessed by us at any one time: there's a limit on access. What is certainly clear from the science is that there's a limit on the number of things that we can hold in working memory and in that kind of access. But what the disagreement is about is whether that limit on access is due to a limit on conscious phenomenology or whether conscious phenomenology is rich and *access* is sparse.

NW: *I'm just trying to get clear what you mean here. Imagine we're standing in front of a picture with a flashlight. Shine this flashlight on bits of the picture and they're highlighted. Is that what visual consciousness is like, highlighting part of the field? Or is it the whole thing?*

NB: It's the whole thing. The opposing view isn't a spotlight view; the opposing view is that there are, at most, four items at any one time in that whole thing that are in working memory and therefore conscious.

NW: *This is really quite difficult because, for me, being conscious is being aware of something and being able to articulate it. My starting point would be that it must be like the flashlight lighting things up, even if it's four points; whereas, I think, you're saying that you can be conscious of something without being able to speak, or recognize, or communicate, exactly what it is you're conscious of.*

NB: Yes. And to some people that sounds as if you can be conscious of something that you're unconscious of, and that *does* sound like a contradiction. The resolution of the contradiction is that the word 'consciousness' is ambiguous. There's a sense that relates to *access*, and there's a sense that relates to the 'what it's like' to have the experience. My opinion is that we're taking in a very large number of things consciously, and we have that 'what it's like' for a large number of things, even though there's only a limited number of things that we can access. My argument for this is based on experiments. I don't think you can tell very easily by introspection whether the sparse view is right or whether the rich view is right. Now, I think people do feel they do see a lot of things at once but the sparse theorists explain that using the refrigerator light illusion. The idea is that someone might think that the refrigerator light is always on because it's on when you look. Similarly, their story is someone might think they have a rich visual field because whenever they attend to part of it, they can report it and access it and think about it. So, they think visual experience is sparse but it only *seems* to be rich because of this refrigerator light illusion. My view is that it really is rich and the limit is a limit on access. But I think that the sparse-consciousness people are motivated by the point you raised originally: that we just wouldn't call it consciousness if it weren't available. Whereas my view is that consciousness is a real kind: it's a real thing that can be investigated scientifically and we can find out something surprising about it.

NW: *On your view, does that mean there's no such thing as a subliminal piece of information or input to consciousness?*

NB: No. On my view, there are three different categories of neural activations in the sensory areas. The bottom level is subliminal, where it isn't conscious in any sense but it does *affect* our behavioural responses: it gets into the brain and it can influence responses—that's the subliminal category. Then, on the other end, there's the straightforward conscious category that everybody would agree to: that you see it, you can think about it, you can plan, you can use it to answer questions. The difficult category is the one in the middle, where you have the very strong activation—this is usually produced by inner tension—that has some of the signs of consciousness, but it doesn't reach your mechanisms of reasoning and reporting. There are a number of such cases that we have some reason to think are actually conscious. The opposition thinks, 'Well, I can't report it so it's not conscious.' That's where the disagreement lies.

NW: *You mentioned earlier the case of the person in a gorilla suit who runs across the basketball court and nobody notices. How would your tripartite distinction explain that?*

NB: The idea would be that the gorilla experience *is* conscious. There is a conscious representation but it lacks the kind of categorization that would allow it to get into the reporting system. So it's consciousness without cognitive access.

NW: *But it's not subliminal because of the level of activation in the brain which you might find out about through some kind of functional MRI scan or something like that?*

NB: It's not just a matter of the degree of activation. There are other features that are involved, including recurrent loops in which one activation is connected to another activation. So, that's important, and it may be also important what the oscillation frequency is. So, there are other factors; it's not just the degree of activation.

NW: *I would never know that just by thinking about my own experience because it just wouldn't be accessible to me. There's no way I can get to 'read' that experience and interpret it because it's not being categorized, as you put it.*

NB: We have to distinguish 'not *accessed*' from 'not *accessible*'. What is certainly true is that there are some very strong activations that are not actually accessed, though it might be that, if you had changed your attention in that gorilla case, you would have fully been able to report that gorilla—maybe even a few seconds afterwards, or half a second afterwards. What is a much more difficult question is whether there might be some representations that are in this category of conscious but are actually inaccessible. The example that I would give is the example of what's called visual spatial extinction. It's usually caused by damage to the attention areas in the right side of the brain which control the left side of space. If these are damaged in a particular way, the subjects, when looking straight ahead at what's called the fixation point, cannot report things on the left side. Yet, surprisingly, if it's a *face* on the left side, they show activation in the fusiform face area—the area that registers conscious perception of faces—almost exactly as if it were a conscious perception, an ordinary conscious perception of a face. Yet, they say they don't see any face on the left. The hope is that more work on these representations will give us a further clue as to whether there might really be a representation of the face on the left that is conscious but still inaccessible because attentional mechanisms that would allow categorizing and reporting are broken.

NW: *Again, using the word 'conscious' there sounds almost contra-dictory. It seems more like a non-conscious experience.*

NB: I agree that it *sounds* contradictory but I think that it's important to get beyond that sounding to the real phenomena involved. It may be that our ordinary categories don't easily allow us to see how that could be true, but if we think consciousness is a real thing, then we have to allow it might be present, even if it cannot be accessed. One way to put it is that our ordinary concept of consciousness has two properties: it's a concept of something that is accessible, but it's also the concept of something that's real. These can come apart. So we have to allow for the possibility that something real might not be accessible.

NW: *What about the Freudian notion of the unconscious? Is there a way in which you can explain the phenomena that psychoanalysts describe as unconscious experience?*

NB: That's a very interesting question. I would argue that Freudian unconscious images might actually be conscious in the phenomenal sense that people actively supress disturbing conscious images, and then, in the Freudian sense of unconscious, they are unconscious, which means that these images are inaccessible. So this is another illustration of how it is that we really have two separate concepts here: a concept that's tied closely to accessibility and a concept that's tied closely to there being something that it's like to have the image.

NW: *Is it possible that people who are in persistent vegetative states are actually conscious in the sense you've just described?*

NB: We do have a few cases found by Adrian Owen and Steven Laureys in which a patient who *is* in a vegetative state by the standard criteria—in a sleep–wake cycle and unable to respond to any commands or track things in the environment—can follow instructions to imagine a certain situation, and when they imagine that situation, they have the brain activation characteristic of imagining it. We think they really have conscious experience, and not just conscious experience, but also some conscious *control* of their imagery involved in that conscious experience. One of these patients later moved up the hierarchy from vegetative to minimally conscious state—which is a higher level—where there seemed to be some indication that she realized that she was getting these questions.

NW: *This is all fascinating, and it could change the way we think about what we are. But beyond that, does it have any impact? Is there any further point to this philosophical speculation?*

NB: Yes, I think it has considerable *moral* impact. One dimension of moral impact is with regard to animals. There has been a persistent question as to whether animals suffer. If they don't have any conscious experience, as some philosophers have claimed, then, according to some philosophers, it's alright to treat them in a cruel way because, after all, you're not causing them any pain. But if they *have* conscious experience, for example if the chicken has conscious experience, then just because of *that* we're obligated not to cause them pain.

A second area where it's important is in the case of patients in a vegetative state, like the ones we've just been discussing. If you had a close relative who's in a vegetative state and there's some discussion as to whether to pull the plug, I think you'd want to know whether they're having conscious experiences or not. You might decide that, even if they were having conscious experiences, their life wasn't worth living, but still it's relevant whether they're having conscious experiences.

9

PATRICIA CHURCHLAND ON
Eliminative Materialism

David Edmonds: *There's a tradition in philosophy, which started in Oxford post-World War II, that insists that to understand mental concepts like belief, or free will, or memory, or desire, we just need to analyse how the concepts are actually used in everyday language. Some people refer to the set of commonly held views about these psychological states as 'folk psychology'. Pat Churchland, who's based at the University of San Diego, is a well-known and contentious critic of folk psychology. With her husband, Paul, she works on the relationship between neuroscience and philosophy. She says that we can't approach folk psychology uncritically; folk psychology can be wrong. As we learn more and more about the brain, we'll need to modify some of our concepts, and even eliminate them.*

Nigel Warburton: *The topic we're going to talk about today is eliminative materialism. Now, to somebody outside philosophy, that's just gobbledegook: so what is it?*

Pat Churchland: The idea of eliminative materialism is really quite simple. When Paul Churchland and I were thinking about the nature of mental states and how they relate to brain states, we were motivated to look at the history of science. One of the things that you can see in the history of science is that there is a progression, and you see it in chemistry, in physics, in biology, whereby certain old concepts get replaced or modified or amplified by new developments in science. So, for example, in the context of Newtonian physics, the old idea of *impetus* got thrown out as explanatorily useless. The concept of *element* was massively modified and amplified as chemistry became a science; ditto for *gene* as molecular biology became a science. One of the questions that we wanted to ask was this: as neurobiology comes to interweave with higher-level concepts, what will those higher concepts look like? Will they look like folk psychology as it has always been, or will there be fundamental changes? We made a prediction that there's likely to be change, and in that sense we were talking about elimination.

NW: *So, the eliminative bit is the idea that you get rid of something. The materialist bit is that the brain is a physical thing, and that's basically what we, as thinking beings, are: physical things.*

PC: Yes. The materialism part of the story is certainly not new with us. The hypothesis that all mental states, including states of consciousness, thoughts, ideas, beliefs, desires, motivations, are all states of the physical brain has increasingly been supported by developments in neuroscience, so that right now, there's very little evidence for the view that there is a non-physical substance, a kind of spooky thing, or ethereal thing, that does the thinking and the feeling and the remembering, and so forth: it looks like these are all part of the physical brain itself. So that's the materialist part of the story. As you say, the eliminativist part of the story was a prediction, a prediction that certain concepts might be modified, developed, might even be eliminated as neuroscience progressed.

NW: *Could you give an example of a concept of folk psychology?*

PC: The concepts that we use in everyday explanations of ourselves and of others, concepts having to do with beliefs, desires, intentions. I think the notion of having a goal is part of folk psychology, but I think that's one of the concepts that's likely to be retained as a high-level psychological concept that really does fit quite well with neurobiological findings. Another concept of folk psychology is the will. There certainly is something that's different between somebody whom we describe as having 'strong will' and somebody we describe as being 'weak-willed', but there isn't a thing in there that is 'the will'. What we find is a whole lot of circuitry, poorly understood at this point, that, in various ways, regulates decision making. But 'will' is sometimes thought of as comparable to a muscle, and there's nothing in there that's like a muscle. In the case of memory, for example, prior to about 1950, people generally thought of memory as a single, unified function. We know now that there are different parts of the nervous system that handle quite different functions that used to be called memory. Remembering how to ride a bicycle is a very different function, and relies on quite different circuitry than remembering your mother's name. It turns out that the concept of memory actually fractionates into many different sub-types, each of which is regulated by rather different pathways.

NW: *Is this a bit like the way in which the concept 'melancholy' has changed? For Elizabethans, the concept of melancholy was quite different from our concept of depression: it could be a creative malady, it had certain causes, in the levels of bile, or whatever explanations were given then, and now we've more or less eliminated that concept of melancholy, and have this different, more medical concept of depression?*

PC: It is rather similar to that. Another example would be the notion of demonic possession. In our culture, we forget how recent the idea of demonic possession was. Consider Huntingdon's disease, in which there is a decline of regulation of motor function, as well as cognitive function, and people make all kinds of movements that they don't, as it were, intend. It used to be thought of as demonic possession. We now realize that is completely wrong. That's an example of outright elimination, as opposed to modification.

NW: *You have this hypothesis that various folk psychological concepts will be eliminated as neuropsychology, and neurobiology progress: what does that mean for philosophy, because there are some styles of doing philosophy where people sit in an armchair and reflect on the concepts that they happen to have? Are they misguided in doing that?*

PC: Conceptual analysis, which has had its heyday in Oxford, really from the mid-1950s onwards, was sustained by the idea that you could find out about the nature of something merely by reflecting in your own mind on the relationships between various concepts, so that you could do it all in an *a priori* way. An American philosopher, Willard Van Orman Quine, suggested that while it's very useful on some occasions to reflect on the meaning of your concepts, the more important question for asking about the nature of things is whether those concepts truly apply to the phenomenon in question. That is what I'm interested in. I'm not so much interested in how people talk about the phenomenon: I really want to know whether those concepts truly apply to phenomena in the brain and in the world. When it comes to understanding perception, decision making, and choice, what it is to be a self, and to be conscious, I'm not so much interested in what you might *mean* by these things, but rather I want to know whether those concepts, rough and ready as they are, apply to the phenomenon in question. I want to know about the nature of things, and this is a very old philosophical preoccupation. I feel that I would have had a lot in common with Aristotle, with John Locke—who, after all, performed dissections—and with David Hume. Increasingly, philosophers are becoming sensitive to the fact that if they want to understand something such as perception, they need to pay attention to both the psychological and neurophysiological results of perception. Here's a really interesting fact: very, very early in the process of visual perception—in early visual cortex, that is in the first area in the visual cortex to which visual signals are sent (V1), there is *valuation*. We know this because there are projections from higher areas of the brain all the way back to V1 that attach a value signal to *this* perceptual signal rather than *that* one. So when philosophers say, 'But you must separate fact and value', we say, *wait*: an interesting feature of the brain is that before we're even conscious of a visual perception, it comes with a valence. Your brain merges fact and value in deciding what to pay attention to.

NW: *So you're suggesting that babies in the act of perception, are at the same time preferring one thing to another, that's the valuation: they attach some kind of qualitative aspect to this, even though they may not be aware of it themselves?*

PC: Absolutely. And learning and being rewarded by interacting with a particular stimulus, the mother, the breast, means that when the baby has a certain smell, or certain visual perception, that already comes to the baby's conscious awareness, as having a 'pro' value. So the separation of fact and value is something that is highly sophisticated, comes relatively late in cognitive development, and we have to be taught that distinction when we do science. This is a very important point, especially in thinking about morality, where philosophers want to assume that the mind has facts, and then value has to come from something else, namely rules. If you look at the nervous system, that is not the way much of valuation happens.

NW: *Does this mean that philosophers have to be scientists?*

PC: I think there is a very particular role for philosophers: it's not to just, as we used to say in San Diego, 'pull it out of your ass'. The more productive strategy is to connect in a very meaningful way with the range of data that is relevant to your question. You could think of the job for philosophers as analogous to the role of theoretical physicists who may, but need not engage in experiments, but who draw upon a very broad range of experiments to try and get a coherent hypothesis about how something works. I think you might say the same thing about certain kinds of philosophical questions, questions about decision making and choice. It's no good just sitting in your office thinking about it. What you need to do is find out what we know about suppressing impulses, about discounting the value for rewards expected in the future, about the role of motivation and choice, about attention, about valuation and perception, that make decision making look the way it is. That means, in addition to a scientific enterprise which is largely vertical—deeper and deeper into the system on a particular problem—the philosopher can have a scientific programme which is *horizontal*. That programme reaches across many labs, across many projects, across many sub-disciplines to try to synthesize and integrate diverse data together in a useful way to sketch a Big Picture. Now, the hypothesis you frame with has to be testable: it's not very interesting if it's true by definition. Sometimes—most of the time, perhaps—you're going to get it wrong. And when you get it wrong, what you're *not* going to say is, 'But this is my position which I defend.' What you say is, 'OK, let's modify the hypothesis in light of the data.'

NW: *Let's take that example of decision making. You could find out all these facts about how people make decisions, and make scientific hypotheses about how decisions are actually instantiated in the brain. But what's the role for a philosopher in this whole world of understanding decisions?*

PC: One of the things we would particularly like to understand is how it is that one desire can be given free rein, and the other suppressed. You can say, if you just reflect in your own mind 'Well, I do it by exercising my will', but we want to know how that really happens, relative to the data that are available now. You could frame a hypothesis about how that happens. What you'd have to do is draw very broadly on data from many projects and you have to talk about it in terms of pathways and interactions and so forth. You would develop a computational model, which may or may not turn out to be true.

NW: *There is a sense in which we need these concepts, the folk psychology of our age, to talk about our relationships with other people: we're stuck with these, we're brought up with these concepts. We're not going to jettison them just because somebody makes a discovery in neuroscience.*

PC: No, that's quite true. Let me make two points, but let me frame those points by saying something about what I mean by a high-level concept. Having a goal, for example, is a high-level concept, and we think that that can be instantiated in a very specific way in circuitry in the brain stem and the limbic system. So the high-level description refers to the behaviour description, and the low-level description would be in terms of neural activity. Now, there's no question that we need high-level concepts. We certainly need to have concepts like 'X has a goal', or 'X is maintaining his goal, despite distractions'—we say that with regard to rats and mice, and babies. The other point really is that there's no question of replacing the high-level concepts that we use from folk psychology until we have a good science to replace them with. (I made this point clearly in 1986 in *Neurophilosophy*, but many philosophers like to assume I did not.) So a concept like trust or attachment turns out to be extremely important in describing the behaviour, not only of humans with regard to their offspring and with regard to their mates and their friends, but also for rats and monkeys and baboons and chimpanzees. Additionally, we know now something about the circuitry and the neurochemicals that regulate bonding and trusting behaviour. So trust is a useful high-level concept. It may get refined and revised as we know yet more, but it's a high-level concept that meshes very beautifully with what we know at the physiological level. Now, there are certain other concepts where we don't know how it's going to work out. Concepts like beliefs are problematic because some beliefs are things that are forefront in our minds as a sentence, such as, 'I believe you are wearing a pair of glasses'; others are in the background of our knowledge. Beliefs are not stored in the brain as sentences—we can be sure of that—so how to characterize them in neurobiological terms remains puzzling. Moreover, many non-verbal animals know things, so what they know will have to be described in some way that does not imply they have language. Finally, notice that whether people in general, apart from science, adopt a new vocabulary depends on how useful it is for them. It was never part of our agenda to say, 'people must change how they talk'. We're very easy-going about that, but what we want to know is how things really are.

NW: *I was just thinking, when you were saying that, of the way that people use the phrase 'left brain' and 'right brain' now. It's very crude, but it's a way of understanding patterns of behaviour, which would have been completely alien 50 years ago.*

PC: I think that's right, and it is rather remarkable how easily people picked that up, muddled though it was. The idea of being 'frontal' is now really becoming very common, so that when someone shows a tendency to be poor in impulse control, to be poor in maintaining a goal, to be easily persuadable by rather goofy ideas, they're often spoken of as being 'frontal'. That's because within the neurological domain, frontality involving lesions within frontal structures is associated with executive dysfunction.

NW: *I know when you first wrote about eliminative materialism, you had some quite strong reactions; this is a radical hypothesis and it annoyed some people.*

PC: Well, we didn't think the hypothesis was radical at all. We thought it was obvious that folk psychology, this sort of ancient bumbling, in many ways incoherent, in many ways inconsistent, but a beloved thing, will change. But there was a certain wilful misunderstanding on the part of philosophers. Some philosophers were terrified by the idea that the sciences of psychology, neuroscience, economics, and so forth, were going to have to play a role in philosophy, and that they needed to think about hypotheses, rather than *a priori* truths. We were caricatured as supposing that beliefs were nothing other than the firing of neurons in the basal ganglia, and I think we were largely written off. We were Americans, we didn't speak the fancy English that people did in Oxford, we were saying the game needed to change if progress were to be made. I don't really know the sociological explanation for why our approach was so vilified, but clearly we were written off. There were occasions when I would give a talk, and someone in the question period would stand up and very aggressively say, 'You're not doing philosophy any more, why are you even here, why are you even speaking, claiming to be a philosopher?' We just got used to it, and we don't care that much. What I'm interested in is finding things out. If there are people who would rather just sit and talk about what they think rationality is without knowing anything, far be it for me to complain.

10

FRANK JACKSON ON
What Mary Knew

David Edmonds: *We're about to introduce you to Mary and a red tomato. Mary's an imaginary person living in bizarre circumstances, of which more anon. Her creator is a distinguished Australian philosopher. When Frank Jackson dreamed up Mary, it was to use her as an intellectual weapon against physicalists—those who believe that the only things that exist in the world are physical. Frank Jackson used to believe there were mental properties distinct from physical states and properties, and that these mental properties were epiphenomenal, i.e. they had no influence on physical states. But back to Mary and what she knew about that tomato...*

Nigel Warburton: *We're going to talk about a very famous thought experiment known as 'What Mary Knew' or 'the Knowledge Argument'. You're responsible for that thought experiment. Could you begin by telling us how you came up with it?*

Frank Jackson: There's a bit of history. I used to be at Monash University, and that was back in the days when nearly all philosophers of mind were materialists. The Psychology Department discovered that there was a dualist in the Philosophy Department and said, in effect, 'Let's ask this dualist over to give us a lunchtime talk and explain how you could possibly not be a materialist' (or so I imagine). So, in the spirit of inter-departmental co-operation, I said, yes, that sounds like a good idea. But then, of course, I had to think of something to say. I thought, well, I've always felt that the sensory side of psychology—the feely bit, the pains and the itches and the tickles and the red sunsets, all that stuff—*that* was the bit that materialism couldn't handle. So I said: right, I'll present the psychologists with the best argument for saying that that gets left out. I just wanted the clearest argument that would spell out exactly why the feely side got left out. The talk I gave was an early version of the knowledge argument.

NW: *So what was the argument that you came up with?*

FJ: Well, the idea that the feely side's left out is the idea that if you tell everything there is to tell in physical terms, everything the materialists talk about—brain states and functional states and information processing and everything that Artificial Intelligence people discuss—if you say everything there is to say in those terms, you somehow leave something out. Now, what's a good way to make that point? Imagine someone who knew everything materialists talk about but had never had an experience of red. Wouldn't they be ignorant about something? And that is the idea behind the knowledge argument.

NW: *The knowledge argument is a bit more detailed than that, isn't it? It's not just a matter of imagining someone who hasn't had experience of red, but of somebody who has had a completely monochromatic experience up to that point.*

FJ: Yes. You imagine a woman who is confined to a black-and-white room. She is painted black and white. She never cuts her hands, so she's never seen any red blood. The room is full of books in black and white. The TV is black and white, and she watches wonderful lectures by the world's greatest neuroscientists on it—all in black and white. That's all inside the room. She's never been outside the room. She's called Mary. Mary becomes the world's greatest functional psychologist and neuroscientist: she's also an expert on physics and chemistry, etc., but she's never had the experience of something looking red to her. You open the door and you let her go out. Won't she say: 'My goodness, there's a whole aspect of reality which I didn't know about'? *That's* the knowledge argument: you can know all there is to know that can be given in black-and-white terms, and yet somehow there's something missing, there's something more to know. But, of course, all there is to know that can be given in black-and-white terms includes everything in materialists' account of the mind, so what's in their account is incomplete.

NW: *Now, when she does go out of the room, philosophers usually describe the experience she has as her experience of 'qualia'.*

FJ: Yes. The basic thought is that she learns something exciting about what the world is like. Being philosophers we want a nice label for this, and the word 'qualia' is just a nice label for it. It's a word for the feely side of looking red and, more generally, the feely side of psychology.

NW: *But in the thought experiment, there shouldn't be anything extra because she knows absolutely everything that you could possibly know about neuropsychology. So she should not be surprised in the least.*

FJ: If physicalism is true, the line of thought in the argument is that she shouldn't be surprised at all. And, of course, she does know, while she's inside the room, that people use the word 'red' on occasion. She reads in her black-and-white books that people say things like 'Sunsets look red', and they say things like 'The experience of red is rather more vivid and exciting than the experience of pale grey.' She knows all that. But the thought is there's something she doesn't know: she doesn't actually know the nature of the state which underlies those remarks she reads about. I hasten to add, of course, that I no longer believe the conclusion of the thought experiment. I'm now a card-carrying materialist—but that's a later part of the story.

NW: *Let's just get to the conclusion that you wanted to deliver when you first gave this paper. You described the thought experiment and presumably there was a punch line?*

FJ: Well, the punch line was that what she learns about are extra properties; and the conclusion was that physicalism is false. But I also said we know enough about how the world works to say that these extra properties don't do any causing. To use the philosopher's jargon, they're *epiphenomenal*. So, that's the reason the original paper was called 'Epiphenomenal Qualia', because the idea is that we've got to believe in these qualia, but we also have to say, as good scientists, that they're epiphenomenal: the extra properties don't affect the words that come out of my mouth, or the movements of my hand, or what goes on in my brain.

NW: *Just to get this straight, what you're saying is that, although I might have these experiences, I can describe brain states and muscular changes and physiological reactions, and so on, in my body without any need to bring in these qualia to explain what's going on?*

FJ: If you ask neuroscientists to explain what happens in our brain and how those happenings lead to changes in our vocal chords and movements in our arms and so on, they never have to invoke anything outside entities and properties they deal with in the neuroscience laboratory.

NW: *I can't believe the materialists just rolled over when they heard your argument. What kind of counterarguments did they come up with?*

FJ: A very large number. The literature is enormous. And, as I often say, although lots of materialists thought there was some obvious error in the argument, I was somewhat consoled by the fact that there was a great deal of disagreement over what that obvious error was. So it cannot have been that obvious. But, yes, they came up with lots of counterarguments. They also said epiphenomenalism is unbelievable. And indeed that was the consideration that eventually made me change my mind.

NW: *So why did you change your mind?*

FJ: Well, the biggest factor was the picture of myself writing 'Epiphenomenal Qualia' but not being *caused* to write 'Epiphenomenal Qualia' by qualia. I said in 'Epiphenomenal Qualia' that you had to be an epiphenomenalist about qualia, and what that meant was that qualia didn't cause the words that came out of my mouth or the movement of my pen on pieces of paper when I wrote the article (this was back in the early 1980s). So that meant that, when I gave the talk defending epiphenomenal qualia, and when I wrote the paper defending epiphenomenal qualia, qualia weren't causing the talk and they weren't causing the writing. I decided that this was unbelievable. Now, of course, 'Epiphenomenal

Qualia' does have a section which says that you can live with epiphenomenalism, with replies to the standard arguments against epiphenomenalism. It also says it's perfectly reasonable to believe that the world is a much more mysterious place than you might have thought, and that one of the mysteries are these epiphenomenal qualia. But I came to think that this section was a triumph of philosophical cleverness over common sense.

NW: *Epiphenomenal things don't do anything. That is the essence of epiphenomenal entities: they don't actually have causal power. So it shouldn't surprise you that they're not doing anything.*

FJ: Oh no, it shouldn't surprise you at all. It's just a bit awkward to see how you can know about them, and, indeed, how you can remember them when you're not seeing anything red, and insist in a lecture that the experience of red isn't captured in the physicalist world scheme. You're remembering the experience of red and the memory is caused by—well, not by the property you're seeking to tell people about at the lecture—but by purely physical goings-on in your brain and its surroundings. And that was the consideration that eventually made me abandon the argument. The other thing that happened is that I became much more sympathetic to representationalism about perceptual experience—the idea that when you have, for example, a colour experience, there's a sense in which there's nothing coloured 'in' your experience: what's happening is that you're in a state which represents the world as being a certain way. And if you think about experience that way, then you can see how you might respond to the Mary argument.

NW: *Well does that mean that you would respond by saying that, actually, if Mary genuinely did have full knowledge she wouldn't be surprised?*

FJ: Yes. What you would say is two things. First of all, she wouldn't be surprised in the sense that she wouldn't learn anything new about what the world is like. She'd be surprised in the sense in which people who are motion-blind and later acquire the ability to see motion would be surprised. They wouldn't think they've discovered a new property, but if you're motion-blind, things don't seem to move. You know there's motion but nothing has that—sort of—'left-to-right', say, look about it, and you can't even imagine what it's like to see motion. And it's no use having someone give you a lecture telling you what it's like to see motion—that's a waste of time. You still won't know what it's like to see motion. And when you subsequently see it, there is a surprise. You come to know what it's like to see motion. But it's not, in any sense, an acquaintance with a new property. So I think what the representationalists can say about what happens to Mary when she leaves the room is that she's not surprised in the sense of learning about a new property but, of course, she's surprised in the sense that she now knows what it's like to see red, in the same sense in which someone who's motion-blind does when they get the ability to see motion—they suddenly know what it's like to see motion.

NW: *Once you'd published this as a paper, what kind of reaction did you get?*

FJ: Well, a lot of it was hostile—in the philosophical sense, I don't mean in the personal sense. But there were always a group of people, of course, that were very enthusiastic about the argument. And I meet them at conferences, now I've changed my mind, and they often come up to me and say, 'We're very sorry you've changed your mind.' I think they feel that I've let the side down. There have been books devoted to the argument and nothing but the argument, and if you look at citation counts, many of the papers on the knowledge argument are cited a lot.

NW: *It would be interesting to know how long it took you to come up with the argument. Was it something that just occurred to you in a minute?*

FJ: I'd read H.G. Wells' book *The Country of the Blind*, and, as you may know, in that book there's a sighted person who lives in the country of the blind. The people who are blind don't believe he is that different from them. They notice he's rather good at winning fights and avoiding falling down holes but they think this is just a behavioural capacity. There's nothing else going on except this rather interesting behavioural capacity. I think that book might have triggered the thought experiment because I thought, 'Hold on, this is quite wrong! This isn't just a behavioural capacity; he has access to a whole range of properties and experiences that the blind people don't have access to—they don't know about them.' But, of course, I was also influenced by the long history of controversy over exactly what it is that people who are blind or colour-blind lack, and by the paper by Paul Meehl I cite in 'Epiphenomenal Qualia'.

NW: *Now that you're back in the world of materialism, are you still left with that mysterious feeling about consciousness and conscious experience that inspires many people to get worked up about qualia in the first place?*

FJ: I've done a reasonably good job of disinfecting myself from my previous opinions, but what I do think, though, is that lots of people who reply to the knowledge argument don't really explain what is wrong with it. They say lots of really interesting, philosophically illuminating things but somehow leave one dissatisfied. Somehow, the redness of reds isn't covered. And the reason I like the representationalist approach is that I think it does allow you to say: 'Look, the redness of reds is not a property of your experience. It's a property of the way you're representing the world to be. So don't think of the redness as some sort of property of a state of you; it's a property that you are ascribing to the world around you. Your visual system is—sort of—shouting out to you, "These objects have got an attention-grabbing vivid property", but don't think that your experience has this property.'

NW: *Does that mean that I can be having an experience which I call 'red' but you would call 'green' if you were having it, and vice versa?*

FJ: Yes. I think it's obviously true that different people might have very different colour experiences. Indeed, if we imagine discovering a tribe in the Amazon jungle whose brains are systematically transposed with respect to ours in the states crucial to having colour experiences, and who have, as it seems to us, rather curious views about which colours go together, I think we might well say: 'My goodness, when they see ripe tomatoes their colour experiences are like those we have when we see grass, and when they see grass, their experiences are like those we have when we look at ripe tomatoes.' And perhaps they say things like: 'Ripe tomatoes are rather soothing whereas grass is rather attention-grabbing, like the sound of a trumpet.' If something like this happened, I think we'd say that they have transposed colour experiences. So I think we should acknowledge that as a possibility. What the materialist has to say, of course, is that at some level— functional, or behavioural, or neuroscientific—you could detect this difference. Indeed, the story I've just told you is a story where you can do the detecting.

NW: *How could you tell that these people were having transposed experiences?*

FJ: Well, I think it would be a combination of three things. You look at their brains and you discover that what happens in their brains when they see ripe tomatoes is like what happens in our brains when we see grass. You also find out exactly which optical properties of the surfaces of objects they are responding to and you discover that the particular properties their visual system responds to when they look at ripe tomatoes isn't the property we respond to; it is some associated property, more like the property of grass which stimulates our responses. And, finally, they'd be behavioural and functional properties to do with how they discriminated one object from another. But I do think that if you found two groups of people who were behaviourally and neurophysiologically and information-processing identical, then you would have to say they have the same experiences.

NW: *You've described how you've changed your opinion about the right conclusion to draw from your thought experiment. Is there any chance you might flip again and go back the other way and say: 'Well, look, actually, I was wrong about physicalism. Dualism is the correct explanation of our state'?*

FJ: No, I don't think so. Since I became a convert to the representationalist picture of the nature of experience, since then, I think I'm bulletproof or iron-clad—or whatever the right phrase is—against sliding back. Which is perhaps a good thing. It would be slightly embarrassing to change my mind, yet again, on the subject.

11

GALEN STRAWSON ON
The Sense of Self

David Edmonds: *'Know thyself' was a popular aphorism with the ancients, but it isn't that clear what this means. What is the self? Is it fixed? And should we spend our lives trying to uncover its nature? Is that being true to oneself? Or is the self, as the existentialists believe, something we create and revise as we go along? And what is the link between the self and character? The one and only Galen Strawson has grappled with these questions, though he lacks—he says—any strong sense of his own self.*

Nigel Warburton: *The topic we're going to talk about is the sense of the self. In your philosophical study of this, what have you discovered? What do people say about their sense of the self?*

    Galen Strawson: Well, one of the most striking things is that people are so different in this respect. Some people think they have a very clear, qualitatively detailed, sense of their own unique personality; whereas others feel that they don't really find anything when they look inside and try to form a sense of what they're like.

NW: *Could you give examples?*

GS: On the positive side, Gerald Manley Hopkins is one of the best examples. He talks of '. . . my self-being, my consciousness and feeling of myself, that taste of myself, of *I* and *me* above and in all things which is more distinctive than the taste of ale or alum, more distinctive than the smell of walnut-leaf or camphor, and is incommunicable by any means to another man'.[1] Well, that's Hopkins describing something that leaves me completely bewildered. I have no idea what he's talking about. I'm more on the side of Iris Murdoch. Here is Iris Murdoch, reported by her husband John Bayley: 'Iris once told me that the question of identity had always puzzled her. She thought she herself hardly possessed such a thing, whatever it was. I said that she must know what it's like to be oneself, even to revel in the consciousness of oneself as a secret and separate person. She smiled; looked amused, uncomprehending.'[2]

NW: *Does that carry across to our knowledge of other people? I might have a sense of what other people are like, even if I'm a bit vague about what I'm like.*

GS: I think we have a very strong intuitive sense of the personality of others; it's just that we don't necessarily have that for ourselves. Ian McEwan talks about the 'glassy continuum of selfhood',[3] by which he means the invisibility of your own character to yourself. And Jean-Paul Sartre puts it like this: 'Character has no distinct existence, except as an

[1] Gerald Manley Hopkins, 'Commentary on the Spiritual Exercises of St Ignatius Loyola', in *Sermons and Devotional Writings*, ed. C. J. Devlin (London: Oxford University Press, 1959 [1880]), p. 123.

[2] John Bayley, *Iris: A Memoir* (London: Duckworth, 1998), pp. 51–2.

[3] Ian McEwan, *Enduring Love* (London: Cape, 1997), p. 187.

object of knowledge to other people. Consciousness does not know its own character.'[4]

NW: *You've mentioned character there. Is character part of what we are as selves? Is that what your sense of self might come from, the sense of what kind of a character you are?*

GS: Yes, I think it would for those who have a strong sense of self. But imagine that you are wearing pink spectacles through which you view the world, and you just assume the world is pink—it doesn't occur to you that you're wearing spectacles. I think your own character is a bit like that. It's something you see the world through, and so it doesn't really feature as an object of experience for you. It just conditions everything and it's invisible to you.

NW: *And yet people around you are likely to make all kinds of attributions about your character and believe that you're an angry person, or that you're a kind person, or whatever.*

GS: Yes. And if I were set the task, I'm sure I could come up with some fairly reasonable description of what kind of person I am, but it's just that it's invisible to me as I live my life.

NW: *But also, I suppose—if you feel that way—if other people are telling you you're one kind of a person, you've got no criteria for judging whether they're right or not if you can't find, within yourself, the thing that matches up with their description of you.*

GS: Well, I could almost go 'behaviourist' about myself at this point. I've got the data about the things I've done

[4] Jean-Paul Sartre, *Being and Nothingness*, trans. H. Barnes (London: Methuen, 1969 [1943]), p. 349.

and I know that people have said 'well that must show that you had a bad temper' and so on. But you're quite right. There's something odd here in the fact that I don't seem to find my character as given in any way from the inside. So I have to, as it were, think about my life, and think about what I've been doing, to see why they might categorize me like that.

NW: *Well, that would fit with the idea that the self is somehow socially constructed, that it isn't anything within me, as well as with a behaviourist account as you suggested.*

GS: I suppose that it would fit with that, but I would want to resist that. I think there are facts about character that are wholly independent of whatever people mean by 'social construction'. It may be that a lot of your character traits only emerge in interaction with others, but I don't think that means that they're socially constructed in the sense that they're not real independently of that. I'd take quite a strong genetic line here—there's a lot of genetic determination in character. If you add early experience on to that, most of it is in place. If you say 'it's socially constructed', I don't think that means it's in some way less than fully objective.

NW: *Now, this seems to me a bit different from what David Hume was seeking when he famously looked within himself and couldn't find a self—an enduring self. Other people had told him that it must be there, as the soul, something that stays there throughout life, and possibly even beyond that. He looked for experience to back this up and all he could find were fleeting impressions; there was nothing that remained fixed.*

GS: I'm trying to write a book about what Hume said on the self because, as usual, I think that people have misreported

him. It's certainly true that he said you didn't find any
enduring self, but he was just applying his empiricism
rigorously in asking 'What are the actual data?', and answering
'What we find when we "enter intimately into ourselves" and
think about our mental life, is just one experience after
another.' One big mistake that people make is to think that
Hume is saying that there isn't a subject of experience at all,
even in the moment. He's certainly not saying that. He does,
of course, think that every one of these fleeting experiences
has a subject. There has to be someone there who's experiencing it. So, that's the big mistake people make about Hume—
to think that he's saying that there isn't really any kind of
subject at all. In fact, as you put it, what he's saying is that you
just don't find an enduring self. There may indeed be one, but
you just haven't got the evidence, and so you've got no right
to assert that there is.

NW: *So what you're saying is that Hume's introspection doesn't reveal
an impression of an enduring self, as he would put it. There's no sensory
or experiential input that tells me there's something there, but that doesn't
mean that there isn't something there.*

GS: Yes, that's right. But I certainly want to put the stress
back on *enduring*. The chapter opens with him saying, 'Look,
all these philosophers around us are absolutely sure that
they have this direct, intuitive, instinctive knowledge of the
existence of the eternal soul.' That's what he's really trying
to attack. These people think that they have direct experience
of having an enduring immaterial soul. But he's saying,
'Where are the data? The evidence simply isn't there.' And
he's right.

NW: *But that seems to me different from character, which is what we were discussing earlier in relation to the self. Hume's not looking in this famous passage for an enduring character—because in his autobiographical sketch 'My Own Life', he describes his character in slightly self-aggrandizing ways. There's a sense in which he recognizes, or at least believes he recognizes, his own character traits.*

GS: Yes, that's completely right. We really have got two different topics here. On the one hand, you've got the self, and whether it exists, and whether it's a thing that endures; and on the other hand, you have got all these issues to do with character. You're quite right that Hume is not concerned with character in his initial discussion of personal identity, but he's certainly not denying that human beings have characters. There are good ones and bad ones and kind ones and mean ones.

NW: *So what's the relationship between the self, the kind of thing that Hume was looking for, and character?*

GS: That's tricky. In my work, I've tried to split these two topics up. In *Selves*, the book that I've just published, I'm writing about whether there is such a thing as the self—metaphysically speaking.[5] The sequel to this book—I'm planning to call it *Life in Time*—is going to be much more about character. The basic difference that I want to consider is the difference between those people who naturally think of themselves as things that were there in the past and will be there in the future, and those people—I include myself as one of them—who have very little sense of its being *them* who was there in

[5] Galen Strawson, *Selves: An Essay in Revisionary Metaphysics* (Oxford: Oxford University Press, 2009).

the further past or who will be there in the further future. What you find is that there's this massive consensus in the humanities, today, about the importance of *narrative*. This is not only in philosophy and literature, it goes even into medicine and law, and it's very important in psychotherapy. It seems to be almost orthodoxy, now, for therapists to say, 'Well, what we've got to do to help this person is to let them develop a narrative of their lives and let them make sense of their lives in that way.' But it seems to me that, while this may work for some people, it's just not the right thing to try to do for others—others like myself. There's variety. We have to stand up for variety in human life: deep difference. There are some people who are not narrative in their outlook, who are just happy-go-lucky, living in the moment, and this is *not* a worse way of life.

NW: *Internal narrative is about the level of consciousness that we have of ourselves, yet it seems that neuroscience and psychology are converging more and more on the idea that much of what we are is either inaccessible to us most of the time, or else is intrinsically inaccessible to us. So, we shouldn't be surprised that some people function efficiently without an elaborate self-consciousness about themselves.*

GS: I quite agree. One famous remark made on the other side was made by Socrates when he said, 'The unexamined life is not worth living.' But I think you can agree with him that we need to be reflective about our lives in certain ways without having to set it out as a narrative. If you're just trying to regiment your life into some satisfying narrative in order to make sense of it, you may just be missing out on almost everything that matters. One remark I particularly like was made by the famous short story writer V. S. Pritchett who said, 'We live beyond any tale that we happen to enact.'[6]

Other people I'd call in support of my view include Marcel Proust. He's a very good example. He has this notion of *le vrai moi*, the 'true me': it's not that you have a continuing narrative that shows what it is. The 'true me' is something, rather, that emerges at certain moments—there's that famous, over-quoted moment when he dips his biscuit in the cup of tea and suddenly he's plunged in memory, back as he was when he was nine. He has this conception of the 'true me' as something that's completely outside of the story of your life. The narrative is just the contingency of your actual life and not the essence of what matters about you.

NW: *So what* does *matter about you then?*

GS: Actually, the more I think about this, the more I'm attracted by the idea that you have a unique essence. I think some people are going to live lives that are really at odds with what their essence is. But if things go well, you find a way to express it in your life. But it isn't as if the narrative details of your life are what matter most. In a sense they matter least.

NW: *So that essence, judging from something you've said in passing before, may be largely given genetically. It may also be something outside your control.*

GS: Yes—and it would be equally outside your control even if it was something that was caused in you by early experience.

NW: *Choosing the word 'essence' makes it sound like the soul, or something mysterious that just is there in us, whether or not we realize*

---

[6] V. S. Pritchett, *The Myth Makers* (London: Chatto and Windus, 1979), p. 47.

it's there. That fits with certain literary interpretations—people not living up to their true selves—and it fits with many people's intuitions, I'm sure. But it also has this arcane, almost esoteric, ring to it. Is this what a philosopher should be examining, this mysterious essence?

GS: Well, I'm already slightly regretting using the word 'essence' like that, but I'm probably going to stick with it. Maybe Sartre could come in again here, because he pointed out that the standard view in philosophy was that essence precedes existence, so that you have your essence and your existence unrolls out of it, as it were. In response, he gave his famous slogan 'existence precedes essence'. For him, somehow, existence, the contingencies of life, were what fundamentally constituted you, and your essence was just that. In contrast with Sartre, I think that it's principally a fact about genetic constitution and early upbringing. We are unique and idiosyncratic—in good ways and in bad ways. There just *are* best ways for our lives to go as a result, but this is because of the way we already are. I don't think experience can change us that radically, beyond a certain point—trauma aside.

NW: *Does it follow from this that we could get a better sense of who we are through introspection? Can we get access to that essence somehow?*

GS: I'm still regretting the word 'essence'. And as for introspection—unsupervised, purely personal introspection—I'm quite dubious about whether it works. I've already mentioned that Socrates said, 'The unexamined life is not worth living', but sometimes I think that the examined life can turn into the over-examined life and be even worse, and it may well be that you need a little help if you want to go into this kind of self-examination.

NW: *If this 'true me', what you've called the essence of the self, is so important to us, how do we go about finding out what it is?*

GS: Every time you use the word 'essence', I'm going to say I regret having brought it into the conversation! I think it may be a bit like what they say in sports psychology, that you have to relax into the shot and not think about it. Maybe you have to do some of that with your own life. You have to somehow just relax. Then perhaps you can hear what's going on, how you are, as it were.

12

ALISON GOPNIK ON
The Imagination

David Edmonds: *Kids like to live in a fantasy world. That much is obvious to any parent. But what's that got to do with philosophy? Alison Gopnik is a renowned psychologist who's intrigued about the role that imagination plays in our lives. She says this is linked to a concept much puzzled over by philosophers—causation.*

Nigel Warburton: *The topic we're focusing on is the imagination. Why do we have an imagination at all?*

Alison Gopnik: That's a good question. Plato thought that the poets should be exiled from the republic because they were not only liars, but they were really bad liars who weren't very convincing. You could think of an evolutionary version of Plato's objections: it's easy to see why understanding about the real world would give us all sorts of evolutionary benefits. But why would an understanding about things that aren't true and that you know aren't true have evolutionary benefits? This is a particular puzzle for developmental psychologists, because two- and three-year-old children spend much of their time in these wild, crazy, pretend worlds.

NW: *For Plato, depictions of reality were at several removes from the real world. We don't have to accept platonic metaphysics to think there's still a problem about how playful, imaginary situations could possibly teach us about reality.*

AG: Yes—the problem becomes more acute if you think about it psychologically and from an evolutionary perspective. We are starting to approach an answer, but the answer actually comes from thinking about a very different philosophical problem and that's the problem of causation. How is it that we can tell the difference between a causal relationship and a mere correlation relationship? And that deep philosophical problem may hold the answer to the problem about why we pretend.

NW: *So what is the difference between cause and correlation?*

AG: Good question. Well, there's been a lot of argument about this over the years. An idea from the twentieth-century American philosopher David Lewis is that, when we know that one thing causes another, we cannot just make predictions about what will happen if one event takes place, but we can make counterfactual inferences. We can say not just that if you smoke a lot then lung cancer will follow, but that if you hadn't smoked then you wouldn't have got lung cancer. Here's an example that nicely illustrates this: having yellow, nicotine-stained fingers is correlated with lung cancer just as smoking is correlated with lung cancer. But we don't think that yellow fingers actually cause lung cancer.

How can we cash out that intuition? Well, we don't think that, for instance, washing your hands will affect whether you get lung cancer. But we do think that stopping smoking will affect it. Now, recently, a philosopher, James Woodward, has come up with what is called the 'interventionist theory of causation'. You might ask, why would we want to know about counterfactuals, why would we want to know about what *would* have happened? After all, counterfactuals just lead to guilt and regret! And Woodward has argued that if you think in terms of the future rather than the past, counterfactuals are really very helpful. So if I know that smoking causes lung cancer, and if I want to know what to do in the future to decrease the amount of lung cancer, I'll know that I should intervene on smoking. So Woodward says that what it means for x to cause y is that if you—to use a technical term!—'wiggle' x, if you change x, than some change will take place in y.

NW: *Though obviously smoking isn't the only cause of lung cancer. So wiggling x—reducing smoking—won't absolutely eliminate lung cancer.*

AG: That brings up another really important aspect of these new philosophical approaches to causation—probability. The picture that comes out of a probabilistic view of causation is this: you are not changing absolutely whether something will happen or not. What you're always doing is messing about with probability. In the past decade or so, in philosophy, psychology, and cognitive science there's been a real revolution in our understanding of human cognition; the new idea is that we are almost always thinking about probabilities, rather than about actual facts. Often, we're not just asking, for instance, is this true or false, but how likely is this hypothesis compared to another hypothesis? And this is the key to the problem we started out with about imagination.

NW: *So it's as if children with their imaginary games are proto-scientists; they are exploring hypotheses which then could possibly be verified or refuted by experience?*

AG: Well, for twenty years developmental psychologists have used the idea that what children are doing is very much like science—they're trying to figure out the casual structure of the world. One thing we've discovered experimentally, for instance, is that two- and three- and four-year-olds are working out theories about how other people's minds work. Three-year-olds, for instance, don't seem to understand that you and I might have really different beliefs about the world, and that that would lead to changes in our actions. But four-year-olds do understand this. And it looks as if what happens is that the two- and three-year-olds go out and do experiments and explore the world and figure out how the world works and develop new causal theories, just like scientists. Children are very concerned about causation; children are figuring out the casual structure of the world all the time. We can do experiments where we show children new patterns of evidence and, sure enough, right away they make causal inferences. So children are pretending a lot and also working out the causal structure of the world a lot. Maybe there's a connection between those two facts?

NW: *Children explore imaginary situations; some elements of those situations will mirror the real world, but others won't. As a child, how can you determine which bits are ones giving you real-world information?*

AG: Well, one of the things that we found out empirically— the developmental psychologist Paul Harris has done this work—is that although children's imagination might look wild and crazy, internally it is quite logical. And that's also true of adult fiction and adult imagination. Children might say, here's a premise that is going to seem unlikely or unusual—'a boy turns out to be in wizard school'. Or a two-year-old might imagine that a stuffed teddy bear is a real person and a real friend. So you start with this extremely unlikely, low-probability hypothesis. But then the inferences that you make from that premise reflect perfectly good causal logic. So you say, well, if Harry Potter were a wizard and going to wizard school, he would have to acquire clothes and books and do all the things that children do. And Paul Harris showed something similar even with two-year-olds. If you say to two-year-olds, 'Here's teddy and we are going to pretend that teddy is having tea and he spills the tea over himself', and you ask the children, 'Will teddy be wet or dry?', they say he'll be wet. And little children can be quite fierce and specific about this: even if you're starting out from a crazy premise, that doesn't mean that you are allowed to have any old consequence, you have to work through those premises in a logical way.

NW: *So that's children. I can understand why they need to discover how the world works. But as adults, do we still need imagination in the same way?*

AG: We don't need imagination in quite the same way—and we don't indulge in imagination as much as children. But when we're in the same position that children are in, trying to figure out new things about the world or create new ways of thinking about the world, then that's exactly when imagination kicks in. You could think about drama or fiction as serving the function of telling us about what the consequences would be of what look like very unlikely probabilities. But what's interesting about human beings from an evolutionary point of view is that we're always exploring very, very low-probability hypotheses. And, in fact, we take things that start out being very unlikely and we actually make them real. So, if you look around this room that we are in right now and think about it from the perspective of a hunter-gatherer in the Pleistocene, everything is imaginary. Not just the computers and the light bulbs, but also the woven fabrics and the right-angle construction of the tables. From the perspective of the Pleistocene, all those things started out as a very, very weird, strange idea in some guy's head: 'Gee, what would happen if we did this?' The 'Gee what would happen if we did this?' is the central question that causal cognition and causal thinking allows you to address.

NW: *The process of imagining something and bringing it into reality assumes that the hypothesis or imaginary situation can be brought into reality. But lots of imaginary situations will be wasted, as it were. They will be explorations which fall by the wayside because they are just unrealizable in reality.*

AG: Well, the difference between children and adults is that the children don't actually have to do anything. A great evolutionary mystery is why humans have this extremely extended period of childhood when, to be blunt, children are completely useless. They don't bring home the bacon, they don't do anything useful; in fact, they're worse than useless because we have to put in so much time and energy taking care of them. And the answer seems to be that there's an evolutionary division of labour. We have this early period in which we can simply explore alternatives, learn as much as we can about the world around us, create and imagine new possibilities, without being under the constraints of needing to get on in the world, and doing the things we need to survive. And then what happens is that as adults we can take all of that exploration and learning that we did as children and put the products of that to use to actually make things happen in the world. So you could think of it like this: evolution has designed children to be the research and development division of the human species and we adults are production and marketing.

NW: *I can imagine an artist or a poet reading this and responding, 'No that's not what the imagination is about; you're just interested in pay-offs, but the imagination has value in itself.'*

AG: Thinking about children is helpful in this regard, because from the grand evolutionary perspective, childhood is absolutely essential; but, of course, from their own perspective, children aren't playing or exploring *because* they are going to be solving this evolutionary project. The interesting paradox is that what enables human beings to achieve our evolutionary goals in the long run is being able to pull ourselves away from achieving goals in the short run. So having this protected period, having a period of play, having a period when you aren't actually trying to accomplish goals, paradoxically turns out to be one of the best ways of accomplishing your goals in the long run.

NW: *So, clearly, every executive board ought to have at least one child playing in the background.*

AG: Well it's no coincidence that my friends from Silicon Valley have beanbag chairs and balls to play in—and if you go to a place like the Googleplex, there are lots of opportunities to play. If your goal is innovation, that child-like sense of exploration is the best strategy to produce innovation.

NW: *What we've been talking about is a mixture of philosophy and psychology; a purist will say, 'Psychology is really interesting but it has nothing to do with philosophy.'*

AG: Well, it's funny because if you think about the great philosophers whom we all admire—like my personal favourite David Hume, or Plato, Aristotle, Descartes, or Locke, they didn't think that what they were doing was this special thing called *philosophy* separate from science. In fact, Hume very explicitly thought that what he was doing was applying scientific methods to the study of the mind. It's only quite recently that there's been this idea of a sharp divide between philosophy and psychology. And my own view is that you should think about philosophy as really very theoretical everything. So if you are doing *very* theoretical art, then you are doing aesthetics, and if you are doing very theoretical law, then you are doing ethics. If you are doing very theoretical psychology, then you are doing what's often called philosophy of mind. And if you are doing very theoretical developmental psychology, then you're doing epistemology. We're all trying to answer the same deep, profound questions, things like how is it that we come to understand the world around us.

The philosopher Quine had a nice image about the giant web of belief; some parts—the scientific parts—are closer to the edges where we make contact with the world and some parts—the philosophical or mathematical or theoretical parts—are closer to the centre of the web. But it is all one web, and finding out something new about the world can change even very abstract ideas we have. And vice versa: thinking very abstractly about things like counterfactuals can tell us something very concrete, such as why three-year-olds have imaginary friends. It's actually very exciting, especially in developmental psychology, to see how work that, to be frank, most philosophers would have turned their noses up at— questions like, 'Why do two-year-olds think that teddy bears will get wet if we poured tea on them?'—turns out to be extremely revealing about deep philosophical issues.

FREE WILL, RESPONSIBILITY, AND PUNISHMENT

13

DANIEL DENNETT ON
Free Will Worth Wanting

David Edmonds: *One way to exercise my freedom would be to act unpredictably, perhaps not to have a typical introduction to a* Philosophy Bites *interview, or to cut it abruptly short mid-sentence. That's the view of the famous philosopher and cognitive scientist, Daniel Dennett. He also believes that humans can have free will, even if the world is determinist, in other words, governed by causal laws, and he . . .*

Nigel Warburton: *The topic we're focusing on is 'Free Will Worth Wanting'. That seems a strange way in to free will. Usually, the free will debate is over whether we have free will, not whether we want it, or whether it's worth wanting. How did you come at it from this point of view?*

Daniel Dennett: I came to realize that many of the issues that philosophers love to talk about in the free will debates were irrelevant to anything important. There's a bait-and-switch that goes on. I don't think any topic is more anxiety provoking, or more genuinely interesting to everyday people, than free will. But then philosophers replace the interesting issues with technical, metaphysical issues. Who cares? We can define lots of varieties of free will that you can't have, or that are inconsistent with determinism. But so what? The question is, 'Should you regret, or would you regret not having free will?' Yes. Are there many senses of free will? Yes. Philosophers have tended to concentrate on varieties that are perhaps more tractable by their methods, but they're not important.

NW: *The classic description of the problem is this: 'If we can explain every action through a series of causal precedents, there is no space for free will.' What's wrong with that description?*

DD: It's completely wrong. There's plenty of space for free will: determinism and free will are not incompatible at all. The problem is that philosophers have a very simplistic idea of causation. They think that if you give the lowest-level atomic explanation, then you have given a complete account of the causation: that's all the causation there is. In fact, that isn't even causation in an interesting sense.

NW: *How is that simplistic? After all, at the level of billiard balls on a table, one ball hits another one and it causes the second one to move. Neither ball has any choice about whether it moved; their paths were determined physically.*

DD: The problem with that is that it ignores all of the higher-level forms of causation which are just as real and just as important. Suppose you had a complete atom-by-atom history of every giraffe that ever lived, and every giraffe ancestor that ever lived. You wouldn't have an answer to the question of why they have long necks. There is indeed a causal explanation, but it's lost in those details. You have to go to a different level in order to explain why the giraffe developed its long neck. That's the notion of causation that matters for free will.

NW: *Assuming that you're not going to rely on Aesop here, how did the giraffe get its long neck?*

DD: The lineage of giraffe-like animals gradually got longer necks because those that happened to have slightly longer necks had a fitness advantage over those with shorter necks. That's where the explanation lies. Why is that true? That's still a vexed question. Maybe the best answer is not the obvious one that they got long necks so that they could reach higher leaves. Rather, they evolved long necks because they needed them to drink because they had long legs, and they evolved long legs because they provided a better defence against lions.

NW: *So that's an evolutionary hypothesis about giraffes' necks. How does it shed any light on the free will debate?*

DD: If I want to know why you pulled the trigger, I won't learn that by having an atom-by-atom account of what went on in your brain. I'd have to go to a higher level: I'd have to go to the intentional stance in psychology. Here's a very simple analogy: you've got a hand calculator and you put in a number, and it gives the answer 3.333333E. Why did it do that? Well, if you tap in ten divided by three, and the answer is an infinite continuing decimal, the calculator gives an 'E'.

Now, if you want to understand which cases this will happen to, don't examine each and every individual transistor: use arithmetic. Arithmetic tells you which set of cases will give you an 'E'. Don't think that you can answer that question by electronics. That's the wrong level. The same is true with playing computer chess. Why did the computer move its bishop? Because otherwise its queen would have been captured. That's the level at which you answer that question.

NW: *We're often interested in intention where this is linked to moral or legal responsibility. And some cases depend on information that we get about people's brains. For example, there are cases where people had brain lesions that presumably had some causal impact on their criminal behaviour.*

DD: I'm so glad you raised that because it perfectly illustrates a deep cognitive illusion that's been fostered in the field for a generation and more. People say, 'Whenever we have a physiological causal account, we don't hold somebody responsible.' Well, might that be because whenever people give a physiological causal account, these are always cases of disability or pathology? You never see a physiological account of somebody getting something right. Supposing we went into Andrew Wiles' brain and got a perfect physiological account of how he proved Fermat's Last Theorem. Would that show that he's not responsible for his proof? Of course not. It's just that we never give causal physiological-level accounts of psychological events when they go right.

NW: *I'm still having trouble understanding what an intention is. We usually think of intentions as introspectible mental events that precede actions. That doesn't seem to be quite what you mean by an intention.*

DD: When discussing the 'intentional stance', the word 'intention' means something broader than that. It refers to states that have content. Beliefs, desires, and intentions are among the states that have content. To adopt the intentional stance towards a person—it's usually a person, but it could be towards a cat, or even a computer, playing chess—is to adopt the perspective that you're dealing with an agent who has beliefs and desires, and decides what to do, and what intentions to form, on the basis of a rational assessment of those beliefs and desires. It's the stance that dominates Game Theory. When, in the twentieth century, John von Neumann and Oskar Morgenstern invented the theory of games, they pointed out that game theory reflects something fundamental in strategy. Robinson Crusoe on a desert island doesn't need the intentional stance. If there's something in the environment that's like an agent—that you can treat as an agent—this changes the game. You have to start worrying about feedback loops. If you plan activities, you have to think: 'If I do this, this agent might think of doing that in response, and what would be my response to that?' Robinson Crusoe doesn't have to be sneaky and tiptoe around in his garden worrying about what the cabbages will do when they see him coming. But if you've got another agent there, you do.

NW: *So, Man Friday appears, and there are problems . . .*

DD: As soon as Man Friday appears, then you need the intentional stance.

NW: *So if you have the complexity of interaction that is characteristic of an intentional system, that's sufficient for its having intentions. So there doesn't seem to be any room for the mistake of* *anthropomorphism. Anthropomorphism, if the situation is complex enough, is simply the correct attitude to hold towards some inanimate things.*

DD: We can treat a tree from the intentional stance, and think about what it needs, and what it wants, and what steps it takes to get what it needs and wants. This works to some degree. Of course, it doesn't have a soul; it's not conscious. But there are certain patterns and reactions. Recently, we've learned that many varieties of trees have a capacity that gives them quasi-colour vision. When the light on them is predominantly reflected from green things they change the proportion of their energy that goes into growing tall. We might say that they have sensed the competition and are taking a reasonable step to deal with the competition. Now, that's a classic example of the intentional stance applied to a tree, for heaven's sake! Fancier versions apply to everything from bacteria, through clams and fish and reptiles and higher animals, all the way to us. We are the paradigm cases.

What's special about us is that we don't just do things for reasons. Trees do things for reasons. But we *represent* the reasons and we *reflect* on them, and the idea of reflecting on reasons and representing reasons and justifying our reasons to each other informs us and governs the intentional stance. We grow up learning to trade reasons with our friends and family. We're then able to direct that perspective at evolutionary history, at artefacts, at trees. And then we see the reasons that aren't represented, but are active. Until you get the level of perspective where you can see reasons, you're not going to see free will. The difference between an organism that has free will and an organism that doesn't has nothing to do with the atoms: you'll never see it at the atomic level, ever. You have to go to the appropriate design level, and then it sticks out like a sore thumb.

NW: *So we can adopt the intentional stance towards a chess-playing computer, and we probably ought to if we want to beat it at chess, but it doesn't follow from that that it's got free will, or agency?*

DD: Exactly. Those beings with free will are a sub-set of intentional systems. We say 'free as a bird', and birds have a certain sort of free will. But the free will of a bird is nothing compared to our free will, because the bird doesn't have the cognitive system to anticipate and reflect on its anticipations. It doesn't have the same sort of projectable future that we have; nor does it, of course, engage in the business of persuasion. One bird never talks another bird out of doing something. It may threaten it, but it won't talk it out of something.

NW: *So let's go back to the original topic. What is the kind of free will worth wanting?*

DD: It's the kind of free will that gives us the political freedom to move about in a state governed by law and do what we want to do. Not everybody has that freedom. It is a precious commodity. Think about promises. There are many good reasons to make promises: some long-term projects depend on promises, for example. Now, not everybody is equipped to make a promise. Being equipped to make a promise requires a sort of free will, and a sort of free will that is morally important. We can take it apart, we can understand, as an engineer might say, what the 'specs' are for a morally competent agent: you've got to be well informed, have well-ordered desires, and be movable by reasons. You have to be persuadable and be able to justify your views. And there are a few other abilities that are a little more surprising. You have to be particularly good at detecting the intent of other agents to manipulate you and you have to be able to fend off this manipulation. One thing we require of moral agents is that they are not somebody else's puppet. If you want the buck to stop with you, then you have to protect yourself from other agents who might be trying to control you. In order to fend off manipulation, you should be a little bit unpredictable. So having a poker face is a very big part of being a moral agent. If you can't help but reveal your state to the antique dealer when you walk into the store, then you're going to be taken for a ride, you're going to be manipulated. If you can't help but reveal your beliefs and desires to everybody that comes along, you will be a defective, a disabled agent. In order to maximize getting what you want in life, don't tell people exactly what you want.

NW: *That's a very cynical view of human nature! There's an alternative account, surely, in which being open about what you feel allows people to take you for what you really are, not for some kind of avatar of yourself.*

DD: Well, yes, there is that. But think about courtship. You see a woman and you fall head over heels in love with her. What's about the worst thing you can do? Run panting up to her showing her that you've fallen head over heels in love. First of all, you'll probably scare her away, or she'll be tempted by your very display of abject adoration to wrap you around her little finger. You don't want that, so you keep something in reserve. Talleyrand once said that God gave men language so that they could conceal their thoughts from each other. I think that's a deep observation about the role of language in communication. It's essential to the understanding of communication that it's an intentional act, where you decide which aspects of your world you want to inform people about and which you don't.

NW: *So freedom, of the important kind, of the kind worth wanting, is freedom from being manipulated. It's about being in control of your life, you choosing to do things, rather than these things being chosen by somebody else?*

DD: Yes. In order for us to be self-controllers, to be *autonomous* in a strong sense, we have to make sure that we're not being controlled by others. Now, the environment in general is not an agent, it's not trying to control us. It's only other agents that try to control us. And it's important that we keep them at bay so that we can be autonomous. In order to do that, we have to have the capacity to surprise agents with our somewhat unpredictable trajectory.

14

FIERY CUSHMAN ON
Moral Luck

David Edmonds: *Suppose on a Monday, we forgot to show up to a* Philosophy Bites *interview and the interviewee was kept hanging around in a furious mood for an hour. Then suppose, on Tuesday, we forgot to turn up for a different interview. But this time the interviewee, by coincidence, also forgot and so wasn't kept waiting at all. Are we more culpable for the former omission than the latter? Fiery Cushman is a psychologist fascinated by philosophy and he's made a special study of what's called 'moral luck'.*

Nigel Warburton: *The topic we're focusing on is moral luck. Could you begin by saying what moral luck is?*

Fiery Cushman: It's best illustrated with a specific case. Imagine that, after this interview, you and I went out for a couple of beers. Then each of us gets into our separate cars to go home. On your way home, you fall asleep at the wheel and you run off the road and run into a pile of bushes and get picked up for drunk driving. (I'll be generous and assume this is your first offence, Nigel). I don't know about the laws in Britain, but in my home state of Massachusetts you could expect to receive a $250 fine.

On my way home, I fall asleep and I run off the road and I hit a person and kill him. In Massachusetts, I could expect 2.5 to 15 years in prison. Those are radically different amounts of punishment for what amounts to identical behaviour. The twentieth-century British philosopher, Bernard Williams, pointed out that in this respect morality seems to depend on luck. That's the phenomenon that I've been investigating.

NW: *So the luck here is whether somebody happens to be by the side of the road when your car veers off on the pavement?*

FC: Exactly.

NW: *Now, that's not the only kind of luck that could be related to morality. It seems to me a matter of luck that I was born in Britain at a time of relative peace and not, for instance, in Nazi Germany.*

FC: That's right. Williams sketched out a number of different ways that luck can impact moral judgements. He calls the one that I have been focusing on, outcome luck. The idea is that some chance variable in the world produces different outcomes based on the same underlying behaviour.

NW: *Can you say something about your work: you're principally a psychologist investigating philosophical issues . . .*

FC: It's a tremendous benefit to psychology to have centuries and sometimes millennia of philosophy to draw on. Philosophers have laid out foundational concepts and, perhaps most importantly, they've identified dilemmas. In other words, they have found situations where our intuitions in different cases seem somehow mismatched. And so I have had some success, I hope, in probing those dilemmas in order to discover the competing psychological mechanisms, the competing systems, that make us feel quite literally 'of two minds', torn between one perspective and another.

NW: *So we have competing intuitions in the drink-driving case we were talking about. On the one hand, it's a matter of luck whether somebody happens to be on the pavement at the very moment that you veer off the road. On the other hand, it does feel intuitively right that people who are drunk and kill people on the way home ought to be severely punished. And those competing intuitions don't match.*

FC: That's right. I would put it like this: on the one hand, it seems absolutely crazy to take a person who ran into a bush and send them to prison for ten years. On the other hand, it seems equally crazy to take someone who killed a person and let them off with a $250 ticket. We've begun to articulate the two psychological mechanisms that are responsible for these competing intuitions. And the surprise is that, in a sense, they track judgements of wrongness versus punishment.

So, if you give people these two cases and you ask, 'How wrong was Nigel?', 'How wrong was Fiery?', 'How wrong was their behaviour?', they will tend to say that the two of us have engaged in equally wrong behaviour. If you ask, 'How bad is our character?', they'll say that we have equally bad characters.

But when we ask, 'How much *punishment* should Nigel get?' and 'How much *punishment* should Fiery get?', suddenly we find that the issue of outcomes matters. So part of the mystery to be explained is why the brain would be designed with different sets of moral intuitions that lead to different answers—one for wrongness or character and another one for punishment?

NW: *When you say that people focusing on judgements of wrongness give the same answer in both cases, that's not just a hunch, is it? This is something that you've discovered through empirical methods.*

FC: Yes, that's right. We've tested literally thousands of people on the web by giving them hypothetical cases to judge. Of course, you don't want to premise your whole argument on a single scenario, so we give them many different cases that manipulate people's intentions and manipulate the outcome of their behaviour. And then we ask people to make judgements of wrongness or character or appropriate punishment.

Now, of course, one concern is whether you can trust what people say on the Internet. People say all kinds of crazy things. So, our next study brought people into the lab. We modified methods used in behavioural economics where people exchange money in rule-structured games. We introduced accidents into those games and looked at whether people would punish and reward even then, based on outcomes. And what we found is this. If I allocate money to you by the roll of dice, then just that roll of dice is enough for you to modulate how you'll reward or punish me. If the dice come up so that I was very generous to you, then you'll sometimes ignore my intent, focus on the dice, and reward me. Whereas if the dice come up in a way that I end up being stingy to you, even if I intended to be generous, you'll turn around and punish me. So that was a nice confirmation in the laboratory of our Internet findings.

NW: *What's interesting about your results is that your conclusions are counterintuitive. I would have expected people's judgements of wrongness to match their judgements of punishment, but you found a split. Why do you think they split?*

FC: It's a really fascinating question, and it's one that we've put a lot of effort into trying to address. It's difficult to explain why outcomes would matter just for punishment, not for other categories of moral judgement. So, for instance, you might say that intentions are very difficult to know, you can't be sure what somebody's intentions are, so you use outcomes as a heuristic. But, of course, outcomes are equally difficult to know, whether you're making a judgement of their character or a judgement of how much punishment they deserve. So the difficulty is to explain what makes punishment unique, such that outcomes would matter more in that case.

The hunch that we have is that it might have to do with the role that punishment plays in teaching people how to behave in the future.

When you make a judgement of someone's character, you're trying to decide, 'Should I interact with them?' You're predicting how they're going to behave in the future. But when you punish somebody, you're hoping to actually change their behaviour. Suppose people just happen to be designed so that they learn better from being rewarded and punished based on outcomes, and they learn worse from being rewarded and punished based on intent. Then you might expect that over the course of evolution our intuitions about punishment would become honed to focus on outcomes.

So, we designed an experiment to test the hypothesis that the way that we punish is matched to the way that we happen to learn. Suppose you and I are participating in the experiment. You're going to be throwing darts at a board and winning and losing money for me. I'm hoping that you aim for the good targets, but the trick is that you don't know which targets are good for me and which are bad. You're going to throw many times, and after each one of your throws I'm going to be rewarding or punishing you to try to teach you.

So if you aim for a good thing and hit it, I'm going to want to reward that; if you aim for a bad thing and hit it, I'm going to want to punish that. Of course, you're not perfect at darts—nobody is—and we demand that you call your shots. That means that, if you say, 'I'm aiming for green', and I know that that's going to earn me a lot of money, but then you hit red and that loses me a lot of money, I face a dilemma. What am I going to do? Am I going to reward you for your generous intent or am I going to punish you for the bad outcome?

So we put it to the test. For half the people we adopted the first strategy. We would always reward or punish based on what they were aiming at. And for half of the people, we adopted the second strategy: we would reward and punish based on what they hit. Here's what we found: by the end of the experiment, the second group of people had learned much better which targets were good and bad. That seems to indicate that it's just a feature of the way that we learn, and that we learn better from outcomes. When we get punished, we don't think to ourselves, 'Oh, gee, I must have had the wrong intent'; we think, 'What happened? What did I do?' So our punishment judgements seem to be adapted to fit the way in which we learn.

Professors talk a lot about teachable moments. It's the classroom moment when things align in just the right way for you to convey an important lesson. You can think about accidents through the same lens. Your child might not have meant to break the teacup, but it's a teachable moment. You have an opportunity to convey a message about what matters to you, and we seem to have evolved to exploit those moments.

NW: *Perhaps we should introduce a third person to your scenario. We've talked about the two of us. I drive home, veer off the road drunk, but don't kill anybody. You drive home, you veer off the road and you kill somebody. What about David here who is holding the microphone? What if he drives home completely sober, sees an enemy, deliberately veers off the road and kills him? How would your approach explain our different intuitions in those three cases?*

FC: I'm glad you asked that question because it highlights an important issue. Although I've been emphasizing the dilemma of punishment—that outcomes seem to matter—there is also an uncontroversial element, which is that intent matters enormously for punishment too. I don't want to give the impression that this story is all about outcome. There is lots of research, including my own, that suggests that David would be punished very, very severely based in part on his malicious intent.

That sensitivity to intentions emerges early in childhood, and grows a lot between the ages of about four and eight. In fact, the very first experiments in moral psychology, by Jean Piaget, identify this developmental change. Four-year-olds are very outcome-based. By the age of eight, they're much more intent-based, and that focus on intent continues to play an important role in the way that you judge punishment for the rest of your life.

It looks like punishment is a composite of two forces. There is a developmentally early emerging, and possibly (we need more evidence for this) innate, reflex that says that if you caused harm, you deserve punishment. Layered on top of that is the capacity that reflects intentions, and which appears to emerge later in development. By the time you're an adult, the intent-based capacity is, in fact, the dominant one. It plays the greater role in determining punishment. Nonetheless, beneath it, creating these moral luck dilemmas, there is still this retributive reflex that can push cases around at the margins.

NW: *There is a great film by Buñuel called the* The Criminal Life of Archibaldo de la Cruz, *in which the central character has malicious intentions. He tries to kill a number of people, but by chance those people get killed in other ways just at the point where he's about to kill them. Now, he's got the intent, but not the outcome. What would you say about that case?*

FC: It's interesting that you ask this. We tested cases that have just that structure. We have examples of people who attempt to kill somebody and fail, and that's the end of the story. We contrast those scenarios with others in which people attempt to kill somebody and fail, but coincidently the person dies. We discovered that if, coincidently, the person dies, people are more likely to let the attempted murderer off the hook completely. If the person doesn't die coincidentally, the attempted murderer is less likely to get let off the hook.

So this is really curious. What seems to explain it is the reflex that I mentioned. You have a reflex to find the causally responsible person and punish them. Thus, if I attempt to kill you and then coincidently you eat a poisoned salad, our reflex asks, 'Where did the poisoned salad come from?' That process diverts our attention. Because we are focused on the kitchen, we ignore the person with the loaded gun who just tried to shoot you. Whereas, if the salad doesn't kill you, that reflex never gets engaged. Thus, that more-developmentally-later-emerging process, the one that focuses on intent, can direct attention to the person with the loaded gun, who tried to kill you.

NW: *So you're claiming that we've evolved with these competing intuitions and there are evolutionary explanations for why that should be so. Let's say your hypothesis is correct. There is a further question though. If a pattern of behaviour or judgement has evolved from, say, the Pleistocene epoch, it doesn't follow that this behaviour or judgement is a good thing. People like sweet food because in the Pleistocene we took all the energy that we could when it was available. But now that's a bad thing because people in the twenty-first century become obese. Is there a parallel here with our views about punishment and culpability?*

FC: That's a wonderful question. The analogy with our diet is a very good one. Think about that child I mentioned who broke the teacup, and whose mother can exploit that event as a teachable moment. In our evolutionary history, she couldn't use language; all that she could do was punish the child to convey the message that broken teacups are bad. In our evolutionary present, she has another option: she can say, 'That broken teacup really upset me', or before the situation even arose she could say, 'Here are the rules: no breaking teacups.' In an interesting way, language gives us an escape hatch from this evolutionary dilemma of needing to punish accidental outcomes. It's one that, at a normative level, I wish we might exercise more often.

15

NICOLA LACEY ON
Criminal Responsibility

David Edmonds: *Suppose in the jungle I shoot a man thinking he was a threatening tiger. Have I killed the man intentionally? It's the sort of conundrum that keeps lawyers, as well as philosophers, happily preoccupied. There appear to be a number of factors that need to be in place before someone is held criminally responsible for an action, such as whether they know what they're doing, and whether they should know what they're doing. These, in a way, are timeless considerations. They apply to a criminal action now, or one hundred years ago, but Nicola Lacey argues that there's also an historical component to criminal responsibility that can't be ignored. The concept of criminal responsibility makes sense only within the particular institutional framework in which it operates.*

Nigel Warburton: *The topic we're going to focus on is criminal responsibility. Could you just begin by outlining what criminal responsibility is?*

Nicola Lacey: We use the term 'responsibility' in lots of different ways when we're talking about the criminal law. Sometimes, if we talk about someone being criminally responsible, we're simply referring to the fact that they've been convicted; but, actually, when lawyers talk about criminal responsibility, they are usually separating out just one of the components that feeds into a justified criminal conviction, and that has something to do with not just the person's conduct, but the attitude or state of mind with which they engaged in that conduct. To show that someone had not only done an act, but was responsible for having done it, certain other conditions would have to be fulfilled. Those conditions are generally thought to be relevant to whether it is fair to hold someone responsible, and whether it is fair, therefore, to convict them.

NW: *So, if I flick a switch on the wall and, unbeknownst to me, it's attached to somebody else, and I give them an electric shock that's fatal, I probably wouldn't be criminally, or morally, responsible for that act.*

NL: Exactly. We draw a rough common-sense distinction between things that are accidental—things that just happen—and things that people make happen, or intend. Take an example I like to use with students. I'm in a crowded underground station, at the top of an escalator, somebody jolts me, I bump into the next person, she falls and she's injured. I'm responsible in some very minimal sense, perhaps, but essentially most people would call that an accident. If, on the other hand, I take a dislike to the person in front of me and give him a shove, intentionally, that is clearly a case where I'm responsible. Lawyers tend to like Latin tags, so it's often known in criminal law as *mens rea* (guilty mind), and it consists in a number of different mental states or attitudes: good examples would be intention—the fact I do something intentionally, purposely, with relevant knowledge of the surrounding circumstances, or perhaps foreseeing a certain outcome. Suppose I don't intend a person I push on the escalator to fall, but I do foresee that there's a risk of that, then that would be recklessness. So there isn't one way of proving responsibility in criminal law, but there is a philosophical idea that arguably holds them all together: that it is only fair to hold someone accountable if they've done something in circumstances in which they had a fair opportunity to do otherwise.

NW: *So, what would that amount to?*

NL: Well, in one very famous and influential account, by the legal philosopher H. L. A. Hart, it consists of two different sorts of components which have to do with the capacities of the person: it's only fair to hold someone responsible if they knew what they were doing, and they had a fair opportunity to do otherwise—they had a fair opportunity to conform their conduct to the law. That implies something not only about their own capacities, but also something about the law itself. The law has to be possible to comply with, and also capable of being known, so reasonably clear. So there's a connection between criminal responsibility and the idea of the Rule of Law.

NW: *So if I commit a crime and fulfil some of this cluster of volition and knowledge of what I'm doing, the sorts of characteristics that you talked about as* mens rea, *then that makes me criminally responsible for what I've done.*

NL: That would be the most common view among lawyers of criminal responsibility. Of course, the capacity-based theory of criminal responsibility, which I've just set out for you, is not the only one within the philosophy of criminal law.

For example, in recent writing, there has been a revival of interest in Aristotelian virtue-centred theories of criminal responsibility, in which the argument is that, when you hold someone responsible, an attribution of responsibility is in effect a judgement that bad character has been exhibited in the person's conduct. That difference between a virtue-ethics approach to criminal responsibility and the more psychological, capacity-based fairness argument is quite interestingly related to different notions of what kind of a thing criminal law is: whether it's a very finely textured, institutionalized form of moral evaluation, or whether it's a practical, regulatory system, which is, however, subject to certain kinds of normative or moral constraints.

NW: *Suppose I'm usually very law abiding, and then somebody treads on my toe at the wrong moment and I swing my fist out in anger and I knock somebody out. It's completely out of character as it happens. How would the two different approaches differ in how they would treat me?*

NL: Things get even more complicated here, I'm afraid, because the character theorists don't necessarily agree. Some character theorists would say, 'Well, if it's out of character, then it's not a real expression of that person's character, and therefore we shouldn't hold him responsible'; whereas others would say, 'But, actually, what's going on here is that a characteristic has nonetheless been expressed: this conduct expresses a bad disposition, and that's what's blameworthy.' On the fairness view, the sort of view Hart endorsed, it's all going to turn on whether we think that the person had a fair opportunity to avoid this conduct, so the question of whether it's out of character or not isn't the relevant question.

NW: *We've been discussing Hart, who wrote in the twentieth century, and we've mentioned Aristotle, who wrote in the fourth century BC, as if they were contemporaries discussing the same issue. Is that acceptable?*

NL: Not from my point of view. I think that's a really good question. Clearly, you can find aspects of the concept of responsibility among which you can see commonalities going back to Aristotle, going through the Christian tradition in Enlightenment philosophers of various kinds, in twentieth-century linguistic philosophy, in liberal political theory, and so on, so it's not as though we can't have a meaningful conversation about the concept of responsibility. However, when we think about criminal responsibility in the sense of how responsibility operates as a component of how we attribute liability in criminal law, there is another factor which is highly relevant to how ideas of responsibility work: that is, how criminal law is institutionalized. We sit here and have a debate about whether someone who injures somebody else when they're very drunk is really responsible. That's a very pure, intellectual, moral argument. If we ask, 'Should that person be held legally responsible?', then we immediately assume a set of institutions, institutions that allow you to prosecute, that formulate rules in relation to which a prosecution takes place, and perhaps, most relevantly, produce a forum in which we have a debate about proof—in other words, a trial. If you go back 250 or 300 years, just in England and Wales, you would see a completely different sort of trial process for the vast majority of criminal cases.

NW: *So how were things different in England in the eighteenth century?*

NL: I can give you an idea of this with something very basic, which is that historians have calculated that the average length of a trial in the late eighteenth century was approximately 15 minutes. You can tell immediately that a 15-minute process was not a process in which it was very likely that cognitive and volitional capacities and fair opportunities of the kind that we were talking about could genuinely be the object of investigation and proof. This was a much more rough-and-ready process. But it's not just the length of the trial: until 1836, felony defendants, in other words the more serious of the criminal defendants, didn't have a right to be legally represented—very often, there were no lawyers present in criminal cases. You didn't have systematic law reporting, you didn't have a hierarchy of appeals, there was no police force until well into the nineteenth century. So how did the criminal law work? Of course, it had some resources that we don't have so much these days—particularly local knowledge. Cases got into the trial process through local information filtered through magistrates. My assumption is that the vast majority of trials operated on the basis of an assumption of guilt and responsibility, in the sense that if somebody had got themselves into the courtroom they were probably a bit of a bad lot. The trial gave that defendant a chance to exculpate himself, usually by calling on character witnesses to speak up for their credibility.

NW: *So that obviously contrasts strongly, we hope, with what goes on in a trial today. What can we learn from that contrast?*

NL: What I'm interested in here is the degree to which, and the way in which, concepts that are operationalized within institutional frameworks actually affect the tone and shape of those concepts. We couldn't have mobilized 'responsibility' as we understand it today, except within certain kinds of institutional infrastructure. I want to put that sort of history of philosophical ideas within much more of an institutional framework. The reason this is important in terms of contemporary criminal law theory of a philosophical temper is that the tendency to take a sophisticated theory, which is in a sense a theory of moral responsibility, and just assume that we can project it onto criminal law, has very often made us ignore aspects of criminal law as a social practice which simply don't match up to those philosophical criteria. We've missed a trick, in terms of looking at the texture of criminal law to see whether there's more than one conception of responsibility at play within this practice, and hence an opportunity to learn something about how law is different as a social practice and a social discourse from moral discourse and argumentation.

NW: *Are you saying that there's more than one concept of responsibility that applies within the realm of the criminal law, or rather that we have one concept that's a moral concept of responsibility, and another that is overlapping with it perhaps, but not exactly congruent with it, which is the area of criminal responsibility?*

NL: There's more than one way in which we structure our practices of responsibility attribution in criminal law. Perhaps the most influential and appealing account is this account based on engaged volitional and cognitive capacities: intention, knowledge, recklessness, and so on. But the criminal law quite often attributes responsibility based on the idea that we have simply caused an outcome. Let's go back to the escalator example, an example where somebody else shoves me, and I accidentally shove the next person, and she's hurt. In terms of the cognitive and volitional idea of responsibility—the fairness idea of responsibility—we don't think that I'm responsible in the same way. On the other hand, here's a thought experiment. Imagine that the person who's injured turns round and remonstrates with me and says, 'That was really bad', and I say, 'Well, it's nothing to do with me, it's just an accident', and just walk away: I don't help her get up, I don't show any concern for her. That, surely, is a morally unappealing position, and we do feel that I'm in some sense related to this outcome in a morally relevant way. Now, the criminal law thinks that's even more relevant: criminal law often holds us responsible for outcomes that we cause, even without these more muscular forms of responsibility like negligence, let alone foresight, knowledge, or intention.

NW: *Could you give an example of that?*

NL: Many road traffic offences, for example, speeding. There's no defence to a speeding offence to say that you didn't mean to do it, or you just didn't look at the speedometer. Over half of criminal offences, on a good calculation, are either offences of so-called strict liability—in other words, no need to prove intention or knowledge or recklessness—or, interestingly, a very important category, they're offences where you don't have to prove so-called *mens rea*—criminal responsibility in the cognitive or volitional sense—in relation to one or more elements. Murder, what many people think of as the paradigm criminal offence, is, you might guess, intentional killing, and it's true, in a sense, that that would be a rough-and-ready definition of murder in English criminal law. But, in fact, the so-called *mens rea*, the responsibility element of the murder, consists of an intention, either to kill or to cause grievous bodily harm. Perhaps an even more clear-cut example would be the case of assaulting a police officer in the execution of his or her duty. I have to have so-called *mens rea* for the assault; but if I'm unaware that it's a police officer in the execution of his or her duty, that's no defence. So there are numerous offences in criminal law in which there is not a complete requirement of proving responsibility. My point is that that makes a real difference to what kind of phenomenon criminal law is, as a social practice, which should be of interest to philosophers of criminal law.

NW: *Is it fair to sum up what you've been saying as this: the notion of criminal responsibility isn't fixed for all time; it's actually partly determined socially and scientifically. What counts as criminal responsibility today is different from what it was in the eighteenth century, and it will inevitably be different in 100 years' time, or 50 years' time even?*

NL: That is a fair summary of what I'm saying, although I don't want to exaggerate it in the sense that I still think there will be family resemblances. It's not that the debates about criminal responsibility will be unrecognizable to a twenty-first-century reader, or in the twenty-third century. As we can see, there's a continuity. For example, some of the issues that neuroscience is now raising were raised within Darwinism and eugenics in the nineteenth century. So there are commonalities. Nonetheless, the changing environment and goals and institutional frame in criminal law make a difference to how we can think about criminal responsibility.

16

VICTOR TADROS ON
Punishment

David Edmonds: *Should we punish an innocent person if by so doing we could stop a riot and so save many lives? Most people would say no. Is it a good thing, positively a good thing, for a guilty person to suffer? I suspect people will have different intuitions about that. What we need is a theory of punishment to help give consistent answers to such questions. And law professor Victor Tadros is the man to supply it.*

NW: *The topic we're focusing on is punishment. What sort of punishment are we talking about?*

> **Victor Tadros:** We're primarily focused on state punishment: punishment of criminal offenders through the state-run criminal justice system. We might also think about punishment in other contexts, where there is no criminal justice system. But we're not primarily focusing on the punishment of children for, say, paternalistic reasons.

NW: *So, we're talking about the kind of things that a criminal comes face to face with in the courts of law, and so on. What are the main philosophical justifications for punishment?*

VT: Most people who work in the field identify two main theories. One of them is consequentialism, which says that you should punish offenders because it does more good than harm. The main way in which it does this is that it deters the criminal from committing further wrongs—and deters other people from committing wrongs. And so, even though it's bad that we punish the offender and that the offender suffers, overall it's good because there will be fewer offences and less harm to other people.

NW: *That sounds convincing. What could be wrong with it?*

VT: Well, imagine that I could punish an innocent person and in doing so I would deter more wrongdoing. Consequentialism looks like it's going to permit me to do that. For example, imagine that a rape has occurred and it's very hard for me to find the rapist. It would take lots of resources. But I've got a person who looks like the rapist and I could punish him. And if I punish him, then it would have a deterrent effect—it would prevent more rapes. Even if it does more good than harm, I think many people would baulk at the idea of punishing an innocent man.

NW: *People who defend consequentialism have a pragmatic response to that criticism: they say that in real life cases, if it became public that an innocent person was punished, that would bring about bad consequences in itself: people would lose their confidence in the law. So although the theory seems to support the idea that you can punish innocent people, in practice, it wouldn't work like this.*

VT: It remains to be seen whether in practice you ever could justify punishment on that basis, were consequentialism true. I don't think we can rule out the possibility that we could do more good than harm by punishing an innocent person. You might be a police officer and be very good at covering up a person's innocence. But also, I think, most people object to this idea, not purely on pragmatic grounds, but on principled grounds.

Most people believe that there are restrictions on harming someone as a means for a greater good. Thus, imagine punishing one innocent person to save five rapes from occurring: the punishment deters five rapes. The consequentialist will have to defend this punishment. But I think many people will baulk at that conclusion, even in circumstances where there are no pragmatic disadvantages in doing this.

NW: *Ok. There goes the consequentialist theory. What's the other common approach in this area?*

VT: The main alternative is retributivism. Retributivism holds that we should punish people because they deserve to suffer. A standard version of this view has two main components. The first is that it's a good thing when wrongdoers suffer, and the second is that the state is permitted to carry out this good thing. Normally, obviously, making people suffer is a bad thing, but retributivists say making a guilty person suffer is good. We can put it like this: the moral valence of making people suffer is altered by wrongdoing. Whereas, the normal moral valence of suffering is negative—suffering is normally a bad thing—in this case, the moral valence is positive; the suffering of the offender turns out to be a good thing.

NW: *Well, psychologically, that seems a very common response. You see it in the playground. You see it in many places. If somebody harms another it seems right to get back at them in some way.*

VT: I agree that many people have the instinctive reaction that it's a good thing when wrongdoers suffer. Think about the bad guy at the end of a cowboy movie who gets what he deserves: we all cheer when this person suffers. We even cheer when the person gets killed. In the mid-twentieth century, many philosophers considered this view barbaric. And my sense is that those people in the mid-twentieth century were just about right—this really is a barbaric view. It's not plausible to think that we should take pleasure or satisfaction at the suffering of other people. But if it's a good thing that offenders suffer, that seems just how we should feel.

NW: *So, although many of us might have the tendency to want to do this, it's something we should try and curb.*

VT: Even if we thought that the suffering of bad people was a good thing, I doubt that the state should bring it about. After all, think about the way in which the state brings about the suffering of people through the criminal justice system—it spends an enormous amount of resources doing this. Now, try and justify spending this enormous amount of resources simply because you think that it's a good thing that people suffer. Haven't we got anything better to spend our money on? Why can't we spend the money making good people much happier?

NW: *So, if straightforward consequentialism fails, and retributivism fails—what are we left with?*

VT: Let's return to the consequentialist thought that we punish people in order to prevent other people committing crimes. That thought seems right: the thought that the most important end that punishment can achieve is to prevent other people suffering the harms and wrongs of criminal offending.

We do this by deterring offenders and others from future offending. So, I'm an enthusiast for deterrence. Deterrence is the right kind of rationale for punishment. And in fact, deterring wrongdoing is the only thing that could plausibly justify the enormous amount of resources we spend on the criminal justice system in the real world. By doing this, the criminal justice system achieves something very important—it protects people from having their rights violated.

Now, return to the weakness in the consequentialist thought which says that you could punish innocent people in order to achieve a greater good—that looks like a deficiency in the consequentialist view.

The remedy for that deficiency, though, is not to think that it's wrong to punish people for deterrence reasons altogether, but rather that it's wrong to punish *innocent* people for deterrence reasons. There might be constraints on punishing innocent people, which don't apply to guilty people. You're permitted to punish guilty people for reasons of deterrence. You're not permitted to punish innocent people for reasons of deterrence. If we could justify that, we would have a view that looks more attractive.

NW: *It's interesting that you focused on punishment to deter other people. I would have thought that the primary role of punishment, in many people's eyes, is to stop the particular individual punished from doing more of the same.*

VT: And I agree that it's permissible to punish people in order to prevent them from committing further crimes, too. The question is whether it's permissible to do more than that: to punish offenders in order to prevent *other* people from committing crimes. That seems more controversial because you're harming one person as a means to prevent other people from committing wrongs. Given that this person isn't responsible for the wrongs the other people commit, this is going to be harder to defend.

But at the same time, it is very counterintuitive to restrict our view of punishment to punishing this person solely to prevent his or her own further wrongdoing. Imagine that I go and commit a very serious wrong. Now I'm a reformed character and I'm unlikely to commit another offence again—well, on this view, there will now be no reason to punish me. Or imagine, even more strongly, that I'm not a reformed character but I just got what I want. Suppose, I want to be rich and, through my crime, I've become very rich. Now, it seems like there's no reason to punish me anymore because I'm not a threat to anyone. I'm quite happy living with all my money that I gained through the crime.

NW: *You could argue that if somebody won't be reformed by the punishment, then punishment is irrelevant. Some people would bite this bullet: 'This person committed this crime; they've had a dramatic character change since then. There's no danger to other people. There is, therefore, no point in punishing them.'*

VT: I don't think this is an attractive position. Imagine a person commits a rape, and they rape the only person that they wanted to have intercourse with. And now, they've had intercourse with that person, they don't want to have intercourse with anyone else. I don't think it's plausible to think that this person isn't liable to be punished anymore. And that is true even if they regret what they did.

Let me try and explore why that might be true. Think about the victim of the crime in this case. This person's had her rights violated by the offender. We might think about what the offender owes to the victim in virtue of having offended. He's made her much worse off. He's harmed her very severely. What does he now owe her? Well, he owes her, at least, compensation. Most people think that that is completely uncontroversial—that when you wrongfully harm a person, you at least need to compensate them for what you've done.

Rape, though, is very hard to compensate for, if not impossible. Monetary compensation seems unsatisfactory. And compensation, even full compensation, were that somehow available, seems an insufficient response on behalf of the offender. What else could the culprit do to compensate the person for the rape that they've suffered? One thing they could do is to protect this person against being raped by other people. Imagine that there are other people around who want to rape this person; the culprit, I think, owes a duty of protection towards the person whom they've raped. As a result, we can justify harming them to deter other people—we can justify this to them in virtue of the fact that they are harmed as a means to the end of protecting people. In virtue of their wrongdoing, they have a powerful duty to serve this end. So we are using them as a means only to serve an end that they are themselves required to serve. I call this the 'duty view' of punishment, because the justification of punishment is grounded in the duties that offenders incur in virtue of their wrongdoing. Importantly, it justifies punishment by thinking about the obligations that offenders have to respond to their own wrongdoing. Justifying punishment to offenders, I believe, requires that we think in this way. In considering how we can act towards them, we should think first about the reasons that they themselves have to respond to their wrongdoing. We punish offenders to protect other people, but we do it only because these wrongdoers must serve the end of protecting people themselves.

NW: *Wouldn't it follow from that, that not only should they be punished, but that they should be seen to be punished? In order for the punishment to be an effective deterrent, other people have to be aware that it is occurring. And the next step down that line is to end up with some kind of public spectacle where the suffering of the criminal is broadcast to everybody.*

VT: I suspect that there was a time when punishment as a public spectacle wasn't completely irrational. I'm not sure that hanging, drawing, and quartering people was ever justified. But if deterrence is going to work, everyone must know that offenders are punished for their crimes. There may have been a time when spectacular public punishments were necessary to achieve this.

But we should think about another consideration to take into account in determining the mode of punishment. On the view that I am outlining, the suffering of offenders is still to be considered a bad thing. If we can punish the person in a way that also benefits that person—say, through rehabilitative techniques—then, we have very good reason to do this. In fact, we're going to achieve a double benefit. We deter criminals because people don't like punishment, even when it's rehabilitative; and we also benefit the offender at the same time, making them better off. Public spectacles are difficult to reconcile with this ambition.

Now, the retributivist view, the view that thinks it is good that wrongdoers suffer, won't see any value in improving the lives of offenders. The view that I'm outlining, which I call the 'duty view', is more humane than the retributivist view in this respect. The retributivist thinks, 'It's great when wrongdoers suffer. And, within the limits of proportionality, we should try and make them as badly off as possible.' The view that I defend says, 'If we can punish the person and deter crime, and at the same time, make them better off—that's what we should aim to do.'

NW: *You've already mentioned that you shouldn't punish the innocent, but what limits do you want to set on the kinds of punishment that you can use to achieve the ends you think are legitimate?*

VT: Another nice feature of the duty view is that it can naturally explain proportionality. There are two ways of understanding the idea of proportionality. One is aesthetic, like when a window is well proportioned to a room. Another idea defends harming a person in virtue of the good that outweighs it. And on the view that I'm defending, it's the second kind of proportionality that we're concerned with. We're permitted to harm people only if doing so is going to bring out about a significant good.

Furthermore, there's a cap on how much you can punish a person. Return to the thought that a person incurs duties as a result of their wrongdoing; what's the scope of those duties? Well, that depends on the gravity of the wrong. Imagine that I steal one of your compact discs. How much do I owe you in return for the compact disc in terms of protection against other people stealing compact discs? Well, not so much that it is permissible to kill me as a result. When we're talking about very serious wrongs, in contrast, we might be able to do much more to the person to harm them in order to bring about a greater good.

NW: *But the key question is, how much more? Some people would say, 'Look, if somebody's murdered or raped, then capital punishment is the correct response and entirely proportionate.'*

VT: I don't think that it's obvious that we can rule out capital punishment on principled grounds, though I do think that the overall case against capital punishment is decisive.

There are some cases where it's permissible to kill a person as a means of preventing them from committing a wrong. And perhaps we can extend that thought to punishment. Imagine that I've hired a hit-man to kill you. The hit-man's coming over the hill with his automatic weapon. The only way in which you can protect yourself against the hit-man is to pull me in front of you as a human shield. Luckily for you, I'm standing beside you. I take it that while it wouldn't be permissible for you to use an innocent person as a human shield to defend yourself against this hit-man, it would be permissible to use *me* as a human shield against this hit-man to save your life. And yet in doing so, I'll be killed as a means to protect you against the hit-man.

Punishment is a few steps further down the line from this kind of case. We're talking about a person being harmed to protect people against threats that other people are going to perpetrate against them. We're talking about a person who's already harmed someone, rather than a person who will cause harm if nothing is done. So, we're not talking about exactly the same kind of case. But I think that the differences between the kind of case that I have outlined and capital punishment may not be decisive in ruling out capital punishment in principle. Just to be clear, it may be that the differences between the kind of defensive case that I have outlined and capital punishment are sufficiently great to rule out capital punishment, but that case has to be made.

But even if that case cannot be made, the death penalty is very likely ruled out on pragmatic grounds. There are very few people, at least in attractive countries to live in, like the UK, who think that capital punishment would be very effective in deterring homicide. The homicide rate is not very high. We wouldn't reduce the homicide rate in any very significant way through capital punishment, so capital punishment is ruled out on that basis. Countries that have high crime rates should probably focus their resources on creating the conditions where crimes are less likely to occur in other ways than on the death penalty.

Finally, let me add that no theory of punishment inherently rules out the death penalty—not the retributivist view, not the consequentialist view.

NW: *So, you're saying that somebody who has a religious prohibition on all killing should revise his or her views in relation to capital punishment?*

VT: I think that sometimes it could be morally wrong *not* to kill people. Imagine that a third party could protect you from the hit-man coming over the hill. I've hired the hit-man. The hit-man is going to shoot you if this third party does nothing. The third party could easily pull me in front of you and prevent you from being killed. I think this person has a moral duty to pull me in front of you. And if they don't do so, I think their failure to help is seriously morally wrong. If it was true that we had a duty to administer the death penalty to provide people with sufficient protection against serious criminal offending, I don't think that religious conviction would provide a person with a good reason not to do their duty. But as I say, I very much doubt that there are good reasons for the death penalty overall.

NW: *In Britain we have a criminal justice system that's partly based on deterrence, partly based on retribution: how would you reorganize this system to make it better?*

VT: One thing it is important to grasp is that moving from a theoretical model of punishment to the pragmatics of punishment is no smooth ride. A reason against imposing the death penalty, for example, is that institutions are not that good at distinguishing between the innocent and the guilty. If we were to try and make them better at this, they would be enormously costly. So while philosophical work on punishment should inform institutional design, we should not draw conclusions about institutions too quickly from accounts of the justification of punishment.

That being said, there are many ways in which the criminal justice system in England and Wales is inadequate. Too much is criminalized, and people are punished too much even when they have violated legitimate criminal prohibitions. I suspect that general deterrence grounds are insufficient to justify the length of penalties that we have in England and Wales. We have long penalties compared with other criminal justice systems in Europe. There really isn't sufficient evidence that this is justified in terms of reducing the crime rate. Most of the evidence suggests that while people are very motivated not to get caught and punished, the length of sentence doesn't make very much difference to people's conduct. So, it may well be that we would retain a similar kind of crime rate with lower sentences. But I am primarily a legal philosopher, and I am quite conscious of my own limitations in speaking about many of the practical difficulties involved in criminal justice reform.

17

PHILIP PETTIT ON
Group Agency

David Edmonds: *Christian List of the London School of Economics and Philip Pettit from Princeton University and the Australian National University in one way constitute a group. They are the group of people who've co-authored a book on* Group Agency. *The book argues that groups, like corporations or political parties or churches or charities, can be agents rather in the way individuals can be agents—they can have goals, they can be held responsible. But groups are not merely an aggregate of their individual components—as the group made up of me, Nigel, and Philip Pettit, discussed.*

Nigel Warburton: *The topic we're focusing on is group agency. What's that?*

Philip Pettit: I think of group agents as a sub-species of groups in general. Groups include the group of red-haired people or the group of people who are the second born in the family. The people in the group share a property, although groups may differ in how far the property is one that members recognize, how important the property is to how they behave and so on.

Group agents are a special sub-set of groups. They all have a property in common, but the feature that makes them a *group agent* is that they mimic an individual agent in how they behave.

NW: *Could you give an example?*

PP: Sure. Suppose the three of us constitute a group—perhaps a group that meets every evening for a drink. But in order to constitute a *group agent*, we would have to endorse some goal or purpose that we want to advance together. And equally we would have to form shared views about the best means to advance this goal, about our sub-goals, about the order of importance of our goals, and about how we could add to or change our goals. We've got to do together what we all do individually when we pursue a goal.

NW: *So would a political party or a company count as a group agent?*

PP: Yes. Groups obviously vary enormously in size and in structure, and any one of them might organize itself as a group agent. Given that the three of us are a group, for example, we could form a group agent in order to further some political purpose. We're speaking in Oxford, and we might set ourselves the goal of advancing a green agenda in the local areas. We would want to agree on sub-goals in that case, on how those sub-goals rank in importance, on what are the best means for pursuing them, and so on. We, as a group, would have to do what I, as an individual, would have to do if I decided on my own to pursue a green agenda.

NW: *Are you saying that as a group we're different from three individuals?*

PP: Yes, I am. There is quite a dominant tradition that says it's just a *façon de parler* to talk about a group as an agent. Only individual human beings are agents, and what happens when group agents seem to exist is just that those individuals coordinate their actions to some purpose.

Now, at a certain level that's true, but it misses something very important. When you ask about the relationship between the judgement or belief of a group on some matter and the judgements of the individuals in the group, people who say groups are just individuals will typically answer, 'The views or beliefs that the group holds are just the views or beliefs held by a majority of the members.'

NW: *That sounds reasonable. What's wrong with that?*

PP: When you begin to see what's wrong with it you gain an insight into why group agency is interesting.

Let me first make an abstract point. Suppose the three of us have to agree on a set of judgements and decisions, because we want to mimic an individual agent. We have to put together our judgements and beliefs, desires and preferences on various matters in order to form shared attitudes. Imagine, then, that we've got to work out our judgements on whether P is the case, and on whether Q is the case, and then on whether P *and* Q—the conjunction of P and Q—is the case.

There are three of us here: me, David, and Nigel. Do we, as a group, believe P? Well, I think P is the case, let us suppose, and David thinks P is the case, so that's the majority. But Nigel doesn't think P is the case. Still, that's OK on the majoritarian approach; as a group we believe P.

Then we vote on Q. It turns out that I think that it is also the case that Q. David this time rejects it: he doesn't think Q is the case. But you, Nigel, accept that Q is the case. The majority, tick off Q, the group believes Q. So the group believes P and believes Q. But now the crucial question. Does the group believe P and Q? Does it believe the conjunctive proposition: P-and-Q?

Let's try the majority vote. David doesn't believe the conjunction because he rejected Q. Nigel doesn't believe it because he rejected P. I'm the only one who accepts it, since I alone accepted P and accepted Q. So if we follow majority voting we're stuck with saying that we believe P and we believe Q, but we reject the conjunction, P and Q.

That's a real problem. If we behaved like that, we couldn't operate as a group agent. We wouldn't be able to get our act together in various situations of choice and we wouldn't be able to present ourselves to others as a group agent with whom they can do business.

NW: *That's really surprising. Does it have applications in real life? Are there really P, Q, and P-and-Q decisions that we have to make?*

PP: There are many examples. I became alerted to this particular paradox through some legal literature on what was called the doctrinal paradox, and I gave it the name of 'the discursive dilemma', arguing that there was a wider problem than arises in the legal case. Christian List and I then went on to establish a more general result. But let us focus first on the discursive dilemma.

Suppose the three of us constitute the board of a housing association. A tenant comes to us with a complaint about a landlord. The heater in his room blew up and caused him great psychological harm.

Imagine that we have to decide on this complaint in the way the courts would decide an issue like this. The landlord will be blameworthy and liable if the tenant was actually harmed by the blowing up of the heater and if the landlord had a duty of care to look after the heater. And if both of those are the case, then the landlord is liable, and maybe some punishment is due to him.

Take the first issue: was the tenant traumatized by the blowing up? David and I might agree he was. But Nigel thinks not. But as a group we think, yes, he was indeed traumatized by the incident.

Second issue: did the landlord have a duty of care for the tenant, being required to look after the heater? David thinks not. Nigel and I think he did. So, again, we agree that as a group he had a duty of care.

But now comes the issue of whether we agree that the landlord should be held culpable or blameworthy. Remember that I am the only one who thought both that he had a duty of care and that the poor tenant was traumatized. Each of you rejected one of those. So you are each going to say 'no' on the issue of whether the landlord is culpable; I'm the only one who is going to say 'yes'. But that means that as a group we are going to be incoherent. We will have to say, 'Yes, the tenant was really hurt', and 'Yes, the landlord was really responsible.' But 'No, he can't be blamed.'

The lesson of all of this is that, if we are to achieve the coherence of a group agent in such a case, then the group views we form cannot each answer by a majoritarian arithmetic to our individual views.

NW: *So what do we do?*

PP: If the three of us are to behave as a group agent, we have to mimic an individual. That means we have to be capable of advancing shared purposes according to shared representations. In order to achieve the status of such an agent, we have to make sure that our representations and our purposes are consistent. What this example shows is that we can't guarantee that the representations, or indeed the purposes, will be consistent if we rely on majority voting within the group. Happily, Christian List and I were able to demonstrate that this is not just an accident of majority voting. There is no simple way of starting with individuals and their views, and then determining the group views by the aggregation of those individual views, whether the aggregation be majoritarian in character or not.

NW: *I'm a bit disconcerted by you using the word 'happily' there, because the result you describe seems to be tragic.*

PP: A very nice point, because it is tragic in a sense. It's what's called in the literature an impossibility result. It's impossible to ensure that the views of a group are coherent or consistent—it's impossible to establish their collective rationality, as we may say—and at the same time meet another condition, which you might call individual responsiveness. This is a condition requiring that a group agent should hold only views that are responsive case by case to the views of members. In order to act as proper agents, groups have to make sure that they are collectively rational, or at least sensitive to the demand for collective rationality, and that means that on one or another issue they have to reject individual responsiveness. They have to be ready to form views that go against the dispositions of members as individuals.

Thus, if we are going to get our act together in the housing case, or the abstract P-and-Q case, then we can't decide by majority. On some issues, we as a group have to adopt one or another view that does not correspond systematically to what we as individuals hold on that issue. We as a group have to be ready to reject the majority view on some proposition. We might decide to accept the conjunction P-and-Q in the earlier example, or to accept that the landlord is indeed culpable, even though a majority of us reject that view. We have to be ready to construct group attitudes, rather than letting those attitudes be determined in a bottom-up way by the attitudes of members.

NW: *This is a fascinating paradox: were you the first to identify it and recognize the ways in which groups can have group agency?*

PP: There is actually a long tradition of recognizing that individuals can combine into units or groups that themselves are capable of acting like agents with common purposes and beliefs. Interestingly, the Romans and the Greeks didn't have a notion of such a corporate entity, at least by many accounts. But it emerged and became very influential in the Middle Ages, being applied to bodies like the guild, the town, and the monastic order—groups that attained a real salience in the medieval world.

As these groups became salient, the lawyers and philosophers began to talk of the corporate entity as an agent in its own right, indeed as an agent that could speak for itself and could count in that sense as an artificial person, a *persona ficta*. Already in the 1300s, there was an influential group of thinkers, mainly legal theorists, who argued that corporate entities are agents in their own right. They've got standing in law like natural persons. They own property, they enter contracts, they can sue and be sued in the courts. It's as if they each have a mind of their own.

NW: *Does this notion of a group mind end in the Middle Ages or does it continue beyond that?*

PP: It figures prominently in many seventeenth-century thinkers, among them Thomas Hobbes. Hobbes thinks that the state or commonwealth is a corporate agent, modelling it, as he says, on a company of merchants. But he misleads his successors by suggesting that what happens when you get an incorporation of individuals—or at least one where there is not a single dictator—is that the members form their views by majority voting. This is the position endorsed later by John Locke and by the Genevan-born philosopher Jean-Jacques Rousseau. And, as we have seen, it is wholly mistaken.

After Hobbes, there are two major developments, practical and theoretical. The practical development occurs in the nineteenth century, with the rise of the commercial corporation. Through most of the 1700s in Britain, it was only possible to form a corporation by means of an Act of Parliament. This measure had been adopted about the time of the South Sea Bubble, when the South Sea Company, founded in 1711 as a trading company, bubbled and burst. Things began to loosen up only in the 1820s. Then over the following 30 or 40 years in the UK and America you get an amazing development; commercial corporations are granted more and more independence. You can form a corporation just by registering it with a notary. The corporation can operate in any area within the domain of the legislation. It can change its sphere of activity without having to go back to parliament, or even go back to the registry. It can enjoy limited liability. And it can own and control other corporations. As a result of these shifts, you get a significant biomass of corporate entities, a biomass that has grown from decade to decade over the last 200 years.

NW: *So that's the practical way in which corporations have evolved—what about the conceptual level?*

PP: Well, very interesting things happen at the conceptual level. One is that in the late nineteenth century, a German thinker, Otto Gierke, goes back to medieval sources and develops a theory of corporate entities, including churches, commercial corporations, political parties, and states. These entities have got a life of their own, he says—they're real, if artificial, persons, as he puts it. This view becomes very influential in the early twentieth century, partly as a result of the influence of a disciple of Gierke's, the English legal historian, Frederic Maitland. But the theory of corporate agency rapidly wanes in influence later in the century, probably because of an association in the popular mind with fascism. As we know, fascism also talks the language of incorporation and corporate entities.

In the fight against fascism you get a cult of what comes to be called 'individualism'. There are many senses in which individualism is fine, but in the form that it assumed in this movement it was taken to commit us to thinking there are no such things as group agents. And frankly we're only recovering from the mid-century hegemony of this denial of group agency, a denial prominent in the work of people like Karl Popper and Friedrich Hayek. They each insisted that there are no group agents, there are just individual agents.

NW: *Group agency usually hits the headlines when something goes wrong; when, for instance, we blame a corporation for a disaster. Does your approach have anything to say about that?*

PP: Yes. There are two normative issues that are very important. One is the question of whether group agents have rights and the other is the question of whether group agents have responsibility. The view that Christian and I defend is that there is an asymmetry. Group agents should have very limited rights, and indeed be subject to certain important checks as to what they can do. On the other hand, group agents should be capable of being held responsible.

Is this inconsistent? I don't think so.

We look to the interests of individual human beings in determining what rights these group entities should have, and equally we look to the interests of individual human beings in determining whether they are fit to be held responsible for what they do. The reason why group agents should not be given, say, equal rights with individual human beings is that clearly this would give an incentive for individuals to coalesce into these group agents, thereby individually profiting themselves at perhaps great cost to the interests of other individuals. But the interests of individuals also argue for holding corporate agents responsible in their own right for the ills they perpetrate. This is important because, as we know, churches, commercial corporations, and the like can do a lot more damage than individuals can. They have great power and often vast resources, they suffer no anxiety, and they have a long time horizon. Thus they should be exposed to the possibility of being called to book for any abuses they commit.

NW: *Yes. I was thinking of particular cases. Recently, British Petroleum has been blamed for the oil-leak disaster off the coast of America. That's blaming a corporation, not an individual. Should we blame the corporation in that sort of situation?*

PP: I believe that that's exactly what you should do. Let me go back to a particular example. In 1987, The Herald of Free Enterprise, a ferry operating in the North Sea, sank, and almost 200 people were drowned. A British government report argued that the company was appalling; it had an extraordinary culture of negligence that had existed for a long time. Essentially, it was that culture, combined with the unusual circumstances of very rough water, that led to a door not having been raised in sufficient time, so that water washed on board and sank the ferry. There was such uproar about that, that a legal case was brought in the criminal courts in Britain against the company.

And, very sadly, in my view, the courts decided that you couldn't hold the company criminally responsible or liable on the grounds, roughly, that only individuals can have liability. And when it came to an individual level of responsibility, well, it turned out that no one individual could be held responsible in any great measure because those who were actually there at the door were just doing what they had been trained to do, and the directors were following routines passed down from their predecessors. Thus the corporation couldn't be held responsible in law and there was what I think of as a responsibility deficit. This case shows why it's very important in general to be able to hold corporate groups responsible for wrongs they do, as well as holding individuals within the groups responsible for their part in perpetrating such a wrong. The point has been acknowledged in UK law with the 2007 Corporate Manslaughter and Homicide Act, although it remains to be seen how effective that Act proves to be.

NW: *You've mentioned Christian List a few times in this interview. Presumably, you are acknowledging a joint responsibility for the ideas that you've been discussing today. Does that mean that the two of you constitute a group, with group agency?*

PP: Actually it does. You two, Nigel and David, have co-authored books, so you must have had experience of this. If you co-author with someone, you often find that as a group you are committed to a view which, individually, you may feel a little bit wary about or you may feel is too timid. You may want to go further. And so, for example, our book has around half a dozen footnotes where we say that on this issue the group agent is prepared to commit thus and so, but the individuals stand differently; but it's important for us as a group author that our views in the book are internally coherent.

NW: Philip Pettit—and I guess Christian List—thank you very much.

POLITICS

18

SUSAN MENDUS ON
Toleration

David Edmonds: *At the core of liberalism is the idea of tolerance:*
individuals and groups should be allowed to live as they see fit. The state
should tolerate people of all beliefs and all lifestyles, so long as other
people are not harmed as a result. But what justification is there for this
degree of tolerance? Should we tolerate everything and everyone? Why?
Merely because doing so might help keep the peace? Or does tolerance have
a moral basis independent *of its consequences? Won't tolerance lead to*
the Balkanization of society—separate communities with irreconcilable
values? Such questions are coming under intense political scrutiny, with
many politicians, such as the German Chancellor, Angela Merkel,
claiming that the multicultural experiment has failed. Susan Mendus,
a leading theorist on tolerance, put up with our gentle grilling.

Nigel Warburton: *We're focusing on the question 'Why be tolerant?'*
Some people talk about 'toleration', some people talk about 'tolerance', do
you have a preference for either word?

Susan Mendus: Well, some people say that 'tolerance' is most properly applied to individuals, whereas 'toleration' is most properly applied to political systems or governments. But I use these terms interchangeably.

NW: *Ok then, what is toleration?*

SM: Standardly, toleration is defined as allowing, permitting, or refraining from interfering with something which you believe to be morally wrong. So, if you behave in a way which I think is morally bad, but I don't prevent you from doing the thing that I think is bad, that counts as tolerating. Of course, underwriting all of that must also be the possibility that I *could* stop you if I wanted to. So the ingredients are these: I need to have the power to stop you, and I need to refrain from stopping you, *and* I need to think that what you're doing is wrong.

NW: *Toleration is very much at the heart of politics. We have to understand how we can live together, and an aspect of that has to be ascertaining the limits of toleration.*

SM: That's right; we have to live together whilst we have different ideas about what's the best way to live. That's what lies at the heart of the problem of toleration. There are two questions that arise which are then absolutely crucial.

First, 'Why might we be tolerant?' As a society, or as a government; why might a government tolerate homosexuality, atheism, Catholicism? These are all real examples of cases where toleration has been very vexed.

Second, 'What are the limits of that toleration?' Because, however tolerant a government, it's not going to be tolerant of *everything*, nor would we want it to be tolerant of everything. I take it we wouldn't want the government to be tolerant of rapists, or murderers, or terrorism. So toleration has got to have its limits.

NW: *Isn't the answer going to vary from case to case? How are we going to have a general theory of toleration if there's such a wide range of things that are up for consideration as possible candidates for toleration?*

SM: There are really two questions there. One is about whether the answer will be different for different cases. Another is a question about the range of cases that there'll be.

Will the answer be different in different cases? Well, a lot of the history of political philosophy is a history of trying to find one answer. If we go back to the seventeenth century, and John Locke's *Letter Concerning Toleration*, Locke's big ambition is to give a principled reason for tolerating people of different religious convictions.

Locke says that in many cases people tolerate not because they think it is right to do so, but simply in order to keep the political peace. Locke, however, is looking for a principled reason for tolerating. He is looking for a single principle of toleration. That's very ambitious, and I don't think he fully succeeds in that ambition.

Then you've got a second question: historically, most questions of toleration were questions of religious toleration. That's where questions of toleration arose in the Western liberal tradition—as in the wars of religion in the sixteenth and seventeenth centuries, when people were killing each other furiously for religious reasons.

So even if it's possible to provide a single answer to the question, 'Why be tolerant as far as religion is concerned?', it may be that that isn't going to give us an answer to the question, 'Why be tolerant with regard to sexuality, or pornography or blasphemy?'

NW: *So what was John Locke's answer to the question, 'Why should we tolerate people with different religions?'*

SM: There's no consensus on the answer, but there are two strong candidates. One very familiar and very powerful argument is an argument from irrationality. Locke's answer is that, in the case of religious belief, what really matters is that each individual believes the right thing to secure salvation. And in that context Locke then says that no amount of political coercion can *compel* you to believe the right thing. He says that fire and the sword are the weapons available to the state, to politics, but fire and the sword will not change your mind.

So it's irrational for magistrates, for politicians, to try to compel people to believe, or to persecute those who don't believe the right thing, because persecuting people isn't going to change their mind.

Another connected thought is that, in any case, trying to interfere with religious belief is not the business of politics. Locke makes a very clear distinction between politics on the one hand and religion on the other. He says that the magistrate is concerned with outward things: how you behave in the world, whether you obey the law, whether you conduct yourself properly, whether you're a good citizen. Religion is a more inward matter and nothing to do with the magistrate.

So it's two thoughts: the magistrate cannot change your mind; and even if he could, he would be doing the wrong thing—he'd be interfering.

NW: *That makes Locke sound very much like a modern liberal. But weren't Catholics and atheists excluded from his account of toleration?*

SM: Yes. Locke is the father of modern liberalism. But it's true that, notoriously, he does not extend toleration to Catholics and atheists. He does not extend tolerance to atheists because he thinks that since they believe in no God their promises cannot be relied upon. It's a kind of Dostoevskian point: if God is dead, anything is possible—people who don't believe in God will do anything. In Locke's day, atheism was a very suspect and radical position to hold.

His position on Catholics is even more interesting; the reason Locke is suspicious of Catholics is because, he says, they muddle together the political and the religious. They bear allegiance to a foreign power, namely the pope. And the pope is a political and a religious power. Locke's thought is that, in so far as they think of the pope as a political power, we should be suspicious of them too because they confuse things that should be kept separate.

NW: *I can see parallels there between Locke's age and ours; in Islam there are clearly connections between the political and the religious.*

SM: That's right. It's one of the problems in any multicultural, multiracial, multi-faith society, where people with very different understandings of the relationship between politics and religion must nevertheless try to live together in something that looks like harmony.

NW: *That brings us to the twenty-first century. We've talked about the seventeenth century and John Locke's position, but where are we now as regards toleration?*

SM: As I said, Locke is really the father of liberalism. So the liberalism that we have now in the twenty-first century is a liberalism that's been handed down to us through the years.

And I suppose its most famous modern advocate is the American political theorist John Rawls. He advances a theory of toleration in his 1993 book, *Political Liberalism*.

The starting point of Rawls' political liberalism is the claim that the aims of political philosophy depend on the society it addresses. Modern society is characterized by what Rawls calls the fact of pluralism. That's to say, societies like Britain, the United States, western liberal democracies generally, are suffused with people who have very different understandings of the best way to lead one's life. There are atheists, there are Muslims, there are Catholics, there are hedonists, there are jazz saxophonists, there are sports people, there are all kinds of different people with different understandings of the best way to lead one's life.

And this pluralism is not going to go away, Rawls says. It is a permanent fact—and what's more, we shouldn't be sorry about it. Rawls doesn't believe that in an ideal world we would all converge on a single truth about, say, religion. Rawls thinks plurality is the natural outcome of the operation of reason under conditions of freedom. So he thinks it's to be celebrated that when we all think about religion we'll come up with different answers. We shouldn't regret the fact that in the world there are lots of people who think very differently from us.

NW: *But even if diversity is inevitable, does Rawls believe that we should tolerate views that we think are false?*

SM: This is the central question, it seems to me. One important answer is that we should allow people to do things which we believe to be wrong because it's important that they should lead their own life in their own way. That's the answer that John Stuart Mill gives: it's important that you cut your suit from your own cloth and not from cloth that I've given you. This thought appeals to what's commonly known as the autonomy of individuals; you should make your own mistakes, and lead your life the way you want to because that has a value in itself, even if it's wrong.

But another thought which is more closely Rawls' thought is that the diversity of opinion doesn't imply that all except one opinion is wrong. He seems to think that it's quite possible that there be a variety of very different views about the way to lead one's life. There is no single right answer to the question, 'Which way should you lead your life?'

Here's an example: suppose you are a Quaker and you have a belief in and are committed to a simple life: no ornament, no decoration, with being self-effacing. There are many virtues associated with such a life. But these are not virtues that are going to lead to artistic glory or that will deliver Florence. This is a point that's made in the film of *The Third Man*. On the Ferris wheel in *The Third Man*, Orson Welles' character says, 'In Florence, there were hundreds of years of bloodshed and murder, and that gave us the Renaissance. In Switzerland, we had 500 years of peace and tranquillity, and what did that give us? The Cuckoo Clock.'

There's a serious point behind that: certain virtues are compatible with certain ways of life, but not with all good ways of life. If you want artistic splendour, and the glories of the Renaissance, then you have to have people who are grand, and proud, and arrogant, and profligate, and overweening. And Rawls' thought is that the Quakers and the Renaissance Florentines exhibit very different virtues. But there's no simple answer to the question, 'Which is the right way to lead your life?', because we don't want a world that's full of Quakers, nor one that's full of Medicis.

NW: *So far, we've talked about why we should be tolerant—and we've presented various views, including Mill's, that individuals should shape their own lives, and Rawls', that there's more than one way of deciding between the different ways of living, so we should just accept that and tolerate diversity. Does that exhaust the spectrum of views on toleration?*

SM: Well, we're discussing arguments for toleration that think of it as a moral good and not just something that's pragmatic or expedient. Let's return to John Locke. Before Locke, there are philosophers who say tolerance is important because otherwise there'll be riots in the streets. So you put up with atheists or Catholics for a bit of peace and tranquillity. But Locke is the father of liberalism because he thinks that there are *moral* reasons for doing this, and Rawls carries on that tradition. Rawls thinks that it's *morally* important to tolerate others.

And so within political liberalism, toleration isn't just what Rawls calls a *modus vivendi*. It's not just a way of muddling along together. It's a moral belief that we owe it to others to allow them to lead their lives in their own way.

NW: *That's interesting because when the German chancellor, Angela Merkel, says 'multiculturalism has failed', she presumably means that it hasn't worked as a pragmatic solution for groups to rub along side by side; it hasn't produced a peaceful outcome free of riots and conflict. But that's not what you're talking about—which is the moral obligation to respect other people's autonomy and to give them space to develop their thoughts and ideas about how to lead their lives.*

SM: Yes. I'm unclear what politicians mean when they say that multiculturalism 'hasn't worked'. Some people think that for multiculturalism to 'work', we must end up with everybody thinking roughly the same—there must be assimilation of some sort. Rawls' thought is the reverse of that. It is that we aren't going to reach consensus, and that's a good thing. The best society that we can aim for is the society in which people retain their different and conflicting conceptions of the good, and where we respect the conceptions of the good that other people have, even though they aren't ours.

NW: *Why should you respect a different conception of the good? Surely, all you need to do is tolerate their beliefs? Respect seems to go further and imply that you think what they're saying is somehow valuable.*

SM: It doesn't seem to me that I need to withhold respect from everybody who has what I take to be the wrong answer; otherwise, I wouldn't respect many people at all. So it's inherent in a liberal society that we recognize that the world is full of people who have different and incompatible beliefs from us. But nonetheless, we respect their right to hold those beliefs.

Of course, you can't respect absolutely everything that people do: Locke and Rawls are both clear about this. Toleration has its limits. As I said at the beginning, we won't tolerate murderers, rapists, terrorists, or thieves. And then, of course, the 64-dollar question kicks in; where *are* the limits of toleration?

NW: *You're obviously committed to toleration. Presumably there have been times when the British government hasn't been as tolerant as you would like it to have been, or hasn't promoted tolerance sufficiently. What would you say could be done to make society more tolerant?*

SM: As a liberal, I find a lot to be sad about in modern British society. What I would home in on is the felt need for separate schools, particularly for separate faith schools. Not because faith is unimportant; on the contrary, I think faith is very important. But the sadness I have is the sadness that Jewish people, Catholic people, Muslim people, Church of England people, wish to educate their children separately from children of other faiths. And it seems to me that the aspiration for a genuinely multicultural society should be the aspiration that we can indeed live together in the same classroom, in the same society, in the same communities, whilst respecting and acknowledging the different beliefs that we have.

NW: *People often accuse philosophers of not making any difference in the world. It seems to me that here's an area where philosophers have a huge potential to affect what actually happens in politics. Do you think they're being heard by politicians?*

SM: Politicians ask philosophers to speak quite a lot; I'm not sure that they listen as well as they should. It's certainly true that here are areas where philosophers can draw attention to the limits of political possibility. So to go back to the case of those politicians who say 'multiculturalism hasn't worked', I'd be interested to know what's meant by 'working' here, what counts as 'success', and what is it appropriate to aim for in a multicultural society. Philosophers have a huge amount to contribute to the question of what we can legitimately hope for. Because if the hope is the hope that sooner or later all immigrants from different societies and different cultures will get to be like me, white and secular and liberal, it's not realistic. And I'm not sure it's even desirable to be in a society of that kind. So politicians need to think about what they mean when they say 'multiculturalism hasn't worked'.

19

HILLEL STEINER ON
Exploitation

David Edmonds: *It's time we at* Philosophy Bites *confess our guilty little secret: we don't pay* Philosophy Bites *contributors the minimum wage. In fact, we don't pay them anything at all. Are we thereby exploiting them? It's often said that desperately poor people who sell their organs for money, or women who sell sexual services, or workers who work long hours for next-to-no remuneration are exploited. But if they've entered these agreements voluntarily, how can it be exploitation? Presumably the low-paid worker believes that some work, however low paid, is better than no work. In exchange for a disquisition on exploitation, we offered Hillel Steiner a glass of water.*

Nigel Warburton: *What is exploitation?*

Hillel Steiner: Well, the most general definition is this: it's an exchange of two things, goods or services, of unequal value. And I should add this: it's a *voluntary* exchange of two things of unequal value.

NW: *Could you give an example?*

HS: Workers in the Third World, who work for multinational food or clothing manufacturers, are generally regarded as exploited when they receive low wages compared to the high value of the products they produce. When you subtract the value of other factor inputs from those products' value, the amount by which that remainder exceeds those wages strongly suggests the presence of exploitation.

NW: *So somebody making a very expensive piece of computer equipment in terrible conditions, paid a pittance, would be a classic case of somebody being exploited?*

HS: Probably. I would want to look at more than just the working conditions *and* the wages to establish whether they've been exploited. It isn't necessarily the case, on my view of exploitation, that they're exploited. But it's very likely that, when we look into the other background circumstances that I'm alluding to, we would find that there's exploitation.

NW: *Where does exploitation sit in relation to other kinds of transactions that we engage in?*

HS: That's a good question and a good way of depicting what's so puzzling about exploitation. Transactions are interactions between two or more people—let's simplify by saying just two—where there are goods or services travelling from one to the other, and possibly also from the other to the first. It's useful here to think of a spectrum of transactions, at one end of which is gifting, and at the opposite end is robbing or theft. Somewhere in the middle is what I would call a fair exchange. In the case of a gift, and in the case of a robbery, there are goods or services travelling in only one direction, from one person to the other—there's no reciprocation. In the middle, in fair exchange, there are goods and services travelling in both directions, and the things exchanged are of equal value, and are exchanged voluntarily.

Somewhere between a fair exchange and a gift is something called a *benefit*. This is where, for instance, I do a week's work for a charity. It's not completely a gift because at the end of the week, they give me a perfectly ordinary ballpoint pen, just as a token of their appreciation. Now in this case, we've each exchanged, voluntarily, but the two things exchanged are not of equal value, and indeed it would not serve the purpose of that exchange if they *were* of equal value. Nonetheless, there are things travelling in both directions in a benefit.

Exploitation is the symmetrical counterpart to a benefit. It lies on the spectrum between the fair exchange in the middle, and the theft or robbery at the end.

NW: *Just to get this clear, let's take an example: suppose I've got a rare book, a first edition of Karl Marx's* Das Kapital, *and somebody steals it from me. That's bad: that's on one end of the spectrum. At the other end of the spectrum, I could give it to somebody—for nothing. And in between we have a fair exchange: perhaps I sell it at auction and receive a decent amount of money for it. And then there's exploitation, where somebody offers me very little money for it, but I voluntarily enter into that transaction.*

HS: That's exactly right. And the question is why? Why would you do that, rather than try to secure the greater amount of money that's involved in a fair exchange. You're presumably not trying to confer a benefit, you're not being altruistic: rather, you're acting in a purely self-interested way—as is the person who's paying this paltry price. So why are you accepting such a paltry price? And the obvious answer is because that's the best you can get. Its *being* the best you can get and its *being*, in your view, paltry, doesn't mean that this is necessarily an instance of exploitation. We need more background facts to the case before we can say for certain that this is an instance of exploitation.

NW: *Well, one obvious fact we'd need, I assume, is the* real *value of that book. Some people would say the real value is just whatever price you can get for it on that day.*

HS: That is what some people would say, and that's why there are many enthusiasts of the free market who insist that it's impossible for exploitation to occur in the free market because every transaction is voluntary and, *ipso facto*, it's fair. I like the theory of value that these people use—I agree with the claim that the highest price that someone would offer *is* the correct measure of the value of something. I don't believe things have an intrinsic value of their own. But I want to add a qualification that free market enthusiasts don't always trouble to add. I want to say that the value of something is the highest amount of money that someone would bid at an auction for, say, your Karl Marx book, provided there were no relevant injustice, no rights violation, in the background... in other words, what price the book would fetch at a *fair* auction.

NW: *What if somebody were prepared to pay a billion dollars for my Karl Marx book—would that really be the correct price?*

HS: Why do you think it wouldn't be?

NW: *Well, it would seem that this somebody was just being crazy, sentimental perhaps, because they could have got it for a fraction of the price.*

HS: I dare say a vast number of the things we buy are driven by our sentiments: certainly, they're not all driven by biological need. If—and here's the big IF—if this person came by his wealth, by his resources justly, and if his sentiments for having a copy of *Das Kapital* were that strong, I can't see any way of gainsaying his valuation of that book.

NW: *You mentioned the sense of there being a rights violation somewhere along the line in the transaction. Could you expand on that?*

HS: Yes, this lies at the core of the theory. Think again about the auction; competitive markets are supposed to be auctions writ large. Suppose that somebody buys your Karl Marx book for £20, but it *could have* sold for £30. However, the guy who was ready to bid £30 was barred at the door from coming into the auction. Now, his being barred at the door isn't necessarily a violation of his rights—we'd have to go into some complex issues to know whether it was or not—but let's suppose it *was* a violation of his rights. Then, by virtue of his rights having been violated, you have lost £10 on your Karl Marx book sale. That's a standard way in which a rights violation provides a necessary condition for an exploitation.

NW: *Would there be a parallel in the job marketplace? What would be the equivalent in terms of somebody being exploited by an employer?*

HS: Exploitation might result in a number of ways. For example, a parallel of the case we've just had with the book and the auction might arise if there are restrictions on the sorts of employer who can bid for that person's labour—for example, if certain people are not licensed to be employers, or if there are various other restrictions on who can bid for that labour—which will lead to some lower than otherwise winning bid and thus result in an exploitation. Such restrictions are violations of the right of free association.

That's the standard model of exploitation that I developed about 30 years ago. Since then, I've realized that there is another way in which, effectively, the same thing could happen: another way in which a rights violation sets up the condition for an exploitation. Suppose a person has been made poorer unjustly: suppose he has been made poorer, not by gambling his money away at a casino, but by being unjustly robbed. Suppose, had he not been made poorer in this way, he would not have accepted a wage of less than £30 a day, but because he has been made poorer, he accepts less than this. I would say that whoever employs him for, say, £20 a day, is exploiting him. That employer is getting him for less than in a just world—in a world in which his rights *hadn't* been violated—he would have received.

NW: *We've been talking as if whether someone's exploited or not is a black-and-white issue—either you're exploited or you're not. But surely, what really matters is the degree to which you are exploited. If somebody exploits me, and I lose 5p a day, that's not a serious case of exploitation. If I lose £500 a day, for me, that would be pretty serious.*

HS: That's absolutely right. Indeed, the whole idea of this particular model of exploitation is to be able to get precise about numbers; how *much* would have been bid for your product or labour or whatever you're selling if that prior injustice, that rights violation, hadn't occurred. And if 5p is how much more would have been bid, in the context of this society it's fairly negligible. So, yes, there are certainly degrees of exploitation.

NW: *And does your theory suggest that a very rich person could be exploited as well?*

HS: Yes. In principle, a rich person could sell something—a work of art or a Karl Marx volume, possibly even his daily labour—and get a lower price than would have been the case if a higher bidder had not been excluded from the auction or the market. Being exploited, on my model, is possible wherever there is a differential between the highest *actual* bid and the highest *counterfactual* bid that would have been made if a rights violation hadn't previously occurred. But we would certainly be less troubled—morally and in other ways—by a millionaire being exploited than somebody below the poverty line.

NW: *In which case, what makes something a really serious example of exploitation—because it sounds like it's not enough that it's exploitation per se?*

HS: I'm assuming that exploitation is intrinsically linked to the idea of injustice—that seems to be its natural home. But if we think about values other than justice—such as benevolence or need-alleviation—we can quite quickly explain why it is that the exploitation of an impoverished worker is far worse than the exploitation of a millionaire, even though the actual *amount* by which the millionaire has been exploited may be many times larger than the amount the worker has been exploited. To use a good Marxist term, the 'surplus value' extracted from the millionaire may be much bigger than the surplus value extracted from the impoverished worker.

NW: *Some people think that there are areas of human transaction which are* essentially *exploitative: that is, there can be no fair price, for example, for a bodily organ, or for your body, when this is sold for sexual purposes. Is that what you believe?*

HS: No, it isn't what I believe. I'm not sure whether my model of exploitation, as we've been exploring it, precludes the idea that transactions for some kinds of goods or services are *necessarily* exploitative. But I wouldn't say so. When it comes to peoples' bodies and their parts thereof, I think it would be unjust to stop them from selling their body parts if that's what they want to do.

NW: *Does it follow then that there is a fair price for everything? If I wanted to sell myself as a meal, for instance, to a cannibal, that's my right, and as long as the cannibal pays the going rate, then I can serve myself up?*

HS: I think there's nothing unjust about your doing that. There may be lots of other grounds on which it might be a morally wrong thing to do, but I don't think it's unjust, and I do think it would be unjust to stop you.

NW: *We've been discussing this at an abstract level. Does it have any real-life implications? If we believe your account of exploitation, should we change the way we structure human interactions?*

HS: I think so. One thing my account shows is that a perfectly voluntary exchange, such as the free market ostensibly sponsors, can, contrary to many of its enthusiasts, be exploitative, and therefore unjust. This is definitely *not* an argument against free markets. On the whole, I think free markets are good things, and very efficient for a number of very well-known reasons. Rather, what this argument supplies is a reason for looking at what economists call the *endowments* that people bring to the market—their goods, services, and money—and seeing whether these endowments—in particular, their magnitudes—are what they are for many people because of some prior injustice, perhaps repeatedly compounded prior injustices that go back a long time and for many generations. When people who are poor—not because of their own doings, irresponsible gambling say, but because they have, in one way or another, been robbed, or previously exploited—come to the market, the price that they get for what they are selling is very likely to be exploitative. The structural change I'm indicating is, then, *not* a curtailment of free markets but rather a redistribution of wealth consistent with the requirements of justice.

NW: *Have you ever been exploited?*

HS: Gosh, I don't think so. I haven't *felt* exploited.

NW: *At least you're not saying we're exploiting you. Hillel Steiner, thanks very much.*

20

RAE LANGTON ON
Hate Speech

David Edmonds: *Should hate speech be outlawed? The use of the 'N word', say? In the US, extensive free speech is said to be guaranteed by the First Amendment, but in Europe there are laws that restrict speech targeting particular groups—racist speech, for example. Should America be more like Europe? Yes, says Rae Langton of Cambridge University. The mistake made by free speech fundamentalists is to regard speech as nothing but harmless words.*

NW: *Could you say what hate speech is?*

RL: I don't want to propose a definition here, but when you see how people have talked about hate speech, one important idea has been that of words or pictures that do something distinctive to members of a certain group of people. So, for instance, the United Nations describes hate speech as inciting or promoting hatred towards members of certain groups, or inciting violence against them. It asks member states to have legislation that will guard against that sort of speech. So that's one idea which we can think of as, roughly, hate *propaganda*. Another idea which is important is the idea of 'words that wound'—where the thought is not so much propaganda but *assault*. In this case, the hateful words are being used directly to attack somebody, rather than to incite third parties to hatred.

NW: *I think I understand what you mean by hate speech as propaganda. This is presumably what was going on in the lead-up to the Second World War with Nazi anti-Semitism, for instance, where Jews were portrayed as rats. Certain sorts of words were used to target that group, amongst others. Now, that's different from what you've called 'words that wound', although obviously it could wound. It typically occurs in a one-on-one situation or is directed at a particular individual. Could you say a little more about 'words that wound'?*

RL: Hank Aaron, the baseball player, at the time when he was about to overtake the famed Babe Ruth, received a huge barrage of hate mail. The hate mail he received was like an assault: it was full of uses of the N-word, of threats—'my gun is watching your every black move'—and of other epithets, 'jungle bunny' and the like. This was 'speech' that was designed to attack him personally and would have been psychologically devastating. But what I want to emphasize is that, quite apart from the appalling psychological effects, those words are being used to *do* something, just *in the saying* of those words. What I have in mind here is a distinction that J. L. Austin introduced, although he wasn't interested in hate speech. Austin wrote a book called *How to Do Things With Words*, and he was interested in three different kinds of things we do with our words. We use words that have certain *meanings*, first of all; and the action we perform when we use meaningful words is the 'locutionary act'. We use words to produce certain effects on our hearers too, and he called that the 'perlocutionary act'. But we also use words to do some-thing very directly: this was the idea that at first he called a 'performative' and later came to call an 'illocutionary act'. What interests me when thinking about these different dimensions of hate speech is how hate speech, both as propaganda and as assault, can be understood as a certain kind of illocutionary act. Of course, it is harmful in terms of its effects, but it's also harmful in itself.

NW: *Could you just clarify that a bit by giving some examples of illocutionary acts?*

RL: Austin had some fantastic examples. Funnily enough, if we're interested in incitement to violence, one of Austin's own illustrations was the utterance, 'Shoot her!' Think about one man saying, 'Shoot her!' to another man, with respect to a woman who's nearby. You could describe that in a number of different ways. You could say he said 'shoot' meaning by 'shoot' to shoot with a gun, as opposed to a bow and arrow. You could say by 'her', he meant the woman nearby. If you describe it *that* way, you are describing what Austin called the locutionary act. You could also describe what happened next. The second man picked up a gun and shot the woman, let's suppose (I'm now embroidering Austin's example). If that happened, and that was your description of what happened, that's about the *perlocutionary* act, in Austin's terms. But Austin would think we'd left out something important: what the first person did *in saying* those words, what *illocutionary* act was performed. Perhaps the first man *ordered* the second. But was it an order? Was it a piece of advice? Was it a suggestion? Was it a joke? There are many different illocut-ionary things that the utterance 'Shoot her!' could have been, and if we don't think about them we're missing out on what Austin took to be one of the most interesting dimensions of language use.

NW: *I'm interested in how this way of thinking about language sheds light on hate speech.*

RL: One feature of many of Austin's examples is that it makes a difference *who* is saying the words, and in what context. Even in the example I just gave, perhaps it could only have been an order if the first man was in a position of authority relative to the second man. And for many of his examples, such as 'I hereby christen this ship the *Queen Elizabeth*', there's a successful christening provided they have got the champagne, and it's the right speaker, and everything else in the ceremony is in order. But, in another nice example from Austin, suppose some 'low type' ('low type' was *his* phrase by the way)—some 'low type' grabs the champagne bottle and smashes it against the ship and says, 'I hereby name this ship the *Generalissimo Stalin*.' We can all agree, says Austin, that it would be 'an infernal shame'; and we all agree that it would not be a christening of the ship. So what this tells us is that certain sorts of speech act can do certain things when they're said by a person in authority, and won't do the same things if they're not.

Now, the reason I mention that example is that we can easily think of cases where what's being done towards members of a certain group is done to them partly in virtue of a kind of authority the speaker might have. We were discussing Nazi Germany before, so when *Der Stürmer*, a major anti-Semitic newspaper, published their hate-filled pictures and essays, it made a difference that it was from an influential paper that, it seems, had the official backing of the government. It was authoritative speech that ranked a particular group as inferior, ranked them as vermin, ranked them as sub-human, and legitimated violence against them. The notion of *ranking* certain groups as inferior, and *legitimating* violence or discrimination—this sort of ranking and legitimating is part of the illocutionary force of propaganda. So, it's worth thinking about who the speakers are, and what their standing is. And it's worth thinking about the possibility that the speech might be doing more than just expressing an unpleasant idea.

NW: *Most discussions about hate speech are about the limits of freedom of speech. Are there consequences from your approach to hate speech? Is it just a matter of understanding it as language?*

RL: There are different reasons why people think that free speech should include freedom of hate speech. One is because they are in the thrall of the idea that speech doesn't do much. You know, the idea that 'sticks and stones may break my bones, but names will never hurt me'. Then another reason sounds like just the opposite: speech does a lot, it's important because it's so powerful, and we need to have this power always available to us. Thinking about speech in general, and hate speech in particular, as a kind of act—a speech act—gives us a way of understanding it as something more than inert words. It helps us think of speech as a kind of 'doing things with words' that's continuous with our other actions. This means that one common way of dismissing legislation designed to restrict certain forms of hate speech is on a losing wicket. Speech is not 'only words', to borrow Catharine

MacKinnon's phrase. It's not inert. When we use words, we're doing all sorts of things, especially if we are in a position of power or authority. Moreover, what we're doing is not simply expressing ideas that might or might not be true. We're acting. We're altering norms. We're making certain things more permissible than they were before. We're making other things less permissible than they were before. We're authoritatively, sometimes, saying that certain people are inferior. That is one of the ways that structures of hierarchy are set up and maintained.

NW: *There are two different models of how this might play out in terms of the law. In Britain, there are quite strict legal prohibitions on what you can say in public. If what you say is racist or homophobic, you may find yourself prosecuted. In the States, it's more complicated because of the history of First Amendment interpretation which protects extensive freedom of speech. Are you saying that the British solution is better?*

RL: The British solution, as you're calling it, is a response to the UN Convention that requires member states to have some laws that will help prevent the spread of racial hatred, which was drafted against the backdrop of a history of racial violence and genocide. More recently, in Rwanda, radio stations were taken over by Hutus calling the Tutsis 'cock-roaches', and that campaign of hate speech was clearly part of what instigated massacre. Now, the US is the outlier on this. The US has *not* adopted this sort of legislation, in part because they think it's in conflict with the First Amendment of the US Constitution. This is odd, because as far as I can see, there is nothing in the Constitution itself that should really prevent the US having laws that were more similar to those that are in force in Europe—especially keeping in mind that they also have the Fourteenth Amendment, which requires them to respect the equality of citizens, and equality is certainly something that anti-hate speech legislation cares about. There are already many restrictions on speech, whether on false advertising, insider trading, or child pornography. There are many things you're not allowed to do with words. But there is still this kind of fairy tale that the First Amendment is absolute—anything goes. But of course, it doesn't. So, to my mind, the UK strategy is part of a relatively sane European policy, that many different democratic countries have signed up to in different forms.

NW: *I'm interested in the part played by intention in so-called hate speech. Hate is usually something you're aware of; it's directed at somebody or something. Do you have to intend to harm somebody by your speech for it to be hate speech?*

RL: There are certain paradigm cases where your description would be completely accurate. Take the kind of assault-like hate speech, the 'words that wound', that were sent to Hank Aaron—those were deliberate, and it mattered that they were deliberate. They were deliberately aiming to be words that wound. But that mightn't always be the case. There will be some cases where what you do with your words might be worse than you mean it to be, and in principle there could be hate speech where people don't know what they're doing. There's so much that you could be unaware of, as a speaker. Sometimes you're not fully aware of the background structures of authority that influence the force that your speech is going to have. If your speech has that force, it might be hate speech, even when you don't mean it to be.

NW: *Generally, what you've been saying is that the way to think about hate speech is not as a series of words that are uttered but people doing things with words. If we think about people doing things with words, we see that it's just another kind of action, and so there isn't really this special category of 'speech' and we don't need to separate out questions about speech from questions about other kinds of behaviour.*

RL: That's a really good way to put part of what I want to say. I do want to emphasize the continuities between speech and our other actions. I do agree with those who think that speech is special, though, in ways that don't quite fit with what you said. I agree with Mill that speech is important, partly because communication is important. Part of what makes me sad about the debates about free speech at present is this. When people wave the flag for free speech, they sometimes make communication harder, instead of easier. When you allow a complete free-for-all for the most powerful or authoritative speakers, this can hurt communication for people lower down in the hierarchy. So if we are serious about free speech, if we want everybody to have a chance to speak more freely, that might mean taking active steps to let other voices be heard.

21

NANCY FRASER ON
Recognition

David Edmonds: *In Britain, Christmas Day is a national holiday, but Passover and Eid are not. In this way, Christianity receives more recognition, and might be seen as having a higher status in British society, than Judaism or Islam. The way a society is run, or the way its institutions operate, can appear to privilege one group or people, or one way of life, over another. Nancy Fraser is an eminent political theorist whose work has emphasized the significance of 'recognition'.*

Nigel Warburton: *Nancy Fraser, we're going to talk about recognition and its link to multiculturalism. What does 'recognition' mean to you?*

Nancy Fraser: Recognition is a concept that is having an important revival in political philosophy. It's a way of talking about forms of injustice, such as disrespect, that drop out of the standard models of distributive justice, which focus on who gets what.

The question of whether the institutions of society express equal respect for everyone can't be analysed in terms of the distribution of resources, and it's in order to analyse that question that we use the term 'recognition'.

NW: *So is 'recognition' just another way of saying 'respect'?*

NF: Recognition has to do with respect, esteem, prestige: the way society values different traits, different activities. It has to do, above all, with what I call patterns of cultural value. For example, do our institutions express in their design, in their structure, the idea that heterosexuality is a valued family form and that homosexuality is not? The focus is on what the institutions are *saying,* implicitly or explicitly, by virtue of the way they're designed.

NW: *Why does this matter? I might think that all I need is toleration, I don't need respect.*

NF: For me, the crucial question is this: 'Is society organized in such a way that everyone has the possibility to be a full member, to participate in social interaction on equal terms with others?' Put differently, does society promote parity of participation? There are two possibilities: in one case, social institutions enable full participation for all on terms of parity; in the other, they prevent some people from participating fully, on a par with others, in social interaction. In the first case, the society promotes reciprocal recognition or status equality, while in the second, it entrenches misrecognition or status hierarchy.

NW: *Is there a psychological element here: if you respect somebody you might actually bolster them in such a way that they're capable of action; whereas cumulative disdain may have the effect of stopping people doing things in the public sphere.*

NF: You're hitting on an important and subtle point. What you say is probably true, but what do we do about it? It could be counterproductive to try to engineer politically correct ideas about other people.

Let's take an example. Suppose we had a society in which the institutions really did adequately respect racial, religious, and cultural minorities, and really did give everyone equal chances of fair participation. But suppose too there were a number of curmudgeonly, backward citizens who still harboured, say, racist or anti-Muslim, sentiments.

I'm tempted to say, 'Well, that's a shame but nevertheless the society in the design of its institutions has succeeded in giving adequate recognition', and my hope would be that ideas would in the end follow institutional change.

There are other theorists of recognition, such as Charles Taylor, who would disagree, and would put much more emphasis on the psychological. But my view is that the essential thing is not whether or not I feel hurt or disempowered by others having a certain view of me.

Consider that I could be wrong in my feelings. On the one hand, I could be oversensitive, imagining I'm being disrespected, when it's not the case. On the other hand, I could be thick-skinned, oblivious to the fact that I'm being denied the standing of a full partner in social interaction, when in fact I am. What these cases show is that the psychological element is not decisive; I don't mean to dismiss it entirely, but it's not crucial. What *is* crucial is how society actually works, whether its organization fosters parity of participation or whether it impedes it.

NW: *How would this issue of recognition arise in a multicultural society?*

NF: We could take examples having to do with religion, with gender, with sexuality. I mentioned the issue of marriage. If society has a legal organization that defines marriage as a relation between a man and a woman, then it denies gays and lesbians the chance to participate fully in social life. That's a clear case of misrecognition or status hierarchy.

But there can also be other, less obvious kinds of misrecognition. Suppose we have social welfare programmes that implicitly favour wage earners over caregivers. This also sends a message about what society values. When welfare institutions work in a way that prevents women or other caregivers from full participation, they too send a message of disrespect or misrecognition.

You could also take the example of whose holidays are treated as public holidays and whose are not, issues about whether you have the public display of Christian crosses, as opposed to Jewish stars or Muslim crescents. In other words, what is given public recognition sends a message about who is a first-class citizen and who, by contrast, is not.

NW: *Well, take the marriage example; if you say a marriage is between two people, that shuts off the religious groups who believe that bigamy or polygamy is perfectly acceptable and even required. How do you sort out whose view of the good life should be recognized?*

NF: This is a truly difficult question. It could be that we have to stretch our minds to get around this question. If I could be convinced—and I'm not at the moment—but if I *could* be convinced that polygamy could be dissociated from male domination and patriarchy and that it was a genuine expression of autonomy of women or men who live that way, then I might feel a lot less worried about it: I might be willing to stretch and say that society should recognize that. Of course, I would also want to make sure that children's interests were protected, and so on.

My idea is that, in so far as possible, we should translate questions about the good life into questions about fairness. Is anybody being dominated? Is anybody having something thrust upon them that is not a genuine choice? Now, I don't think that every question can be translated into a fairness question. There are still going to be value questions to decide. But I don't think it's the role of the political philosopher to give us the answer to those questions. What we as political philosophers—or even as citizens and activists—should do is to work to create conditions in which citizens can themselves decide these value issues—through deliberation and argument, negotiation, and contestation. But, and here's the crucial issue, these decision-making processes will be legitimate, and the results will be valid, only if the participants can interact as peers, only if their discussions proceed on fair terms. And this is not the case today. On the contrary, the debates that we have about these questions now are tainted by severe power asymmetries; not everyone can really participate on equal terms.

NW: *One asymmetry arises in the democratic voting process—between majority and minorities. Even if the majority of the minority vote in favour of a certain outcome, they might still lose: they're not going to have their particular way of life acknowledged by the wider society. Is it all going to come down to a democratic vote? In which case, aren't minorities going to be exploited?*

NF: The key is to figure out what sorts of issues allow for the peaceful co-existence of different forms of life and which do not. In cases of the first sort, it is possible to pluralize institutions, whereas cases of the second type require a common public framework. So, for example, take the question of nature. We have a general tendency, part of modern western rationalism, to think of nature as relatively valueless, as a supply of resources for human exploitation.

But at the same time, we have various religious communities, or in first-world nations, native communities, that have a much thicker, more value-laden ethical view of nature. Now it's an interesting question as to whether these two can co-exist. Because if the hegemonic view of nature as a valueless pool of resources for exploitation is allowed free rein, it will surely drive out the possibility that small communities of native peoples can maintain ways of life that are based on different ideas of nature.

That's an example of a case where separation alone will not suffice to ensure equal recognition. But where there are different ethical conceptions that *can* co-exist and where all pass the test that no one's being dominated or exploited, then I don't see any reason why we shouldn't just pluralize and let people choose which one to affiliate to.

NW: *I know you said that philosophers shouldn't decide particular cases, and that it should be done through negotiation of the people involved. But there are practical issues where an agreed conclusion will be impossible. For instance, with holidays: you can't argue that every group should be recognized by having their own public holidays—then every day would be a holiday.*

NF: Sounds good to me! There may be practical considerations and constraints that prevent absolute symmetry. In cases like that, in which you must institutionalize, say, a majority preference, you will have to find ways in which the minorities are not penalized—in which they are provided compensation, exemptions, alternatives, etc.

NW: *Doesn't structuring society in a way that recognizes different groups emphasize and entrench difference? It tells you that these people need to be respected in this way and these other people need a different kind of recognition?*

NF: Well, every society necessarily institutionalizes some recognition order, some specific pattern of cultural value. So we will always live with value hierarchies: with some sense of what a first-class and second-class citizen looks like.

It follows that the choice is not between recognition or no recognition—it's, rather, *which* recognition, or, if you prefer, what counts as a fair symmetric equal respect form of recognition? That said, I share your concern about not wanting to promote separatism. That's why I've avoided analysing recognition in terms of *identity*, and why I've analysed it instead in terms of *status*. For me, in other words, what requires recognition is not one's identity, but one's status as a full partner in social interaction. That might sound purely verbal or semantic, but it's not. By putting the emphasis on *interaction*, it discourages us from associating multiculturalism or recognition with separatism. What we should care about is that people can *interact* with one another on fair terms. The aim is not to encourage them to act in little separated enclaves only with their own kind, but to ensure that they can interact across differences as peers.

NW: *Well we care about that, but there are presumably groups who don't care about that and would like to be separatists, would like to keep a corralled area for their own way of life and not have any interference from outside.*

NF: Absolutely right, and my approach does not entail that everyone *must* participate in everything. What it does entail is that we have an obligation to remove entrenched obstacles that prevent people from participating, if they want to.

NW: *So do you have a name for your approach?*

NF: I call it the status model of recognition, where the question is equal status, as opposed to identity. So my approach offers an alternative to the standard identity model of recognition, which focuses on the psychological and which encourages identity politics.

Analysing recognition as a question of status raises all sorts of interesting questions about the relation between status and class, and that brings me back to what we started with: the relation between questions of distribution, which I think of as class questions, and those of recognition, which I think of as status questions. In my view, these represent two analytically distinct orders of equality/inequality, which do not always coincide. They are practically intertwined, and they interact causally, but they can't be neatly mapped on to or reduced to one another.

I oppose efforts to talk about multiculturalism in a way that disconnects it from questions of socio-economic equality and inequality.

NW: *What you're saying is that recognition of status is incredibly important, but it has to be seen in connection with economic inequalities. But what is the connection? Could you not have one without the other?*

NF: You could. Think about the very simple societies that anthropologists used to analyse: the societies they called 'primitive' societies. They were societies in which you could say everything was recognition: everything was organized in terms of orders and structures of prestige, and what you got—the question of distribution and economy—simply followed from that recognition hierarchy.

And you could take the other extreme. Imagine a society in which everything was determined by the market—prestige simply followed automatically from how much you had. Our society is not like either of those two extremes. We have to deal with something more complicated: two analytically distinct, practically intertwined orders of stratification or domination. Too many current discussions of multiculturalism ignore the dimension of distribution and class, the political economy side, and if you really want to understand and redress inequality, you have to think about both orders together.

NW: *Some European politicians have been very pessimistic about the future of multiculturalism in Europe. Do you share that pessimism?*

NF: That's a complicated question. It is true that we've seen a huge backlash in recent years against diversity, against toleration, against equal respect. I am indeed pessimistic that this will turn around anytime soon. But I firmly believe that it *should* turn around at some point. The backlash is connected to the high levels of socio-economic insecurity that people are currently experiencing, which again brings me back to the relation between recognition and distribution. One way in which these two dimensions of justice/injustice can be related is this: people who feel that they're on the losing side of, let's say, economic globalization—who feel that their forms of life and their standing in society is threatened, will often react defensively by insisting on their superiority in some other respect. In the United States—where we have a long history of racism—white racism gave poor white Southerners a sense of being superior to somebody else, even though their economic circumstances were miserable.

22

C. A. J. COADY ON
Dirty Hands in Politics

David Edmonds: *The former US Secretary of State for Defense,*
Robert McNamara, an instrumental figure in the Vietnam War, offered a
list of principles for the conduct of foreign policy. Number nine was this:
in order to do good, you must engage in evil.

The idea that politicians have to follow a different moral code from the
rest of us has been explored by political theorists from Machiavelli in
the early sixteenth century to, in modern times, Princeton University's
Michael Walzer. But what exactly is the claim being made here? Sure,
politics is messy, but does it really have its own specific moral realm? Here,
to tease out the arguments, is a renowned professor of moral philosophy,
Tony Coady.

Nigel Warburton: *The topic we're focusing on is dirty hands in*
politics. Could you explain what the problem is?

Tony Coady: Well, there's a technical problem of dirty
hands; there's also a popular sense of dirty hands, which is
somewhat related. In the popular sense, people say, 'We're
really in a difficult situation now with the so-called "War on
Terror", it's a time for tough measures and we've got to get
our hands dirty.' That can mean any one of numerous things:

it can mean, for example, we've got to take more risks than we would previously have done, or that we've got to do distasteful things though they're morally demanded.

But this is actually related to the philosophical topic, because sometimes people mean, 'The emergency is now so great that we have to get our hands *morally* dirty. We have to do things that we would normally regard as deeply immoral, perhaps absolutely prohibited, but in this crisis, to avoid some great evil, what we have to do is to break the moral law in order to avert a disaster, or to achieve some very great good.' And the technical sense of the term 'dirty hands' has been made popular by Michael Walzer, who wrote a very influential article about this in the early 1970s. Walzer has spent a good deal of time since then trying to work out the implications of his position, or what he actually meant.

There's a difficulty in knowing how to characterize the dirty-hands problem. It sounds like it's saying that it's morally right to do what's morally wrong. That appears to be a flat contradiction. Michael Walzer once said to me, probably as an ironic comment on the way he thinks philosophers have misunderstood him, 'Oh philosophers use my article to show students basic philosophical mistakes!' Well, I'm not sure it is a contradiction, but it has certainly got an air of contradiction about it, and one of the things I want to do is work out a satisfactory way of stating the problem.

NW: *The dirty-hands problem sounds like something Machiavelli said: that to be a good leader, a leader must be prepared to do things that other people would consider immoral—the morality of the leader is different from the morality of other people.*

TC: Well, Machiavelli is certainly part of a dirty-hands lineage, but even your account of Machiavelli raises the problem of unravelling what we mean by dirty hands. Is the leader required to do something that other people think is morally wrong, but actually it's not wrong at all? In which case all that is being said is that popular morality may be misguided. That's not paradoxical at all.

But sometimes it's the second point you made: that politics is different from ordinary life, that the political leader has obligations of a special sort, and therefore that these obligations allow him or her to do things that would be morally wrong for other people to do. That's a version of what's called, in the jargon, role morality. The idea is that the special features of the leader's role are such that what would be morally wrong for ordinary people, or for anyone in a different role, isn't morally wrong for the leader. Now, this is not stepping outside morality, but it is fracturing morality. It is saying there's this morality, that morality, and then there's political morality.

I think this is a very bad way to go. There's some descriptive truth in it, and some normative truth, in that there are different roles in society, and we attach specific moral permissions and prohibitions to these different roles—to doctors and to lawyers, and so on. But that's still within the framework of a general morality which is more universal and deeper, and in terms of which you can judge the role. If you stated the dirty-hands problem in that way, then you'd still be in the moral orbit. It would still be possible to say, 'Alright, you've got a different role, political leader, but it doesn't license you to torture someone', for instance.

NW: *So what is the real problem of dirty hands in politics?*

TC: I think what Walzer usually means is that the political order is such that sometimes a certain sort of *necessity* overrides genuine morality. The conflict doesn't occur within morality, as it were, as in the story told about different professions and groups having different roles. Rather, it takes place, somehow, outside morality. In certain extreme circumstances, there's something higher or bigger, something more determinative. Machiavelli uses the term 'necessity' too.

Let me give an example, one that Walzer himself uses in his original article. A political leader is facing terrorist threats. This leader thinks torture is deeply immoral, as many of us do. But now he's got hold of a terrorist who knows where a bomb is hidden. There's limited time before this bomb detonates, and he doesn't believe he has any other options for finding the bomb. This is now known as 'the ticking bomb' example. In spite of his strong moral objections, the leader has to order the torture of the person. According to Walzer, he should feel very torn about this, and remorseful, for that shows that there really is a moral thing that's being overridden. Nonetheless, it's the *right* thing to do, in some sense of right.

I think this position makes a certain kind of sense if you take the view that morality is not the whole of what's to be considered when you're deciding what's right or not right to do.

NW: *The way you've described it there, it's a problem that can only arise in really exceptional circumstances: it's not an everyday occurrence. And it's a particular problem for politicians because they're the ones with huge responsibility for the fate of nations.*

TC: Yes, that's right. Walzer doesn't rule out the possibility that it can occur in a non-political context, and once you push the argument hard, it'll turn out that it isn't specific to politics. For instance, a mother in a war-ravaged situation may be in a position where she thinks she has to violate some deep moral constraint in order to save a child. So the stress on politics is not as convincing as it normally sounds. But it's always put in political terms, and, as you say, politicians have big responsibilities. So it's plausible that though the dirty-hands problem is not restricted to politics, it's very prominent there. As to your more general point about exceptional circumstances, Walzer has moved somewhat from his original article, since now he restricts the application of dirty hands to what he calls 'supreme emergencies', whereas one of the examples he gave originally was a more commonplace one of a 'good' political leader bribing a corrupt ward boss to deliver him vital votes with the promise of improperly delivered school-construction contracts.

NW: *So do you think this is a genuine problem? Or do you think that morality never comes into conflict with this other force?*

TC: That's a good question. I've spent a lot of time teasing out this dirty-hands problem, and I began, and remain, somewhat sceptical about it. I'm sceptical for a number of reasons. One is that even if there *are* situations in which the dirty-hands story makes some kind of sense, and is actually true for somebody, it opens up a can of worms. Politicians can start saying, 'I'm a special kind of chap and I face these big decisions and these supreme emergencies so I can violate deep moral constraints with the blessing of philosophers.' I'm very nervous about that, and I'm particularly nervous about it with the example I gave of torture. That's a case where people have resorted to the dirty-hands story far too readily and in many, many cases, implausibly: the ticking bomb scenario is a very implausible one when carefully considered, but it is initially appealing to many people.

It's also true that people sometimes confuse dirty-hands situations with what philosophers call moral dilemmas. They're different. A moral dilemma is a situation in which some dreadful emergency, or circumstance, arises, and moral considerations of a deep kind pull in two different directions. You're then in a position where it looks as though morality can't decide for you, and whichever way you go, you'll have done a wrong. You might think that about *Sophie's Choice*, for instance. In the famous novel and film, the Nazi officer said to Sophie, 'You've got these two children, you decide which one will die, and then I'll let you and the other one live.' That's a case where there isn't a right decision. Walzer and others who tell the dirty-hands story always go one way: they always say, 'The deep moral constraint is overridden by the necessity.' If they had couched it more in terms of a dilemma, I'd be happier: but they always favour the governmental or state decision—and that disturbs me.

NW: *Given that the ticking bomb scenario is pretty far-fetched, do we ever get real situations where the problem of dirty hands does arise?*

TC: The sort of cases that look as though they're the most plausible candidates for dirty hands are what I call cases for extrication morality. These are situations where there is an ongoing wrong that the politician has inherited. It may be an unjust war that's been waged by a predecessor. The politician has decided it's wrong and should stop. But immediately stopping it would be disastrous for all sorts of innocent parties. So, perhaps the right extrication strategy is to continue with this moral wrong for some short time, under the governance of the idea that it is actually morally wrong, and we've got to do something to extricate from it.

One of the criticisms of the Walzerian position is that it's too static. It makes it seem as though there's this horrible wrong that necessarily must be done by the ruler, and that's it; whereas I think that if it were true that a horrible wrong *had* to be done, then it would be terribly important to start looking around for changing the circumstances, for changing the institutional background, so that it didn't happen again or was less likely to occur. It ought to be an ongoing moral enterprise, in other words. One ought not just to throw up one's hands and say, 'Oh, we're politicians, we get dirty hands.'

The extrication case makes that a little bit clearer because what's to be done is governed by the consideration that this is a deep wrong. I've got to stop doing it, but maybe the *way* I stop doing it is something that commits me to doing more wrong. Take an imaginary President Obama early in his period of office: suppose he thinks that the Afghan War is profoundly wrong; he hasn't told anybody yet, and it's getting worse; and the soldiers are saying, 'You must put more troops in.' Now, he's got a real problem. Let's suppose he wants to stop the war. He's got to have popular support behind him to do this; he's got to get the generals on side too. So maybe he's got to do what he thinks is actually wrong, and keep the war going for a bit longer, before ending it, which means a lot of people are going to die while it continues.

Such cases might be genuine dirty-hands cases. But the ticking bomb scenario—'Oh, the school is going to be blown up by the terrorist and I've got this fellow, and I know for certain that he knows where the bomb is, and I know for certain that he'll succumb to the torture, and I know for certain that he won't mislead me long enough for the bomb to go off somewhere else'—there are all these insane hypothetical aspects to the story. There's something corrupting about the way people focus on such examples.

NW: *I'd imagine somebody who said, 'Look, these exceptional circumstances allow me to torture somebody', might be more prone to make that move faster in the future.*

TC: I think people can be corrupted by engaging in evil with the best of intentions, and they can be corrupted by endless consideration of these things. There's a certain kind of exercise in philosophy, unfortunately, which then leaks out into the wider world. You imagine all these bizarre and extreme circumstances in which people do the most hideous and horrible things. Now, I don't think this means one of the philosophers is immediately prone to torturing some passer-by, but there's a corruption of the intellectual environment that can go with this, which can help promote rather awful things.

NW: *In a previous interview, we talked to Raimond Gaita about torture. He said that even to consider the possibility of torture is to have taken a morally significant step in a bad direction.*

TC: Yes, I have sympathy with that. There is something dangerous in the political climate that influences the way many intellectuals have fallen in behind the torture brigade, and produced these arguments—some of them of the dirty-hands kind, some of them just consequentialist—to provide a moral rationale for this practice which we know is operating not in supreme emergencies, but in all sorts of situations. That's pretty alarming. I don't think it can be considered a purely intellectual exercise to go around saying people can torture a child because of some perceived political 'necessity'.

NW: *So should we wash our hands of dirty hands?*

TC: If you say you want to wash your hands of something, you're always put in the same boat as Pontius Pilate, and I don't want to be in that category! People sometimes say, 'Oh, you're worried about your soul', and all this stuff. Well, yes, I think you ought to worry about your soul. I don't mean your 'soul' as an abstract object—and whether it gets to heaven or not—but rather what sets of significant dispositions you have towards action. I think people ought to be careful about getting too deeply into the dirty-hands business. Walzer himself seems to have become more cautious about the category of dirty hands in his more recent writings. He says for instance, 'As hard cases make bad law, so supreme emergencies put morality at risk. We need to be careful.'[1]

NW: *Does that then mean that we shouldn't be electing politicians who use dirty-hands rhetoric?*

TC: Well, unfortunately we don't always know what kind of politicians we're electing. But I think we should aim to elect politicians who are skilled at political craft, and have good

[1] Michael Walzer, 'Emergency Ethics', in *Arguing About War* (New Haven, Conn.: Yale University Press, 2004), p. 33.

character, and can be trusted to do good things. Walzer says that we want political leaders who will get their hands dirty when the time comes—I don't think we do. If the time comes, and it really is a situation that calls for dirty hands, then the guy will have to make up his or her mind, but it shouldn't be done, as it were, in advance.

METAPHYSICS, MEANING, AND REASON

23

KIT FINE ON
What is Metaphysics?

David Edmonds: *Although Aristotle did not himself know the word, the term 'metaphysics' was first used after his death by an editor to describe a collection of his writings that we now think of as Aristotle's Metaphysics. 'Meta' means after or beyond, and there is speculation that the editor meant to deter students from reading Aristotle's Metaphysics, until after they'd read his Physics. The term is notoriously hard to define, so when modern philosophers describe themselves as working on metaphysical questions, what exactly do they mean? A question for leading metaphysician, Kit Fine, from New York University.*

Nigel Warburton: *The topic we're going to focus on is what is metaphysics? Now, a simple view of metaphysics is that it's just about reality: it's the study of reality. Is that fair enough?*

Kit Fine: Almost. It's the *philosophical* study of reality. Of course, many disciplines study reality. Metaphysics is the philosophical study of reality, and of course, reality is a big thing: you might think of it as including everything. So metaphysics is the study of the most general features of reality.

NW: *How does that differ from science, because for many people, science is the best way we have for discovering anything about the nature of reality, whether it be the size of a planet, or the nature of a microorganism?*

KF: The main difference from science is that the philosophical study of reality is *a priori*. That means that it is independent of observation. So, whereas the scientist will work in the laboratory or rely on the results that issue from the laboratory, the philosopher will not be so heavily dependent on such results: he'll just sit in his armchair, or her armchair, and think about the nature of reality. The kinds of questions they'll consider will be the nature of space and time, the nature of causation, what a person is, and so on and so forth. These are just very general questions about what you might call the fabric of reality.

NW: *But if you're just speculating from your armchair, how could you possibly know that you are right, for instance, about the nature of time, or space and time? It seems to me that you'll want to get out of the armchair and find out about things in the world if you're investigating reality.*

KF: This is a fundamental question facing the study of metaphysics: 'To what extent is it possible to gain *a priori* knowledge of the general nature of reality?' However, there do seem to be questions of great interest that can only be answered by *a priori* means. Let's take the question of the nature of cause. David Hume thought that causation was just a matter of regularities: what it is for one thing to cause another is for the one thing, or things of that type, to be followed by things of the other type. Other people have thought, well, there must be more, there must be some kind of necessary connection. The one thing, in a real sense, must make the other thing happen. There are no experimental methods that could settle that question—at least on the face of it, there don't appear to be—so if we are to have any hope of settling the question, it seems that we can only do it by thinking about it in the armchair.

NW: *Let's take Hume's example: one billiard ball rolls against another one, there's a click, the second ball moves. The first ball causes the second one to move. Many people would think that if you want to understand cause and effect what you have to do is investigate the nature of that collision scientifically. Why is it a philosophical problem in the* a priori *way you described?*

KF: The actual detailed mechanism of the cause and effect of how one billiard ball hitting the other would impact on the other is a scientific matter, of course, but the question now is this: if you do want to say, and maybe you don't, but if you do want to say that the first billiard ball hitting the second *causes* the second to move, then the question is, well, what is the nature of that causal relationship between the one event and the other? We're not interested in the actual details here of how fast the one would move, given that it was hit by the other, or what have you.

There's a big divide here. Some people think that all we have in the universe is just one thing following another, so if

there is causation here, it just must be a matter of this
particular event following the other particular event, and
similar events following from similar events. Other people
have thought causation cannot just be a matter of one thing
following another, there must be some kind of necessary
connection in the world. Somehow, it must be necessary if the
one event happened that the other happened if there's to be
genuine causation. This is a very general question about the
nature of causation; it's not one that, it seems, science can
answer.

NW: *Given that this isn't an empirical question, once you've got these*
two candidate explanations or descriptions of cause and effect and how
they're related, how do you discriminate between them?

KF: So, if you're a Humean, or what now is called a
regularity theorist, you have to try to distinguish between
so-called accidental generalizations—generalizations where
one thing just happens to follow another—and genuine causal
generalizations. So it may well be, for example, that at five to
twelve, some people leave a classroom at one school, and
at twelve, some other children leave a classroom, but there's
no causal connection between the two, so this is a purely
accidental generalization: the one happens to follow the other.
If someone is a Humean, they have to try to account as best
they can for that distinction between accidental generalizations and the causal generalizations. On the other hand, the
non-Humeans have to give an account of what this necessary
connection might be, of how it can do the kind of work that
we want it to do, and so on and so forth. We can frame the
question in terms of how adequate these answers are.

NW: *So, in your example, with the school children leaving at five to twelve and the other group leaving at twelve, this always seems to happen: whenever one group leaves, five minutes later the other one does. Now there's probably no causal connection between those, yet it looks like there could be because there is this pattern of regularity. Now, what you're saying there presumably is that that's merely an accidental coincidence. The thing we're trying to investigate when we're looking at cause and effect is something which isn't accidental, which seems to be a necessary connection.*

KF: Right. So certain generalizations are just accidentally true: one thing just happens to follow another, but not for a causal reason. There are others that seem to happen for a causal reason. If you have a regularity view, according to which causation is a matter of one thing following another, you have to distinguish between the accidental cases of one thing following another, and the genuinely causal cases. The question is whether there's enough resources within the regularity theory to make the kind of distinctions we think actually exist.

NW: *Let's take another example of a metaphysical question. You mentioned the nature of a person; how could that be a metaphysical question? Superficially it seems like a psychological question.*

KF: Yes. We're asking what is a person, and, if you like, what is a person by his or her very nature. Perhaps we can get a feel for the question by considering some of the answers that might be given. You might think a person is simply his or her body, or you might think that a person has something like a soul, so the person is a soul, or you might think a person is some combination of a soul and a body, or you might have a view according to which there's no more to a person than his or her experiences. These are all very different views about the nature of a person, a person as such, if you like, not the nature of a person's psychology or personality or what have you.

NW: *So, again, this is operating at a very general level, and that seems to be a characteristic of metaphysics—that it's not the kind of very specific investigation of a particular individual, but more like the question: 'What is an individual?', 'What is a person?', 'What is causation?', 'What is free will?' Those are all big metaphysical questions.*

KF: Yes. There's a great deal of generality in the question, so we're not interested in the nature of men as opposed to women, for example—that wouldn't be general enough. We're also interested in the nature of these things in themselves, that is at the most abstract level, abstracting from the very particular features they might just happen to have.

NW: *A further example of metaphysics is the question, 'What is a number?' What are the candidates there?*

KF: There are a number of candidates. Some people have just thought of numbers as the same as the signs for numbers, the so-called numerals; other people have thought that numbers are something abstract in some sort of platonic realm existing independently of us; other people have thought that numbers are some kind of mental construction, perhaps somewhat like a fictional object that's made up by the mathematician in the way that a fictional character is made up by an author. So these are three views, but there are many, many others as well.

NW: *It seems that the mathematician is doing something quite close to what a metaphysician might be doing. He or she thinks about abstract entities, reasoning in a way that doesn't necessarily relate back to actual individuals. Often mathematicians are thinking about the nature of an equation, or trying to find some kind of entity that doesn't seem to have any direct connection with the real world as we experience it.*

    KF: Well, yes, mathematics is like metaphysics in being an *a priori* investigation into reality. One of the reasons one might have for thinking metaphysics is possible, is that mathematics is possible. I should emphasize that mathematics is an *a priori* study of reality. I'm not sure it's the *a priori* study of the *nature* of reality: mathematicians are not interested as such in the nature of numbers or what have you: they're interested in number. Mathematics doesn't have the generality of metaphysics, so mathematics is interested in a very specific subject matter.

NW: *Now, there's a great tradition of metaphysics from the pre-Socratics onwards, but in the twentieth century, it came under radical attack, particularly from the logical positivist movement.*

    KF: Yes, it did and it's only recently, actually, that philosophers recovered from those attacks. They were taken very seriously, and for a very long time, many philosophers, as a result of those attacks, just dismissed metaphysics as so much idle talk.

NW: *So, let's just run the sort of argument that A. J. Ayer popularized in* Language, Truth and Logic, *against metaphysics: he said for anything to be a meaningful statement, it has either to be true by definition, like 'All cats are animals', or else it's got to be empirically verifiable, in the sense that you could do some kind of scientific experiment to show that the statement that you made was true or false.*

Anything that didn't pass that two-pronged test for meaningfulness, ended up in the category of meaningless statements which he pejoratively labelled 'metaphysics'.

KF: Yes, that's true, he did make that attack, and Hume made a similar attack before him. Behind that attack is a very serious question, which is the question you started out with, namely, 'How can philosophers hope from their armchair to discover anything about the nature of the world?'

NW: *Given this quite vigorous assault on metaphysics as traditionally conceived, how did it recover? You said it recovered, and in recent years it's been flourishing. How could it possibly recover from that attack?*

KF: There are two explanations. One is just the intellectual argument that identifies what is wrong with Ayer's attack, and there were many criticisms of Ayer. I'm not sure that many philosophers actually subscribed, a decade or two after the positivists' attacks, to the so-called verification criteria of meaning, but still it wasn't clear that there was a viable enterprise in doing metaphysics. Part of the reason had nothing to do with the positivist attacks, but with the fact that the quality of metaphysical discussion seemed to be very obscurantist. So even if the positivist objections weren't correct in principle, they did seem to point to something that was wrong in the discipline itself. Metaphysics often involves very difficult concepts, and one might wonder whether these concepts have any real application. So metaphysicians, for example, claim to be talking about the fundamental nature of reality, but what is this notion of fundamentality, or reality? Another difficulty is that metaphysicians often seem to be just disputing what's a matter of common sense. They might say, look, everything is mental, or everything is physical, and this just seems to fly in the face of common sense. There are a number of things that made metaphysics seem suspicious, and what's happened is that slowly philosophers realized that the questions of metaphysics were real questions and were worth studying.

NW: *I can imagine a sceptical listener here who's saying to himself, or herself, 'This is all very interesting for you, and your colleagues, but why should any university be funded to have such people?' Why do metaphysicians exist at all, given scarce resources?*

KF: For one thing, these questions are interesting in themselves. There can be hardly a person who has not thought about the nature of mind, or the nature of physical reality, and how the two might relate. But also these very general concepts are employed, or are pre-supposed, in many other disciplines, and so by being clearer about these concepts through metaphysics, we can be clear about their role in these other disciplines. For example, the notion of cause is pervasive throughout many different subjects. We talk about cause in many different ways—in the social sciences, the physical sciences, and what have you—and so one might hope that the general study of these concepts could actually be of real benefit to these other disciplines.

NW: *I wondered if there's one, single discovery or theory in the whole history of metaphysics that you think encapsulates what can be achieved with metaphysics?*

KF: A good example is the distinction between primary and secondary qualities which had a huge impact on science. The thought was that the primary qualities were somehow really in the objects themselves, so the primary qualities would be things like length, or mass, and the secondary qualities would be things like colour or taste. It was thought that the secondary qualities were a reflection of the human mind, how we reacted to the primary qualities. That distinction suggests that science should be about the primary qualities rather than the secondary qualities. In so far as scientists are interested in the physical world itself, rather than our reaction to it, then that's what this distinction would suggest. And making that distinction had a huge impact on the study of science.

24

DAN SPERBER ON
The Enigma of Reason

David Edmonds: *Philosophers have traditionally celebrated reason: Aristotle defined humans as 'rational animals'. It is our ability to reason, he thought, that sets us apart from other animals. But why did humans evolve with a capacity to reason? What function does reason serve? The obvious answer is that it helps us get at the truth and that has survival value. But according to the French social and cognitive scientists Dan Sperber (who is with us) and Hugo Mercier, it's not as simple as that.*

Nigel Warburton: *The topic we are going to focus on today is the enigma of reason. What's that?*

Dan Sperber: Well, reason is puzzling because, on the one hand, it's a cliché that this is what makes humans superior to all other animals and that some of the greatest achievements of mankind from science technology to law are based on our capacity to reason. So you'd expect reason to function particularly well. But when you do experiments on reasoning, people, it seems, are rather bad at it. Another puzzling aspect is that reason is supposed to be our best path towards truth, and so it should cause people to converge on the same views and ideas, but on the contrary it very often tends to polarize positions and disagreements.

NW: *Could you give an example of the kind of errors in reasoning that people are prone to?*

DS: Suppose I ask you to solve the following very simple problem. A bat and a ball together cost £1.10. The bat is worth one pound more than the ball, so how much does the bat cost?

NW: *I guess £1.*

DS: Well, are you sure? If it were £1, then the difference between the two would be 90p, and I said that the difference has got to be £1, and the total £1.10. So that can't be the right answer.

NW: *So I guess the bat costs £1.05 and the ball costs 5p.*

DS: Very good. The answer you've given now is given as the first answer by only about 30% of the participants in experiments where we pose that kind of problem. So intuition doesn't give us the right answer. What's surprising is that even if you give people time to reason before they give the answer, what they do, instead of correcting their mistaken first intuition, is use reason to confirm it. Across lots of experiments, you give tasks that are logically fairly simple to resolve like this one, and not only do people fail to give the right answers, but if you give them time to reason and rethink their answers they use reasoning just to confirm their initial hunch, which is not what reasoning should be doing if it were a path to a better solution or towards the truth. This is an example of what is known as the *confirmation bias*. Once you have a certain view, an opinion—either because that is what you have been told or because it is your first guess—you use reasoning to confirm this opinion, not to correct it, not to go beyond it, but just to find further arguments to reinforce your own bias.

NW: *That makes it sound as if the role of reason is rationalization, not the discovery of truth.*

DS: Well that's the suspicion! People use reasoning to confirm the biases or opinions they already have. The issue is why would you do that?

NW: *Given the fallibility of reasoning and the difficulty of explaining what its role is, has anybody come up with a plausible account of what its purpose is?*

DS: There are several hypotheses. First, some psychologists are content to assume that human reasoning is just not very good, and that's that. We may think of ourselves as great reasoners, but in fact we are not. But that does not make much sense: why should we deploy this costly mental activity in reasoning? In contrast, intuition is fast and almost effortless and, it seems, is not more error-prone than reasoning itself.

Apart from the idea that reasoning is just not very effective, another answer that has been suggested is that the biases we exhibit in reasoning in many situations serve us well: it is only in special situations that reasoning fails to provide the right answer. That view is correct to a certain extent, but more about inference in general than about reasoning proper. Our mechanisms of inference on the whole serve us reasonably well, but they sometimes fail abjectly. The problem, again, is that our low-cost mechanisms of *intuitive* inference serve us well in ordinary situations and that reasoning proper does not seem to do better. Reasoning is a costly mental activity which we seem to use just to confirm our intuitions.

NW: *So what is your solution? What is the way out of this enigma?*

DS: The enigma comes from the underlying assumption that reasoning is something that serves individual cognition, that it is a way for each of us in our individual thinking to reach higher and better levels of understanding, a better grasp of the way the world is, and better decisions. What Hugo Mercier and I have tried to argue is that the function of reasoning is not to enhance individual cognitive capacities, it's to play a role in *social* interaction, more specifically in communication.

Humans depend massively on communication with others. To become a competent adult and to lead your daily life, you typically depend on communication with others in lots of ways, from moving around to deciding what to eat, where to go, and so on. You probably read the newspaper this morning, looked at news on television or the Internet, discussed what's going on with your friends or your partners, and we do that all the time. So we depend massively on communication with others.

Other people have a lot of information that we don't have and we can benefit immensely from them. On the other hand, they each have interests that are, at least in part, different from our own. They communicate not just out of sheer altruism, to serve our interests, but to influence us—sometimes for our good, but also so that we will see them in a better light, agree with them, do what they want us to do, and so on. So in order to get the best out of communication, we have to exercise some degree of what can be called 'epistemic vigilance' to try to believe all the information that is given in good faith by competent speakers, while remaining aware of the possibility of speakers being incompetent or aiming to deceive us, or at least manipulating us.

So, if I am vigilant, how can you convince me of something that I won't believe just on trust, just because you said it? Well, you can argue for it, you can present reasons. That is where reasoning comes on the scene. You can give me highly acceptable premises and show me that if I accept these premises, the conclusion that I would not accept at first follows from them. That is what reasoning does: reasoning often allows us to go beyond the bottleneck of insufficient trust. On our view, the basic function of reasoning is to produce arguments and to evaluate arguments in order to overcome trust bottlenecks in communication.

NW: *I can see there's a social role for giving reasons, but if giving reasons doesn't reliably lead to the truth, why would this social encounter be more likely to produce truth than just an individual on their own making mistakes due to relying on their reasons?*

DS: We are not thinking of reason as a way to take us to the truth, but reason as a way to convince others, and, from the point of view of an audience, as a way to be convinced on good grounds but not otherwise. From the point of view of the communicator, reasoning is a way to convince a reticent audience. From the point of view of the audience however, reasoning is an ability to evaluate arguments, an ability that may help both eliminate a number of errors or misleading information and recognize good arguments.

So, again, the claim on this view is not that reasoning is there to get at the truth: reasoning is for overcoming trust bottlenecks in communication. But it does have relevance to resolving the enigma of reasoning and to explaining the fantastic achievements of reasoning, for instance, in the sciences. What happens in a dialogical situation, in a situation where people have different views and argue in order to convince one another is that you get a kind of social division of cognitive labour. You present arguments which may not be that good and I will criticize them; I will perhaps present other arguments which you will criticize. And if we have a common interest in truth, the chances are that we will converge on it, and, in fact, there is experimental evidence to that effect. This is the same kind of reasoning experiment as the bat and ball problem which people are pretty bad at solving individually, when you put them in a group of three or four people none of them necessarily has the solution initially. They start producing their own solutions while criticizing those of the others, and they are not satisfied as a group until they've found the right solution. Groups perform much better than individuals in resolving these reasoning problems.

NW: *That sounds like an ideal philosophy seminar. Philosophers are often caricatured as thinkers in ivory towers on their own scratching their heads, but in reality they are often in dialogue, as we are now.*

DS: Absolutely—and not just philosophers, but scientists too. These are highly competitive activities, where people are trying to argue for the hypotheses that they put forward as well as they can, and also to find fault with the hypotheses of others, and where only the best hypotheses tend to survive. I want to stress that I'm not trying to say that the function of reasoning is to ensure a collective convergence towards the truth, but the function of reasoning is to allow us to provide and evaluate arguments in communication which can *under certain conditions* cause a group of people to converge on the truth, move towards better knowledge. Under other conditions it can create polarization. So if you take a group of people who start with near-identical views, let's say a religious group, and now they start reasoning, they reason in favour of the same opinions and against people of different opinions who are not there to respond. What will happen is polarization: they will just become more fanatical, set in their views, and are highly susceptible as a group to the confirmation bias.

NW: *Does your theory have any practical implications?*

DS: Let me give you two examples where it does have an impact. One is in education. There's a lot of wonderful work showing that children learn much better if they are given the chance to argue about the subject matter at hand. If you just teach them what they should end up knowing, they are not that good, but if you put it in a problematic form and encourage them to take different points of view, and then to argue among themselves, not only do they tend to come to a better solution, but they also learn it and internalize it much, much better. The second example is from the political sphere. There's great interest in what's now called deliberative democracy and the precise importance of discussion, debate, and so on. Political engagement is not just voting and delegating your power and authority to an elected official, but involves deliberating as much as possible on the issues.

25

STEPHEN NEALE ON
Meaning and Interpretation

David Edmonds: *'How do you feel about Women's Rights, Groucho Marx?' 'I like either side of them', he replied. 'A child of five could understand this', said Groucho. 'So get me a child of five.' Sometimes it seems that a sentence can semantically mean one thing and so be interpreted in one way, but is intended to mean something else. A central theme in the philosophy of language is working out what 'meaning' means, what it is for a speaker or writer of a sentence to mean something by a sentence. Can I just read off the meaning of a sentence by the definitions of the words I use and the order in which these words are placed? Or are the words just clues to what I mean? Is the meaning of a sentence dependent on its context? Stephen Neale is at the City University of New York.*

Nigel Warburton: *We're going to focus on the topic of meaning and interpretation. It would be quite useful to separate out those two. What are they? What's meaning? What's interpretation?*

Stephen Neale: To *interpret* is to draw an interesting conclusion about something. A geologist is interpreting when she draws conclusions about a volcanic eruption on the basis of facts about lava composition, stratigraphy and ash distribution. An archaeologist is interpreting when he draws conclusions about a disinterred object on the basis of its shape and material composition, the archaeological context, and stratigraphy again. And you and I are interpreting when we draw conclusions about what a speaker means by uttering something, which can be quite different from what the sentence he uttered means.

NW: *I'd like to ask you to clarify the meaning–interpretation distinction in connection with language. Let's say I utter the words, 'The cat sat on the mat', to describe something that happened in my house last night. That sentence has a straightforward literal meaning which is, presumably, connected to what I mean by uttering it. But an interpretation is not something the sentence has; interpretation is what somebody does: they hear me utter those words, or see that I wrote those words down, and then they try and work out what I meant.*

SN: That's exactly right. When I'm working out what you meant, I'm engaged in *interpretation*. And the conclusion I reach is *an interpretation* of your utterance. We use the word 'interpretation' to describe both an *activity*, as you said, and also the *product* of that activity. (We do the same thing with the words 'writing' and 'painting'.) But two important distinctions are needed to make everything clear. The first is between a *sentence*, which is an abstract object, and particular *utterances* of that sentence, which are events taking place in space and time. Think of the difference between a symphony and various performances of it. The performances are events, but the thing they are performances *of*, the symphony itself, isn't an event, it's an abstract entity. The second distinction is between two kinds of meaning: *linguistic* meaning, which concerns what *words, phrases,* and *sentences* mean; and *speaker* meaning, which concerns what people mean by uttering words, phrases, and sentences. Right before we started recording this conversation, you said to me, 'We're ready.' What you meant was that *you and David* were ready *to begin recording*. So what you meant was closely related to the meaning of the sentence you used, but not identical to it. The meaning of the sentence, 'We're ready', doesn't concern *you* or *David* or *recording*.

NW: *So what the sentence means is less specific than what I meant in this example because of the pronoun 'we' and the lack of specificity surrounding 'ready'?*

SN: That's right. Another way to put the point is to say that the meaning of the sentence is more *abstract* than anything a speaker will mean in uttering it. The sentence meaning is really a *blueprint* for the *sort* of thing a speaker can mean in uttering it. To interpret your utterance, to work out what you meant, I needed more than this blueprint because I needed to infer *who* you meant by 'we' and *what* you meant you were ready for. In a different context, you might utter, 'We're ready', and mean that *you and Barry Smith* are ready *to perform the Monty Python dead parrot sketch*, and this would conform to the sentence's blueprint too. Many distinct possible speaker meanings conform to a sentence's blueprint, just as many distinct possible buildings conform to an architectural blueprint.

NW: *If interpreting an utterance is drawing a conclusion about what the speaker means, the goals of a theory of meaning and a theory of interpretation will be connected. Could you explain what the goals are and how they differ?*

SN: Yes, it irks me how often the goals get run together in contemporary philosophy and cognitive science. To ask about the *nature* of something—'What is justice?', 'What is truth?', 'What is meaning?'—is to ask a *constitutive* question in metaphysics, a philosophical question about the nature or *constitution* of something. For speaker meaning, the constitutive question is 'What determines what a speaker means by uttering something on a given occasion?' Or, 'In virtue of what facts does a speaker mean whatever he or she means?' When you said, 'We're ready', you meant that *you and David* were ready *to begin recording*. What determined that? What made that the case? A theory of speaker meaning should provide a fully general answer, one that applies to every case of speaker meaning. There's nothing about the meaning of 'we' or the meaning of 'ready' that made it the case that you meant *yourself and David* by 'we', or that you meant *ready to begin recording* by 'ready'. The meaning of 'ready' is just a blueprint for the sort of thing a speaker can mean by it. So is the meaning of 'we', which dictates only that someone using it should mean himself or herself and at least one other person—monarchs notwithstanding. It doesn't dictate that the other person has to be *David Edmonds*! So something other than linguistic meaning made it the case that you meant David and yourself by 'we'. And it's hard to see how it could be anything other than your *intention* to be talking about yourself and David. You intended and expected me to recognize that you meant yourself and David by 'we'. The linguistic meaning of 'we' merely constrained the *sort* of intention you could have if you were using the word with its customary meaning. I had to *infer* whom you meant by 'we'. It wasn't *hard*, but just knowing English, knowing the customary meaning of 'we' wasn't enough. I had to draw upon facts about the context too. If I had interpreted you as meaning that you and Barry Smith were ready to perform the dead parrot sketch, then I would have misread your intentions and got you wrong on two counts. I would have *misinterpreted* you.

NW: *You said what question a theory of speaker meaning should answer. Could you say what question a theory of interpretation is meant to answer?*

SN: It's a question in cognitive science, a very different type of question from the constitutive question about the nature of speaker meaning. It's this: 'How do interpreters come up with the interpretations they come up with about what speakers mean?' Somehow, we manage to do it, and typically it involves no effort, or training, or conscious reflection. It's spontaneous. We have no choice unless we plug our ears. I hear an utterance of 'We're ready', and Bingo! An interpretation pops into my head. Cognitive science aims to explain how this happens, how I bring together information about linguistic meaning, information derived from context, and all manner of background information and beliefs stored in memory, how I assess and integrate it, and finally reach a conclusion about what the speaker means. The cognitive processes involved are fast, automatic, largely beyond the reach of conscious thought. I can't choose to hear an utterance of an English sentence as just sounds. I organize the sounds into words and phrases, whether I want to or not. I can't choose to hear those words and phrases as devoid of meaning. And I can't decide not to *interpret*, not to draw a conclusion about what the speaker means. All of this makes utterance interpretation importantly different from the other sorts of interpretation I mentioned at the beginning, interpreting on the basis of lava samples or erosion patterns, stratigraphy, pottery sherds, bone arrangements, and so on, where special skills must be acquired on the basis of training.

NW: *So when somebody does utter some words, where does the meaning come from? Humpty Dumpty in Lewis Carroll's* Through the Looking Glass *famously said that he could use words to mean anything he liked. That clearly wasn't true.*

SN: Right. And there are important lessons to be learned from understanding exactly what Humpty Dumpty got wrong. I'd like to come back to that if I may. But first I want to separate the constitutive question about *speaker* meaning—*In virtue of what facts does the speaker mean whatever he or she means?*—from the constitutive question about *linguistic* meaning—*In virtue of what facts does a word or sentence mean whatever it means?* The answer seems straightforward for sentence meaning: *the meaning of a sentence is determined by the meanings of its words and by principles governing the positions those words occupy in the sentence's grammatical structure*—'Tom loves no one' doesn't mean the same thing as 'No one loves Tom', for example. We can think of a sentence meaning as a kind of structure whose basic elements are word meanings. That structure is effectively a blueprint for the sort of thing a speaker can mean in uttering it. But this still leaves *word* meaning unexplained, so we certainly haven't explicated linguistic meaning yet—we haven't said what it *is*, we haven't explained its nature. And we *won't*, I claim, until we explicate *speaker* meaning.

NW: *Can you explain why you say that? Some people might believe, perhaps naïvely, that what determines the meanings of words are their dictionary definitions. When you utter certain words in an appropriate*

order they just have a fixed public meaning. It seems counterintuitive to
say we need to explain the nature of speaker meaning to explain the
nature of linguistic meaning.

SN: Yes, it does at first. Words *do* have reasonably fixed
public meanings—*reasonably* fixed because a word can change
its meaning over time—the word 'starve' used to mean *die*, for
example. But at any given time, a word means whatever it
means independently of how any particular speaker plans on
using it. If a theory of the relationship between word meaning
and speaker meaning is to have any intuitive plausibility, it
must respect the fact that what a word means at a given time
imposes pretty serious constraints on what a *speaker* can mean
with it at that time. But there's another fact the theory must
respect: that the meaning of the word at a given time is the
product of the myriad ways it has been used *prior* to that time
in *acts of speaker meaning*. If that weren't the case, words
couldn't change their meanings over time. But they do.
Meaning change usually takes place slowly, like tectonic shift,
but with the pressure for movement coming from acts of
speaker meaning piling up. So a word's meaning at a given
time is effectively its *potential* for use in acts of speaker
meaning at that time. To know the word's meaning is to know
that potential. And what makes this potential something we
can get our heads around is the *systematicity* imposed on it and
honed by prior acts of speaker meaning. (This can be
modelled using evolutionary game-theory.) So there's
something right in the naïve view about word meaning. A
dictionary definition of a word is, in effect, an attempt to
capture facts about the word's potential in acts of speaker
meaning, a potential that derives from its history in acts of

speaker meaning. You can't keep speaker meaning out of the picture! It's the *source* of meaning: *people meaning things by doing things*. As far as I'm aware, there's no remotely plausible alternative picture of word meaning. But we can't provide an account of word meaning along these lines without an account of speaker meaning, obviously.

NW: *So what is the nature of speaker meaning? What determines what a speaker means by an utterance?*

SN: I think Paul Grice was basically right: what the speaker means is determined solely by certain complex intentions he or she has in producing the utterance. The easiest way to appreciate this idea is to start with a case in which the speaker means something very different from what the sentence he or she utters means. People speak ironically; they talk metaphorically; they imply or insinuate things rather than stating them outright. A famous example of Grice's concerns a professor who has been asked about the suitability of one of his students for a philosophy job. His only comment is, 'Smith has wonderful handwriting and he's always on time.' That's it. What he means is that *Smith is not suitable for the job*, which is not what the sentence means.

NW: *The professor is 'damning with faint praise'.*

SN: Right. And we can provide a philosophical analysis of the damning. *Stating* and *implying* are really two ways of *meaning* something. The professor is *implying*, by omission really, something that he would rather not *state* outright. He *means* that Smith is not suitable for the job, though this is not what the sentence itself means and not what the professor states. (Maybe he also means that Smith has wonderful handwriting and is always on time, maybe not, depending upon how the example is filled out, but that doesn't matter here.) If the listener doesn't realize that the professor means Smith is not suitable for the job, then she fails to grasp what the professor means: she *misinterprets* him. This example underscores some important points about interpretation. In most everyday situations, when we interpret we end up latching onto what the *speaker* means—we don't care that much about what the *words* mean, or what the whole *sentence* means. In fact, most of the time, we don't remember the exact words the speaker uses, even when we remember the gist of what he meant. Words are simply *means to ends*. So are their *meanings*. We've evolved to recover what *speakers* mean and chuck out the rest. (I doubt you remember the *exact* words the professor uttered in the example. Did he say 'excellent handwriting' or 'very neat writing' or something else?) *What determines what the professor meant by uttering 'Smith has wonderful handwriting and he's always on time'?* The natural answer is that what he meant is what he *intended to communicate*.

Now Grice had a brilliant insight: if we can characterize the nature of such intentions—which are often called *communicative* intentions or *meaning* intentions—we will have a fully general account of speaker meaning. A little philosophy of mind is needed to understand Grice's insight. We have mental states—beliefs, desires, intentions, expectations, and so on—about all sorts of things, including the mental states of other people. We have beliefs about their desires, desires about their beliefs, intentions about their desires, beliefs about their intentions, and so on—higher-order mental states, they're usually called. A communicative intention is a spectacular type of higher-order intention. For you to have a communicative intention in uttering something is for you to utter it intending to produce a specific *reaction* in your addressee—his *thinking* something or *doing* something—partly in consequence of his recognizing that *that's* the reaction you intend him to have. What you communicatively intend your addressee to think or do is what you *mean*.

NW: *That sounds complicated. Could you run through an example to bring it down to Earth?*

SN: Let's start with one that doesn't involve language. Suppose you and I are at a party. I've promised to give you a lift home, and I know you want a reasonably early night. I'm trapped talking to a terrible bore and want to get away. I catch your eye across the room and yawn quite ostentatiously. You nod discreetly and come over. 'Goodness!', you say, 'look at the time. We need to go.' What I mean by yawning ostentatiously—it's my story, so I'm allowed to stipulate the facts—is that you should come over and rescue me so we can leave. What was my *communicative intention*? Well, I yawned intending you to come over and rescue me so we could leave, partly in consequence of your recognizing that that's how I intended you to react. And it worked! This is a case of 'speaker' meaning without linguistic meaning. Humans have developed the capacity to form and recognize intentions of this complexity. It's a remarkable capacity, one that separates us from the rest of the animal kingdom. We do it all day, usually effortlessly, automatically. It's often claimed that *language* distinguishes us from other species, but that claim's too vague to evaluate, and it could be trivially true or trivially false, depending upon what you mean by 'language'. I think we've got much clearer conceptions of *speech*, *communication*, and *co-operation* (for which we can give a game-theoretic analysis). There's a lot we don't yet understand about their emergence in human history, but the capacity to cooperate and the capacity to have and to recognize communicative intentions must have been instrumental in the emergence of systems of gestural representation and speech, forms of which have been around for tens of thousands of years.

NW: *Are you saying we have such complex intentions even when using language?*

SN: It's controversial, but I think the answer is basically, 'Yes'. A language like English or Japanese is essentially *a shared system for generating reliable shortcuts to communicative intentions*. Let's go back to the party. Instead of yawning, suppose I come to you and say, 'I'm leaving soon.' I mean that I'm leaving the party soon, but I also mean—it's my story, I can stipulate— that you should get ready to leave (if you still want a lift home). I intend you to think that I'm leaving the party soon and to get ready to leave, partly in consequence of your recognizing that these are the reactions I intend you to have. Once we reflect on *why I'm justified* in thinking you will recognize how I intend you to react, we get a fix on the precise role linguistic meaning plays. I expected you to know the meaning of the sentence 'I'm leaving soon', a *blueprint* for the sort of thing a speaker can mean in uttering it. We can make this more precise by invoking the stating–implying distinction again. I'm *stating* that I'm leaving soon and only *implying* that you should get ready to leave. But I *mean* both things. To *state* something with a sentence is to mean something that conforms to its *blueprint*. When I utter, 'I'm leaving soon', and mean that I'm leaving *the party* soon, I mean something that conforms to the sentence's blueprint. But I could use the same sentence, in a different situation, and mean that I'm leaving *London* soon, and that would also conform to the blueprint. We use the blueprints but we customize all the time when talking, and sometimes the blueprint itself *demands* customization, as the blueprint for 'leave' does. When I use 'leave', there must be *somewhere* or *something* or *someone* that I mean I'm leaving. No one can just leave *punkt*. We can use your utterance of 'We're ready' to make the point clearer. The meaning of 'We're ready' specifies nothing about recording or about you or David. But what you meant by uttering it was that *you and David* were ready *to begin recording*. When you use the word 'ready', there must be *something or other* that you mean you're ready *for*. No one can be just ready *punkt*. If I'm ready to *eat* but not ready to *go to bed*, am I *ready*? If I'm glad about *getting a pay raise* but not glad I'm *stuck in traffic*, am I *glad*? These are silly questions unless understood as filled out.

NW: *Those are all cases where the sentence's meaning, its blueprint, demands customized speaker meaning. Are there cases where something else demands it, common sense for example?*

SN: This is controversial too, but again I think the answer is basically: *Yes*. Suppose you come into my house and you look very thirsty, and I open the fridge and say to you, 'Take anything you like.' Now something's gone very wrong if you walk off with the fridge door, or the thermostat, or the cat.

I didn't *tell* you those weren't among the options I was offering
you. You just knew they weren't—you knew that what I
meant by 'anything you like' was quite narrow. The sentence,
'Take anything you like', has a *meaning*, but you, the
interpreter, spontaneously imposed some constraints on how
far you thought I intended my utterance of 'anything you like'
to stretch. The meaning of the sentence didn't reveal to you
what the relevant constraints were; you had to infer them. But
what counts as getting the *right* constraints? Answer: *getting the*
constraints I, the speaker, intended. That's why I say something's
gone wrong if you walk off with the fridge door or the cat:
you've done something which doesn't square with my
communicative intentions. There's a degree of flexibility in
the precise content of my communicative intention, and
neither of us have to spell it out mentally in massive detail. If
you pour yourself a drink from a cold bottle of lemonade
that happens to be standing next to the fridge, or take tap
water, or take a yogurt from the fridge and a banana from a
bowl and make a smoothie, that would be fine. That's because
it's tacitly appreciated by both of us that the content of my
communicative intention is to some extent malleable or
sensitive to various social norms and relations, contextual
factors, and subtleties of various kinds.

NW: *Lots of jokes are based on that kind of literal misunderstanding,*
where somebody takes the words with fixed meaning and interprets them
without taking the context into account.

SN: That's right. Context is one of the things speakers
expect interpreters to take into account in reaching
conclusions about what they mean. Normally, interpreters do
this automatically, without conscious effort. The sorts of jokes

you're talking about trade on someone's manifest failure to do this. That's what makes the jokes work. A theory of interpretation must explain precisely what context is and how it affects our mental processes. The context was something I used—and something you tacitly *expected* me to use—in identifying whom you meant by 'we' when you uttered 'We're ready.' You *exploited* the context without even realizing you were doing it. So did I, in a reciprocal way. We do this sort of thing effortlessly. Most of the time, at least.

NW: *Can you bring the various pieces together by explaining how the speaker's expectation about the role of context in interpretation is connected to the speaker's communicative intention?*

SN: Good. It's really important to understand this. Unfortunately it gets overlooked in the literature. When you said, 'We're ready', you intended me to think that you and David were ready to begin recording, partly in consequence of my recognizing that that's what you intended me to think. And that communicative intention *alone* constitutively determined what you meant. So *context* did not constitutively determine what you meant, not even partly. You, the speaker, tacitly *expected* context to play a part in my coming to a conclusion about *whom* you meant by 'we' and *what* you meant you were ready for. The meaning of the sentence itself didn't tell me *those* things. So I tacitly drew on the context, just as you tacitly expected me to, in identifying the content of your communicative intention. In fact, you tacitly took context into account in *forming that communicative intention*. So context has a dual theoretical role: it figures in a theory of utterance interpretation—which is also called a *pragmatic theory* or *pragmatics*—and it also figures in a theory of utterance construction and intention formation, which I have called a *formatic theory* or *formatics*—which has been my main interest of late. A pragmatics answers the question: *How do interpreters come up with the interpretations they come up with about what speakers mean?* A formatics answers the reverse or mirror question: *How do speakers come to form the communicative intentions they have in producing the utterances they produce?* Sentence meaning has the same dual theoretical role. It figures in a pragmatics because of its role in the interpreter's reaching a conclusion about what the speaker means. And it figures in a formatics because of its role in the formation of the speaker's communicative intention in uttering whatever he or she uttered.

NW: *That brings us back to Humpty Dumpty. It's sometimes said that intentionalist theories of meaning must be Humpty Dumpty theories.*

SN: The people who make this claim—literary and legal theorists, linguists, and philosophers of language—are as confused as Humpty Dumpty. Intentionalism is not committed to the view that speakers and writers can mean whatever they like using any words they like; and the reason is obvious to anyone who's reflected on what's involved in having an intention: *you can't intend what you believe to be impossible.* Or, if you prefer: *you can't intend to bring about a state of affairs that you know you can't bring about.* It's an old point that's often missed by opponents of intentionalism. I can't intend to swim to Australia tonight, because I know I can't succeed. Similarly, I can't utter the sentence. 'Fred reads two novels a week', right now and mean that Paris is the capital of France—unless I'm speaking to you in some kind of code that we have set up in advance. Anyone who claims that intentionalism entails Humpty Dumptyism just hasn't thought about what's involved in having a genuine intention. There's a more general moral here: you can't really do the philosophy of language properly without doing the philosophy of mind.

NW: *In a conversation like the one we're having, there are all sorts of non-verbal aspects of communication, the tone of voice, the speed at which somebody speaks, hand gestures, I may be communicating all kinds of things. But when it comes to the written word, it strikes me many of the cues about a writer's intentions are just not present.*

SN: That's right, and it's what makes interpreting written texts, tape recordings, even friends on the phone, more difficult. In a typical speech situation, the speaker utters something, and the words used form a crucial part of the evidence we use for identifying what the speaker means. As you said, there's also *perceptual* evidence—hand gestures, vocal and visual clues and cues. And prior utterances and all sorts of background knowledge provide further evidence. In principle, we can draw on anything we like in trying to work out what speakers mean. But when we interpret writing, the range of *evidence* we can draw upon is typically narrower, for the reasons you gave. Another difference is that more thought, more effort, more time, often goes into writing and interpreting writing. Even texting allows for editing before messages get sent.

NW: *Of course, not everyone agrees with you about the emphasis on intention. Presumably, some people would put much more stress on the public meaning of, particularly written words, so that the interpretation that you give is based on the text in front of you, not on the presumed intentions of the writer.*

SN: Yes. This gets debated in legal theory. But there's often a serious misunderstanding of the sort of intentionalist position I hold. I don't claim that we base our *interpretations* on the presumed communicative intentions of the writer, or that those intentions are part of the *evidence* for a correct interpretation. In fact, that gets everything backwards. The writer's communicative intentions aren't evidence; they're the things we seek evidence *for*. I claim (a) that *what the writer means* is settled by those intentions; and (b) that an *interpretation* is a conclusion about what those intentions *are*, a conclusion based on the available evidence. The text itself is often the best evidence we have for them, and sometimes it virtually exhausts the evidence. And that raises an important issue in legal theory: *What do you do when there's a genuine interpretive question about a statute that needs resolving and the text itself doesn't provide enough evidence to resolve it?* The fact that the legislators who enacted it may not be present to be questioned about what they intended by this or that phrase is not the real issue. Even if they *were* present, they'd squabble, and most likely wouldn't agree on an answer. Some voted against the Bill, some wanted a different word here or there, one even managed to get a phrase deleted at the last minute in exchange for some shady land deal, and most of them never read the thing in the first place. Perhaps some of it was drafted by influential lobbyists or corrupt clerks attempting to thwart the will of the legislators. So another question is: *Whose communicative intentions could we, or should we, be trying to ascertain when reading a text that is meant to be understood as produced by a legislature?* It's hard to provide a satisfactory answer to this question, and that's one reason some legal theorists think the aim of statutory interpretation cannot be

identifying anyone's intentions. So-called textualists say we
should stick to the language of the text without considering
anyone's intentions, and resolve any looseness or ambiguity by
interpreting as an ordinary, reasonable person would. But
there's an element of fantasy in this idea. It's based on a naïve
picture of what we're capable of doing. We're not *built* like
that. We treat writing we encounter as the product of an
agent with *communicative intentions*, whether we want to or
not, and whether it's a legal text or a sentence we know was
just produced randomly by some computer program. And
that applies just as much to writing produced by committee.
We are built to approach it as the product of a single agent.
Why? Because *natural languages are evolved systems for generating
reliable shortcuts to communicative intentions*—that's really the
Gricean insight.

A lot of anti-intentionalist rhetoric is oblivious to facts
about the mind and about our use of language. It fails to
appreciate the special nature of communicative intentions, the
fact that linguistic meaning can provide at most blueprints for
speaker meaning, the ubiquitous role of inference in ascertaining meaning, and the nature of the cognitive processes
involved in ascertaining it. Of course, when something seems
very wrong, we can make conscious decisions to *reject* the
interpretations served up so automatically and effortlessly by
these cognitive processes. And when we have time to reflect,
as when reading, we can run through a range of possible
interpretations and choose one that suits the purpose at hand.
That's what really happens in much legal interpretation. We
can go over the same ground time and again, bringing
different considerations to bear: traditional canons of interpretation, prior decisions, considerations of absurdity, the

legislators' expressed or assumed goals in enacting a particular law. And different legal theorists have different opinions about what counts as legitimate evidence.

NW: *I know you're in the unusual position for a philosopher of language of having been involved in legal cases that turned on the meaning of words. Could you say a bit more about that?*

SN: In a sense, it's a natural outgrowth of work that's been going on in the philosophy of language for the past twenty or thirty years. It's *applied* philosophy of language—the application to areas outside philosophy of ideas, distinctions, arguments that have been worked over by philosophers of language. I was asked by the US government to help in a case some years ago, and one thing led to another. I'm still appalled by some of the things judges, officials, lawyers, and legal scholars say about language and its use. Distinctions that seem obvious to philosophers are routinely missed, and blatant falsehoods about language and about intentions are presented as fact. Speaker meaning and linguistic meaning get conflated; vagueness, ambiguity, and underspecification are run together; constitutive and evidential notions of determination get conflated; so do different notions of context; and an unbelievable amount of nonsense gets talked about 'plain meaning' and 'ordinary meaning'. This intellectual embarrassment is set to continue until the philosophy of language gets onto the law school curriculum.

NW: *Could you give an example of a case where there's a problem?*

SN: *Smith v. the United States* is a good one. John Angus Smith traded a firearm, a modified MAC-10 and silencer for, I believe, two ounces of cocaine, and was found guilty of a drug-trafficking offence, which should have landed him a few years in prison. But since he was also found to have 'used' a firearm 'during and in relation to' a drug-trafficking offence, he got thirty years. On appeal, Smith argued that since he had used the firearm as *barter*, and not *as a weapon*, he had not 'used a firearm' in the sense meant in the statute. The US Supreme Court disagreed. It upheld the original decision by six votes to three. But both sides tied themselves in knots talking about language and its use. The Justices did not understand that the linguistic meaning of a sentence falls short of fully determining what it is being used to state, and so inevitably falls short of determining its contribution to statutory content. Justice O'Connor, for example, said that if the legislature had intended a narrow interpretation of 'use a firearm', it could have indicated as much in the statute, but it didn't and it isn't the job of the Court to impose this 'additional requirement'. *If* she means the Court can't just add the *words* 'as a weapon' after 'uses a firearm' in the statute, then obviously she's right. But that's not the issue. It's whether 'uses a firearm' is meant to be understood as *using a firearm as a weapon*. O'Connor says it shouldn't, but her rationale is confused. She says that when a word is not defined in a statute, it's standard practice to understand it as having its 'ordinary' meaning, which means understanding 'use' broadly enough to include using a firearm as barter. But the issue isn't the *meaning* of 'use'—'ordinary' or otherwise—the issue is how 'use a firearm' is meant to be understood, which is certainly constrained by the meaning of 'use'. It's similar to the case of your utterance of 'We're ready', which we've got plenty of mileage out of already. I understood you as intending 'ready' to be understood as *ready to start recording*, and I was right. Just as there's no such thing as just being *ready*, so there's no such thing as just *using* something. We can't seriously interpret someone's use of 'use a firearm' as applying to every conceivable thing one could do with a firearm!

Did I use gravity yesterday? Did I use the big bang? Did I use a bike? I can't answer without adding some detail. I didn't *ride* a bike yesterday, but I did arrange for a small package to be picked up by a courier who arrived on a bike, so it seems fine to say I *used* a bike to get a parcel to Holborn. If I had told my daughter that I would cancel the order for her new bike unless she behaved, would I have been *using* a bike? I'd have been using one to influence her behaviour, I suppose. O'Connor just doesn't grasp the distinction between the meaning of a word and how a speaker or writer intends it to be understood, which is only *constrained* by its meaning.

We find the same basic problem in the dissenting opinion written by Justice Scalia, who's officially a textualist. He agrees with O'Connor that non-technical words occurring in statutes should be understood as having their 'ordinary' meanings, and then goes on to claim that the 'ordinary' meaning of 'use a firearm' is restricted to ways firearms are *intended* to be used (by their manufacturers, I suppose), which does not include bartering. So Smith didn't 'use' a firearm. This happens to coincide with the interpretation most people tend to come up with if asked, and that's primarily because it's the one served up by the largely automated, non-conscious cognitive mechanisms of interpretation I was talking about earlier—they are highly sensitive to contextual considerations precisely because they are geared to ascertaining speakers' and writers' *communicative intentions*. But Scalia believes the object of statutory interpretation is never to identify anyone's intentions, and any information interpreters have about legislators' intentions is irrelevant. So he can't support his interpretation by saying it captures the intent of the legislature, or even that it accords with the interpretation ordinary speakers take to capture the intent of the legislature. At most, Scalia can say it accords with the interpretation ordinary speakers tend to *come up with*. And he can't attribute this to their loyalty to the 'ordinary' or 'plain' meanings of the words in question because the meanings of words are much thinner, just blueprints.

Scalia has boxed himself in completely, made it impossible for himself to justify the interpretation he favours, which is the one automatically foist upon the intentionalist without bogus appeals to 'ordinary' meaning and 'ordinary' speakers. Scalia and O'Connor both claim to reject the idea that it is the Court's job to infer the full content of the statute from the blueprint provided by the statutory language itself. But it's what both of them actually do! On the highest court in the land, no less.

NW: *So this whole case turned on the meaning of the word 'use'. If you use a gun in a drug-trafficking offence your tariff is immediately much higher. Yet the intentions of the people who drafted that legislation clearly weren't that you can't use it as the equivalent of money. They meant you mustn't threaten people, you mustn't shoot a gun at somebody or fire it over someone's head.*

SN: It turned on the difference between the meaning of the phrase 'use a firearm', which is just a blueprint, and how it was intended to be understood in the statute, which is only constrained by its meaning. But it's not that easy to say precisely what the legislators intended by 'use a firearm', even for someone convinced that Smith's barter doesn't count. Discharging it? Pointing it at somebody? Threatening?

Does hitting someone with a rifle butt count? It's not clear-cut what counts as using a firearm in the intended sense. O'Connor argues that what matters is whether it's used in a way that is material to the execution of the crime. But it's not clear-cut what that amounts to. Using a gun to scratch an itch that is so intense that not scratching will scupper the entire transaction?

NW: *One interpretation of this case you mentioned is that it was just a badly drafted law, that's the weakness; it wasn't that it turns on the meaning of 'use'.*

SN: There's a sense is which all laws are, and forever will be, badly drafted. Inevitably, there will always be ambiguity, vagueness, underspecification, various ways in which things aren't nailed down precisely by the meanings of the words themselves. It takes pages and pages to say 'Thou shalt not steal' in statutory language because getting it 'right'—which just means reducing the leeway or slippage to an acceptable level—requires piling words onto the page. So legal prose is always going to be drawn out and convoluted in the Anglo-American world. A French law is different: it's more like a set of guidelines within which judges may operate, so there's no need for such wordiness. There appears to be a fantasy in Anglo-American law that if you just get enough words on the page, enough people working on it for long enough, you can nail things down so there's no slippage at all. But that's nonsense. There's always going to be interpretation that goes beyond identifying linguistic meaning. When you hear a sentence, when you read a sentence, you're not simply involved in recovering linguistic meaning on the basis of the meanings of the words and their syntactic arrangement. You're automatically involved in interpreting, in working out what the producer of that sentence meant.

The existence of perfectly good traffic signs shows that we don't always have to pile on the words. A sign that says, 'No Parking', or displays the letter P with a red diagonal line through it, can work perfectly well, even though it does not specify *where* you can't park. The person who put it up, or ordered it to be put up, intended somewhere or other and the driver is expected to infer where. There's nothing in the sign to indicate that it refers to itself—besides, the sign isn't telling you not to park on the *sign* or on the *wall* it's attached to! It's more complicated than that, and the driver will draw upon the physical context and all sorts of beliefs about cars, their sizes, shapes, and so on. There'll always be interpretation, and there'll never be a choice about that.

NW: *Mightn't it be said that the way language is used in the legal context is that people draft legislation for a completely literal reading of the text? So this is a special area of language use.*

SN: It is. And you're right, that does make a difference. We don't want irony and metaphor in our laws or in our traffic signs; that would produce chaos. If we don't treat legislation as drafted literally and carefully, then we're essentially undermining the very idea of law. The law has to be accessible in some public form or other, and judicial responses must be reasonably predictable, otherwise the whole legal system becomes a mockery. To that extent at least, written law is quite different from ordinary speech. Now I don't think we have a good story yet of precisely what the difference amounts to. To enact a law is to change the rights and obligations of citizens, and the language the legislature selects to state that change is the language the legislature is officially using to communicate those changes to those to whom the changes apply. There's no way of squeezing communicative intentions out of the picture. Utterances and inscriptions of words are things we produce *intentionally*. So are the laws and poems we use words to fashion. And so are the tools, weapons, pots, ceremonial items, cave paintings, and jewellery that archaeologists interpret. The types of intentions with which we produce such things fit into an interesting hierarchy with communicative intentions at the top. Archaeology shades into palaeography, which itself shades into semantics, pragmatics, formatics, and the philosophy of language. There's no flight from intention!

26

SUSAN WOLF ON
Meaning in Life

David Edmonds: *Sisyphus was a figure in Greek mythology,*
condemned by the Gods to roll a huge stone up a hill, only to watch it roll
back down again, and to repeat this process ad infinitum. *Even if poor*
old Sisyphus came to terms with his fate, and ended up enjoying it, his life
doesn't sound very meaningful. This Philosophy Bite *is about meaning*
in life—with the eminent philosopher Susan Wolf. To say of someone that
they're living a meaningful life, she says, it's not enough that they're
happy. Nor does it necessarily mean that they're especially moral—
devoting their lives to others. Meaning is a separate category from
fulfilment or morality. To live a meaningful life requires engagement in
activities or relationships that are objectively valuable—*and it's not*
valuable to spend your life in the equivalent of Sisyphean stone pushing.

Nigel Warburton: *We're going to focus on the topic of meaning in*
life. What does 'meaning in life' *mean?*

> **Susan Wolf:** It's a dimension of a good life. We tend to think
> that some people's lives are more meaningful than others'.
> Sometimes we feel that there's something missing in our lives
> and it's not just pleasure, it's something more difficult to get a
> handle on—and 'meaning' is the word that comes up to try to

express that. We want something that will be more rewarding in a special way.

NW: *And is asking about the meaning in my life a question about morality?*

SW: First, I should mention that it's not the same question as 'What is the meaning *of* my life?' When we talk about the meaning *of* life, we are often asking, 'What's the purpose of life? What am I put on this earth for?' That sounds almost like a religious question. Asking whether my life is meaning*ful* is different. I am asking whether my life has something—or more than one thing—in it that gives it a point.

I started reflecting on this subject because it occurred to me that philosophers, and maybe everybody else, tend to think of life in terms of two categories, and meaning doesn't fit into either. The two categories are, first, happiness or self-interest— that what I want out of life is to be as happy as possible. One dimension of a good life is for it to be happy, or go well for oneself. Second, there's morality or being good from an impersonal standpoint. But it seems to me that many of the things that we do in life, the things that really drive us, don't fit into either of those categories.

NW: *I'd really like to hear an example of something that does give meaning to someone's life.*

SW: There are two kinds of examples: they're familiar things around which people structure their lives. One kind has to do with personal relationships, and another with non-personal activities that play a central or deep role in your life, like a vocation or a political or social cause that you're committed to.

Let's start with an example of doing something for your child, making an elaborate Halloween costume for her. I can remember spending hours, and actually losing tremendous hours of sleep, trying to get the costume just right for my daughter's Halloween parade the next day. And I remember thinking, I'm not doing this because it's in my self-interest—it's not making me happy, and if I had more hours to sleep, I would be better off. On the other hand, I'm certainly not doing it because it's better for the world or because I have a moral duty to make an elaborate Halloween costume. I'm doing it for my daughter. But, having this relationship with my daughter, loving my daughter, doing things out of love for her, that's one of the things that gives meaning to my life.

Another kind of example is writing a philosophy article, and working very hard on it. Suppose I've written two drafts but I keep struggling to make it better. This can be painstaking and it can make you nauseous, and again you can lose sleep over it. If you've got tenure, not many people are going to notice the difference in the quality of the work and I'm not sure that I'm better off by making it that little bit better. Certainly, the world doesn't care that much, and I could do much more good if I were raising money for Oxfam, or whatever. But I'm doing it to get it right; I'm doing it because of an attachment to philosophy and the values of good, clear writing and the quest for truth.

NW: *So is that a subjective value for you or are you suggesting that there is an objective value in the relationship of a mother to her child or of a philosopher to her article?*

SW: Well, in my view, it's essential to meaningfulness that it has both of those things and that they're appropriately linked. The idea of meaning is the idea of doing something that you're subjectively very attracted to, engaged by, excited by, but the thing to which you're devoting all this energy and attention is also objectively valuable. If I didn't love philosophy then it wouldn't give meaning to my life to keep banging my head against the wall to write a better article. On the other hand, if what I loved was not philosophy but Sudoku, and I was just spending hours on end trying to solve an ultra-hard Sudoku, that wouldn't be objectively valuable, and so that also wouldn't give meaning to my life.

NW: *But what makes philosophy better than Sudoku? A critic might say that philosophy is just like Sudoku—solving little problems and a good way of passing the time. But beyond that there's nothing objectively valuable about philosophy.*

SW: Actually, that's a good question. There's a worry that there's nothing objectively valuable about philosophy. It's easier to say why Sudoku isn't valuable than why philosophy is. Sudoku is not doing anything good for anyone else and it's not creative. Obviously, in answering your question in this way I'm showing that I don't have a theory of objective value in which everything with objective value has property X and Sudoku doesn't have this property. I'm starting from our communal intuitions about what's valuable and what isn't. We recognize a lot of things as valuable, and I'm guessing that we're on the right track with that. Then I look at Sudoku and say, 'This has none of it.' This is based on personal experience, of course, having wasted a lot of time doing Sudokus myself.

NW: *So in answering the question, 'What will make life meaningful?', you're not telling people the actual ingredients—but you're providing a structure. You're saying it's going to be subjectively pleasurable, you will*

*be personally committed to it, and it is going to have objective value.
'Meaning' is going to take that form.*

SW: Yes, that's right. One way to look at the issue is against
the background of what, in the US, is a very familiar view
about meaning—find your passion and go for it. So when
people ask how to live a meaningful life, the answer is not to
go for conventional success, but to look for something you're
passionate about and engage in that, and that will make your
life meaningful. My view is that there's something right about
that, but it's not enough. Because if your passion is for
Sudokus, or for rolling a stone up a hill, it doesn't seem to me
to be sufficient to be meaningful. So really, the advice, which
is very limited, is to find your passion, but before you
go for it, stop and think—is there anything worthwhile about
spending my life engaged in this activity or promoting
this goal?

NW: *And your notion of what's worthwhile is far beyond morality; it
doesn't have to be altruistic, good for other people—there can be other
worthwhile values, such as aesthetic values, which might not be good for
anyone else?*

SW: Right. Moral values are among the really valuable
things that you can have and for a lot of people the projects
that give their lives most meaning are moral ones. There's a
moral component to advancing political causes, assisting
people, and, of course, in relationships with loved ones—these
give a lot of meaning to our lives and they involve helping
people other than ourselves. But in addition to that, there's
creating works of beauty, advancing knowledge—scientific
and philosophical inquiry—and maybe even the pursuit of

excellence in any number of ways. Being an Olympic athlete is a meaningful activity, even though it doesn't contribute to any moral good in any particular way.

NW: *That example of athletics is an interesting one because some people see no point in just being the fastest runner, and some people disparage kicking a football around—why kick a bit of leather or plastic around a field? You might do it really well, they say, but it doesn't have a significance in the universe.*

SW: You're right. The meaning that I tend to see in those activities doesn't come from the fact that you are running a race or putting the ball in the hole or whatever, but instead from two other kinds of things. One is doing something as well as you can, and especially if you do it as well as you can and it's very well indeed. This does involve the exercise of virtues of various kinds, like discipline. Additionally, there are various social aspects that go with being part of a team or being part of a community of people; so it's not the particular game or the particular movements that are valuable, but the meaning of the whole activity or the realm of interest which plugs you in to other kinds of relationships that are valuable.

NW: *Does luck play a part in whether your life is meaningful or not?*

SW: Certainly, you are dependent on a certain amount of good fortune in order for your life to be meaningful, or at least in settling how meaningful life is. One example is a scientist who is spending his time trying to discover something that will cure a disease. Imagine that just before he comes out with the discovery, someone else working in an independent laboratory produces the cure, so that all of that work was in some sense wasted. Had he been the person who discovered the cure, his life would have been tremendously meaningful, but instead there's a sense in which it was all a waste of time. For sure, I think his life is less meaningful than it would have been, because of this misfortune.

NW: *And is meaningfulness a social phenomenon or could a recluse achieve meaning in his or her life?*

SW: A recluse could do something that then goes off to other people and helps them anyway; that's one way which it could indirectly have a social impact. There's also the possibility of someone who writes great poetry but the poetry is lost or destroyed, perhaps even destroyed by the poet himself—was his life still meaningful if no one could appreciate his poetry? I would say it was; the production of something beautiful is itself a valuable activity and a valuable accomplishment.

NW: *We have the real-life case of Gerard Manley Hopkins who asked for his unpublished poems to be destroyed after his death, and his executor didn't do that. Now, in one scenario, he's written the poems and they're wonderful poems but nobody gets to read them. In the other one, he becomes a major figure in the history of poetry.*

SW: Well, on one level, I would think that what he accomplished was much greater as a result of people having actually been able to benefit from reading the poetry; so there's some sense in which you could say there's more meaning to his life in this case.

NW: *Those seeking meaning in their lives obviously want some meaning: but does that mean that there are people alive who have no meaning in their life?*

SW: Well, I know it sounds harsh but, yes, I think it does. On the one hand, there are people whose lives are just very hard—they face so many obstacles, they have to work so hard in order to feed themselves and their family. From a certain point of view, it's a luxury to be able to live a meaningful life, and so there are people who are deprived of the opportunity. And then there are the people who actually have the opportunity but spend their lives doing the equivalent of Sudokus or rolling a rock up a hill, who are wasting the chance to do something valuable. Their lives would have very little meaning also.

NW: *John Stuart Mill said something like the best way to achieve happiness is by not pursuing it too aggressively, and by pursuing something else that matters to you. Is it the same with meaning in life; do you somehow scupper your chances of having meaning in your life by obsessing about it too much?*

SW: Absolutely. From a philosophical point of view, it's good to remember that meaning is a dimension of the good life, so that when we're writing about how to live, we don't forget that whole realm. But when it actually comes to living, it would be a terrible mistake to be concerned whether this or that was adding meaning to your life—because it certainly won't if you have that too much in your mind.

27

SAMUEL SCHEFFLER ON
The Afterlife

David Edmonds: *I've just heard from senior sources that Planet Earth will self-combust in exactly a year from now and all of life will be destroyed. Sorry to bring you this rather gloomy news. The question is, can* Philosophy Bites *now be bothered to transcribe this interview? Samuel Scheffler, of New York University, will help us reach an answer.*

Nigel Warburton: *The topic we're talking about is the afterlife. I know you don't believe in the religious afterlife, in which people go to heaven or hell and carry on existing in some form forever. So what do you mean by the afterlife?*

Samuel Scheffler: I use the term 'afterlife' in an unconventional, perhaps even misleading sense. The afterlife I'm concerned with is not the personal afterlife—it's not the hope or belief that one will continue to live in some form after one's death. I'm concerned with what it means for us to think about the survival of other people after we ourselves have died. Most of us take it for granted that other people will live on after we have died. And I refer to that as 'the afterlife'.

NW: *Most of us don't imagine that other people cease to exist when we finally lose consciousness.*

SS: That's right. And my thought is that although we don't often reflect seriously about that assumption, it plays a surprisingly significant role in our lives.

NW: *But given that our conscious experience will end, why should we care about things that happen after our death?*

SS: The short answer is that we don't care only about our own experiences. One way to bring out this point is to imagine certain things happening after your death and to see how you now respond to the prospect of those things happening, even though you know you won't be there to witness them. It's easy to show that there are lots of things that we can imagine happening after our own deaths that would horrify us now. For example, you can imagine horrible things happening to people you care about: you wouldn't think, 'Oh, I'm not going to be around, it doesn't matter to me.'

NW: *Presumably, a way of investigating that would be to imagine a scenario in which people don't exist for very long after I die.*

SS: Right. Imagine, for example, that you knew that although you personally would live a long life, say as long a life as you were going to live anyway, thirty days after your death the earth would be destroyed in a collision with a giant asteroid. Let's bracket questions about how you know this and whether anybody else knows it. Just imagine that you knew that this was going to happen. And then think about how this would affect your thinking and your choices about what to do with your life now.

NW: *It's quite a profound exercise. Negative utilitarians believe that the important thing is to reduce as much suffering as possible. So they* *might think that if everyone were painlessly removed from existence that would be a good outcome! For then there would be no more suffering in the world.*

SS: Well, people with certain theoretical commitments might say that. But I think it would be a minority reaction among people generally. Most people would find the prospect that everything was going to be destroyed thirty days after their own death horrifying. This would partly be because people they know and care about would be destroyed. So too would things that they care about: beautiful works of art, features of the natural environment, practices that they are attached to and regard as valuable. What this brings out is that we want the things that we value to be sustained. We want them to survive. We want them to persist. We are not indifferent to the destruction of things that we care about. And the fact that they will be destroyed after we're dead doesn't really change that.

But another question raised by this doomsday scenario is what we would want to do with our time and how it might affect our choices about how to live. Suppose I'm a cancer researcher, or someone whose life's work is trying to devise techniques for strengthening bridges so that they will hold up during an earthquake. If I know that the whole world is going to be destroyed thirty days after my death, I might find activities like that pointless, for two reasons. One reason, especially prominent in the cancer case, is that I don't necessarily think that the cure for cancer is going to be found by me, or even in my lifetime. I think I'm making a small contribution to an ongoing project that may take a very long time to complete. Second, I think that the value of the project derives from the benefits that it will eventually provide to people over a very long period of time. If the world is going to be destroyed in a very short period of time, then the point of activities like that might be considerably reduced. And there are quite a lot of activities like that—activities whose point, surprisingly, derives to a great extent from what will happen after we're dead.

NW: *I can see that it would be hard to sustain the motivation to do cancer research in this scenario. But there is a range of activities: aren't there some activities that you would plausibly want to continue?*

SS: That's an excellent question. I'm sure there are some activities like that, but one has to think through the cases one by one. The most obviously threatened activities, the ones most likely to seem pointless under these conditions, are goal-orientated projects when you don't expect the goal to be achieved in the very short term. Those projects would be rendered pointless, or arguably pointless. And a lot of our projects are like that.

But there are other things too. For example, I'm a philosopher. I'm working on a couple of articles at the moment. The activity of writing a philosophical article is not goal-orientated in the same way that cancer research is. But would I still have the motivation to finish writing the article that I'm working on now if the destruction of humanity were imminent? I'm not sure that I would. And that's not because I expect the article to have a great impact in a 100 years. It has more to do with some implicit sense that I think of myself as participating in an ongoing historical enterprise. And if you cut that enterprise short, then who cares if I finish this article? It somehow deprives it of the conditions that make it a sensible-seeming thing to do.

Of course, I'm sure that there would be a lot of variation in the way people would react to the doomsday scenario. But I think that the range of activities that we would find compelling would be drastically reduced—more than we might think.

NW: *Take something like the football world cup. I'm English. Would I like England to win the very last world cup? Or would the fact that history wouldn't record that for very long stop us caring about it?*

SS: Sports, and games more generally, have their own rules; they set up their own criteria of significance. Internally to the world of a given sport or a given game, some things just matter. If the world were coming to an end, would they stop mattering? Maybe not. But to me it doesn't seem at all obvious that they would continue to matter as much as before.

NW: *Aren't there some pleasures that are 'in the moment', like listening to music, which wouldn't be affected by whether or not other people existed after my death?*

SS: That's a great question. A natural first thought is that there are certain activities whose rewards are completely available in the moment, and listening to music is a good example. It might not seem, at first, as if our capacity to take pleasure in music should be at all affected by the knowledge that human beings are dying out.

But on second thought it's not obvious that this is right. It may well be that people would find some pleasure or consolation in listening to music. But the rewards of listening to music aren't just brute sensations that have an effect on us independently of our other mental states. In ordinary circumstances, it's a familiar fact that one's appreciation of music can be blocked on any given occasion by anxiety, by preoccupation, by stress. This suggests that even though the rewards of music appear to be available fully in the moment, our ability to access these rewards is not independent of other things going on in our lives. And it's at least not self-evident that if one were faced with the prospect of humanity's imminent disappearance, one would continue to find pleasure in listening to music as consistently as one previously had.

NW: *As a parent, I care about what happens to my children. That's one of the reasons I sometimes think about what will happen after my death. I might think about my children's inheritance or their continuing happiness, or about what they will do with their future. Is that something that's relevant here?*

SS: Certainly, one powerful element in our reactions to the catastrophe scenario we've been discussing is that it involves the sudden horrible death of everyone we care about who will be alive thirty days after our own death. That is a terrible prospect; family, friends, children all wiped out in an instant. And it's natural to think that that's the primary source of our distress in contemplating the scenario. But you can vary the scenario in ways that eliminate that factor and it still seems that we would react quite strongly to the prospect.

For example, in her novel *The Children of Men*, P. D. James imagines that the human race becomes infertile. When the novel starts, human beings have been infertile for over 25 years—and so no baby has been born for this period. The human race is gradually dying out because no new people are being born. But no one who is already alive has to die any younger than they otherwise would. And yet it still seems that the disappearance of humanity under these conditions would be a profoundly depressing prospect to many people.

NW: *Is the philosophical point that by contemplating these scenarios we reveal to ourselves that things that we do, that seem to be in the moment, actually have the presumption that other people will continue to exist and do something in relation to those things in the future?*

SS: That's exactly right. The central philosophical point is that, to an extent that we rarely recognize, our capacity to find value in our activities depends on an implicit assumption that life will go on after we ourselves are gone. Or, to put it more generally, that we are part of an ongoing historical chain of lives and generations. And if you cut that chain short in thought, it suddenly begins to seem that lots of things that we regard as worth doing no longer seem so clearly worth doing.

NW: *I find that fascinating. And the idea sounds plausible. Does it have implications for how we act now?*

SS: I think it does. Or, more fundamentally, it has implications for how we think now about the future. There are obviously lots of concerns that people have about the impact of our activities on future generations of people. Are we spoiling the environment? Are we destroying the earth's atmosphere? There are questions about population size. There are all kinds of questions about the impact that we and our activities have on the future. And many people believe that we don't give enough weight to the interests of future people in deciding what we're going to do now.

But in making that case, it seems that they have to appeal to some sort of moral obligation. We're obligated to take into account the interests of future people. And there are well-known puzzles about why we should do that and how we should do it, and about how to think about who the future people are, and about what we owe to these non-existent people.

One of the interesting implications of thinking about the issue in the terms in which I've posed it is that it reverses the order of concern. It's not that we have a moral obligation to these powerless, vulnerable, future people, and so we should impose some burden on ourselves and restrain ourselves in certain ways for their sake. It's rather that we desperately need them to come into existence and to persist. It's not that they depend on us—although, of course, they do—but that we depend on them! Without an ongoing humanity, our capacity to find value in our own lives would be, if I'm right, substantially reduced.

NW: *The scenarios that you've talked about—the doomsday scenario, of an asteroid hitting the earth, and the P. D. James' case of humans gradually dying out because there is no further procreation—these are short term. But the truth is that humanity won't last forever. There will be a point where the sun burns out and humanity dies out. And yet we still find value in things that we do now. Why does it matter that in your examples catastrophe happens in a short period of time, when in the long term the same result will occur?*

SS: That's a fascinating question and poses a real puzzle. I like to think of this as the Alvy Singer problem, named after a character in Woody Allen's movie *Annie Hall*. Alvy, at age nine, is taken by his mother to the doctor because he's refusing to do his school work on the grounds that the universe is going to be destroyed some day. The doctor assures Alvy that this won't happen for billions of years. And that's supposed to convince him that he should go ahead and do his school work. And yet if I'm right, if it were going to happen in thirty years, Alvy might have a point. Why is that? Why would it have such a devastating effect on our capacity to find value in our lives to know that humanity was going to disappear in the short term when it doesn't do that in the long-term case?

There are several possible solutions to this problem. One natural thought is that there's rational pressure to standardize our reactions in the two cases. And there are two different ways we could standardize them. The Alvy Singer solution is that we should lose confidence in the value of our activities now, even if we don't think the universe will be destroyed for a long time. The second solution goes in the opposite direction. We shouldn't lose confidence in the value of our activities even in the short-term case; we should apply to that case the lesson that Alvy's mother and doctor wanted him to apply to the long-term case. So those are two possibilities.

But another option is to deny that there really is rational pressure to standardize our reactions to the two cases. Maybe there's some relevant difference between the cases.

NW: *What sort of difference could there be?*

SS: One thought is that we don't react strongly to the eventual disappearance of the human race partly because we think that someone will find a way around this problem, the destruction of humanity, somewhere down the road: our successors will figure out a solution. A different answer is that we think that the human race has a certain potential and so long as it survives long enough to achieve most of the values that it's capable of achieving, it might not be so terrible any more if we disappear.

Still another possibility is that our reactions to the long-term case are simply unreliable. We just don't know how to think about things happening in billions of years—it's not part of the temporal frame of reference within which we ordinarily operate. So it's misleading to compare our reactions in the short- and long-term cases.

In the end, I'm not sure what the right answer is. But I do think that it's an extremely interesting puzzle.

NOTES ON CONTRIBUTORS

Ned Block is Silver Professor of Philosophy, Psychology, and Neural Science at New York University. He is co-editor of *The Nature of Consciousness: Philosophical Debates* (1997). The first of two volumes of his collected papers, *Functionalism, Consciousness and Representation*, came out in 2007.

Noël Carroll is a Distinguished Professor of Philosophy at the Graduate Center of the City University of New York. He has written fifteen books, of which the most recent are *Art in Three Dimensions* (2010), *Living in an Artworld* (2012), and *Humour: A Very Short Introduction* (2014).

Patricia Churchland is U.C. President's Professor of Philosophy at the University of California, San Diego. In various projects, she has focused on issues concerning the neurobiological basis of consciousness, the self, and free will, as well as on more technical questions concerning to what degree the nervous system is hierarchically organized.

C. A. J. Coady is a prominent Australian philosopher, well known for his writings on epistemology and on issues to do with political morality. One of his current research projects concerns the role of religion in politics.

Fiery Cushman is Assistant Professor in the Department of Cognitive, Linguistic and Psychological Sciences at Brown University. His research investigates the cognitive mechanisms responsible for human moral judgement, along with their development, evolutionary history, and neural basis. His work often draws on classic philosophical dilemmas, and has focused in particular on the psychology of punishment and the aversion to harmful action. He received his BA and PhD from Harvard University, where he also completed a post-doctoral fellowship.

Daniel Dennett is the Austin B. Fletcher Professor of Philosophy at Tufts University, and co-director of the Center for Cognitive Studies. His most recent book is *Intuition Pumps and Other Tools for Thinking* (2013).

David Edmonds is a BBC World Service radio documentary maker and a senior research associate at Oxford's Uehiro Centre for Practical Ethics. His books include the international bestseller, *Wittgenstein's Poker* (co-written with John Eidinow, 2001), and *Would You Kill the Fat Man?* (2013).

Kit Fine is University Professor and Silver Professor of Philosophy and Mathematics at New York University. He is a member of the American Academy of Arts and Sciences and a corresponding fellow of the British Academy.

Gary L. Francione is Board of Governors Professor, the Distinguished Professor of Law, and Nicholas de B. Kaztenbach Scholar of Law and Philosophy at Rutgers University School of Law in Newark, New Jersey. He blogs at <http://www.abolitionistapproach.com> and conducts a discussion forum at <https://www.facebook.com/abolitionistapproach>.

Nancy Fraser is Loeb Professor of Philosophy at the New School for Social Research in New York, an Einstein Fellow of the city of Berlin, and holder of an international research chair in Global Justice at the Collège d'études mondiales in Paris. A specialist in social and political philosophy, she has written on social justice, the welfare state, feminism, the public sphere, globalization, capitalism, and multiculturalism.

Raimond Gaita is Professorial Fellow in the Faculty of Arts and the Melbourne Law School, University of Melbourne and Emeritus Professor of Moral Philosophy at King's College London. Gaita's books include *Good and Evil: An Absolute Conception* (2004); *The Philosopher's Dog* (2002); and *Romulus, My Father* (1998), which was made into a feature film of the same name (2008).

Alison Gopnik is a Professor of Psychology and Affiliate Professor of Philosophy at the University of California at Berkeley, author of *The Scientist in the Crib* (1999) and *The Philosophical Baby* (2009), and writes the 'Mind and Matter' column for the *Wall Street Journal*.

Thomas Hurka is Professor of Philosophy at the University of Toronto. He works in moral and political philosophy, with special interest in the theory of value, or in questions about what is intrinsically good and intrinsically evil.

Frank Jackson is Distinguished Professor of Philosophy at The Australian National University. He has taught at Adelaide University, La Trobe University, Monash University, and Princeton University. His most recent book is *Language, Names, and Information* (2010).

Nicola Lacey is School Professor of Law, Gender and Social Policy at the London School of Economics. Nicola's research is in criminal law and criminal justice, with a particular focus on comparative and historical scholarship. She is currently working, with David Soskice, on American Exceptionalism in crime, punishment, and social policy.

Rae Langton is Professor of Philosophy at the University of Cambridge, and Fellow of Newnham College. She works in the history of philosophy (especially Kant), metaphysics, epistemology, feminist philosophy, ethics, and political philosophy. She testified to the Leveson Inquiry in 2012 about liberal principles governing free speech, and their implications for the objectifying treatment of women in the media.

Jeff McMahan is Professor of Philosophy at Rutgers University. He is the author of *The Ethics of Killing: Problems at the Margins of Life* (2002) and *Killing in War* (2009). He has several other books forthcoming from Oxford University Press.

Susan Mendus is Morrell Professor Emerita in Political Philosophy at the University of York, UK. She has been associated with the Morrell Centre for Toleration at York for over 30 years and has published extensively on problems of toleration and also on modern and historical liberal political theory.

John Mikhail is Professor of Law and Professor of Philosophy (by courtesy) at Georgetown University, Washington DC.

Stephen Neale is Distinguished Professor of Philosophy and Linguistics, and the John H. Kornblith Family Chair in the Philosophy of Science and Values at the Graduate Center of the City University of New York, and was formerly Professor of Philosophy at Rutgers University, the University of California, Berkeley, and Princeton University. He works primarily on questions in the philosophy of language and their intersection with interpretive questions in neighbouring fields, particularly law and archaeology. He is the author of *Descriptions* (1990) and *Facing Facts* (2001), a forthcoming book entitled *Matters of Interpretation: Pragmatics, Archaeology and Law*, and numerous research articles. He has been a Guggenheim Fellow a Fellow of the National Endowment for the Humanities, and of the Rockefeller Foundation Bellagio Center, and was the first Chandaria Laureate at the School of Advanced Study, University of London.

Philip Pettit, Irish by background and training, is L. S. Rockefeller University Professor of Politics and Human Values at Princeton and Distinguished Professor of Philosophy at the Australian National University. Among his recent books are *On the People's Terms: A Republican Theory and Model of Democracy* (2012) and *Just Freedom: A Moral Compass for a Complex World* (2014). *The Robust Demands of the Good: An Ethics of Attachment, Virtue, and Respect* is forthcoming in 2015 from OUP.

Samuel Scheffler is University Professor in the Philosophy Department at New York University. He is the author of *The Rejection of Consequentialism* (1982), *Human Morality* (1992), *Boundaries and Allegiances* (2001), *Equality and Tradition* (2010), and *Death and the Afterlife* (2013).

Dan Sperber is a French scholar who has worked and published in anthropology, linguistics, psychology, and philosophy. He has developed in particular an 'epidemiological' approach to culture and, with Deirdre Wilson, a cognitive approach to communication known as relevance theory. Lately, with Hugo Mercier, he has been working on a new, evolutionary approach to reasoning.

Hillel Steiner is Emeritus Professor of Political Philosophy in the University of Manchester and a Fellow of the British Academy. He is the author of *An Essay on Rights* (1994), co-author of *A Debate Over Rights: Philosophical Enquiries* (1998), and co-editor of philosophical anthologies on freedom and on left libertarianism.

Galen Strawson is Professor of Philosophy at the University of Texas at Austin. He has taught at Oxford University, Reading University, New York University, Rutgers University, the Graduate Center of the City University of New York, the Massachusetts Institute of Technology, and Princeton University. His most recent book is *Locke on Personal Identity* (2011).

Victor Tadros is Professor of Criminal Law and Legal Theory at the University of Warwick. He is the author of *Criminal Responsibility* (2005) and *The Ends of Harm: The Moral Foundations of Criminal Law* (2011). He is currently working on a book entitled *Wrongs and Crimes* for Oxford University Press.

Michael Tye encountered philosophy at Oxford, and taught at Temple University, St Andrews, and London University, before coming to the University of Texas at Austin in 2003. He is the Dallas TACA Centennial Professor in Liberal Arts.

Nigel Warburton is a freelance philosopher. His books include *The Art of Question* (2002), *Thinking from A to Z* (3rd edn, 2007), *Free Speech: A Very Short Introduction* (2009), *A Little History of Philosophy* (2012), and *Philosophy: The Basics* (5th edn, 2013). With David Edmonds, he hosts the Philosophy Bites podcast.

Susan Wolf is a Professor of Philosophy at the University of North Carolina, Chapel Hill. Her work ranges widely over topics in ethics and its close relations in philosophy of mind, philosophy of action, political philosophy, and aesthetics. She gets meaning from friends, family, and philosophy.

FURTHER READING

Joy and Pain

CHAPTER 1: PLEASURE

Fred Feldman, *Pleasure and the Good Life: Concerning the Nature, Varieties, and Plausibility of Hedonism* (Oxford: Oxford University Press, 2006).

Justin Gosling, *Pleasure and Desire: The Case of Hedonism Reviewed* (Oxford: Oxford University Press, 1969).

Thomas Hurka, *The Best Things in Life* (Oxford: Oxford University Press, 2010), Chapters 1–3.

CHAPTER 2: PAIN

David Chalmers, *The Conscious Mind* (Oxford: Oxford University Press, 2004).

Michael Tye, *Ten Problems of Consciousness* (Cambridge, Mass.: MIT Press, 1997).

Michael Tye, *Consciousness Revisited* (Cambridge, Mass.: MIT Press, 2009).

CHAPTER 3: HUMOUR

Reginald Adams, Daniel Dennett, and Mathew Hurley, *Inside Jokes: Using Humour to Reverse-Engineer the Mind* (Cambridge, Mass.: MIT Press, 2013).

Noël Carroll, *Humour: A Very Short Introduction* (OXFORD: OXFORD UNIVERSITY PRESS, 2014).

John Morreall, *Comic Relief: A Comprehensive Philosophy of Humour* (Chichester: Wiley-Blackwell, 2009).

Morality

CHAPTER 4: MORAL STATUS

Jeff McMahan, *The Ethics of Killing: Problems at the Margins of Life* (Oxford: Oxford University Press, 2002).

Peter Singer, *Practical Ethics* (2nd edn, Cambridge: Cambridge University Press, 1993).

Mary Anne Warren, *Moral Status: Obligations to Persons and Other Living Things* (Oxford: Oxford University Press, 2000).

CHAPTER 5: UNIVERSAL MORAL GRAMMAR
Paul Bloom, *Just Babies: The Origins of Good and Evil* (London: Bodley Head, 2013).

Noam Chomsky, *New Horizons in the Study of Language and Mind* (Cambridge: Cambridge University Press, 2000).

John Mikhail, *Elements of Moral Cognition: Rawls' Linguistic Analogy and the Cognitive Science of Moral and Legal Judgment* (Cambridge: Cambridge University Press, 2011).

CHAPTER 6: TORTURE
Alan Dershowitz, *Why Terrorism Works: Understanding the Threat, Responding to the Challenge* (New Haven, Conn.: Yale University Press, 2002).

Raimond Gaita, *A Common Humanity, Thinking about Love & Truth & Justice* (London: Routledge, 2000).

Raimond Gaita, 'Torture: The Lesser Evil', 68(2) *Tijdschrift voor Filosofie* (2006), pp. 251–78.

David Grossman, 'Terror's Long Shadow', *Guardian* (21 September 2001), <http://www.theguardian.com/world/2001/sep/21/afghanistan.writersreflectionsonseptember11>.

David Sussman, 'What is Wrong with Torture?', 33(1) *Philosophy and Public Affairs* (2005), pp. 1–33.

Jeremy Waldron, 'Torture and Positive Law: Jurisprudence for the White House', 105(6) *Columbia Law Review* (2006), pp. 1681–750.

Simone Weil, 'Human Personality', in *Letter to a Priest*, introd. Raimond Gaita (London: Routledge, 2013).

CHAPTER 7: ANIMAL ABOLITIONISM

Gary L. Francione, *Animals as Persons: Essays on the Abolition of Animal Exploitation* (New York: Columbia University Press, 2008).

Gary L. Francione and Anna Charlton, *Eat Like You Care: An Examination of the Morality of Eating Animals* (Kentucky: Exempla Press, 2013).

Gary L. Francione and Robert Garner, *The Animal Rights Debate: Abolition or Regulation?* (New York: Columbia University Press, 2010).

Mind, Self, and Imagination

CHAPTER 8: CONSCIOUSNESS

Ned Block, *Functionalism, Consciousness and Representation* (Cambridge, Conn.: MIT Press, 2007).

Ned Block, Owen Flanagan, and Güven Güzeldere (eds), *The Nature of Consciousness: Philosophical Debates* (Cambridge, Conn.: MIT Press, 1997).

CHAPTER 9: ELIMINATIVE MATERIALISM

Patricia Churchland, *Braintrust: What Neuroscience Tells Us about Morality* (Princeton, N.J.: Princeton University Press, 2011).

Patricia Churchland, *Touching a Nerve: The Self as Brain* (New York: W. W. Norton, 2013).

Robert M. McCauley (ed.), *The Churchlands and Their Critics* (Cambridge, Mass.: Blackwell, 1996).

CHAPTER 10: WHAT MARY KNEW

David Braddon-Mitchell and Frank Jackson, *The Philosophy of Mind and Cognition* (2nd edn, Oxford/Cambridge, Mass.: Blackwell, 2007).

Jaegwon Kim, *Physicalism, or Something Near Enough* (Princeton, N.J.: Princeton University Press, 2007).

Peter Ludlow, Yujin Nagasawa, and Daniel Stoljar (eds), *There's Something about Mary* (Cambridge, Mass.: MIT Press, 2004).

CHAPTER 11: SENSE OF SELF
Barry Dainton, *Self: Philosophy in Transit* (London: Penguin, 2014).

Marcel Proust, *In Search of Lost Time*, trans. C. K. Scott Moncrieff and Terence Kilmartin, revised D. J. Enright (New York: The Modern Library, 1992).

Galen Strawson, *Selves: An Essay in Revisionary Metaphysics* (Oxford/New York: Oxford University Press, 2009).

CHAPTER 12: THE IMAGINATION
Alison Gopnik, *The Philosophical Baby* (New York: Farrar, Straus and Giroux, 2009).

Alison Gopnik, Andrew Meltzoff, and Patricia Kuhl, *The Scientist in the Crib* (New York: HarperPerennial, 2001).

Paul Harris, *The Work of the Imagination* (Oxford/Malden, Mass.: Wiley-Blackwell, 2000).

Free Will, Responsibility, and Punishment

CHAPTER 13: FREE WILL WORTH WANTING
Daniel Dennett, *Elbow Room: The Varieties of Free Will Worth Wanting* (Oxford: Clarendon Press, 1984).

Daniel Dennett, *Freedom Evolves* (new edn, London: Penguin, 2004).

Robert Kane (ed.), *Free Will* (Malden, Mass.: Wiley-Blackwell, 2001).

CHAPTER 14: MORAL LUCK
Fiery A. Cushman, 'Crime and Punishment: Distinguishing the Roles of Causal and Intentional Analysis in Moral Judgment', 108(2) *Cognition* (2008), pp. 353–80.

Fiery A. Cushman, 'Should the Law Depend on Luck?', in Max Brockman (ed.), *Future Science: Essays from the Cutting Edge* (New York: Random House, 2011), pp. 197–209.

Fiery A. Cushman, Anna Dreber, Ying Wang, and Jay Costa, 'Accidental Outcomes Guide Punishment in a "Trembling Hand" Game', 4(8) *PLOS* One (2009), e6699.doi:10.1371/journal.pone.0006699.

CHAPTER 15: CRIMINAL RESPONSIBILITY

Peter Cane, *Responsibility in Law and Morality* (Oxford/Portland, Ore.: Hart Publishing, 2003).

H. L. A. Hart, *Punishment and Responsibility: Essays in the Philosophy of Law*, introd. John Gardner (2nd edn, Oxford: Oxford University Press, 2008 [1968]).

Nicola Lacey, *Women, Crime and Character: From Moll Flanders to Tess of the d'Urbervilles* (Oxford/New York: Oxford University Press, 2008).

CHAPTER 16: PUNISHMENT

Antony Duff, *Punishment, Communication, and Community* (Oxford/New York: Oxford University Press, 2001).

Michael S. Moore, *Placing Blame: A Theory of the Criminal Law* (Oxford: Oxford University Press, 1997).

Victor Tadros, *The Ends of Harm: The Moral Foundations of Criminal Law* (Oxford: Oxford University Press, 2011).

CHAPTER 17: GROUP AGENCY

Peter A. French, *Collective and Corporate Responsibility* (New York: Columbia University Press, 1984).

Christian List and Philip Pettit, *Group Agency: The Possibility, Design and Status of Corporate Agents* (Oxford: Oxford University Press, 2011).

Frederick Schmitt (ed.), *Socializing Metaphysics: The Nature of Social Reality* (Lanham, Md: Rowan and Littlefield, 2003).

Politics

CHAPTER 18: TOLERATION

John Horton and Susan Mendus (eds), *John Locke: A Letter Concerning Toleration in Focus* (London/New York: Routledge, 1991).

John Stuart Mill, *On Liberty* (London: Penguin, 1974 [1859]).

Bhikhu Parekh, *Rethinking Multiculturalism* (London: Macmillan, 2000).

CHAPTER 19: EXPLOITATION

Andrew Reeve (ed.), *Modern Theories of Exploitation* (London: Sage, 1987).

Hillel Steiner, *An Essay on Rights* (Oxford: Blackwell, 1994), esp. Chapter 5.

Hillel Steiner, 'Exploitation Takes Time', in J. Vint et al. (eds), *Economic Thought and Economic Theory: Essays in Honour of Ian Steedman* (London: Routledge, 2010), pp. 20–9.

Alan Wertheimer, *Exploitation* (Princeton, N.J.: Princeton University Press, 1996).

CHAPTER 20: HATE SPEECH

Miranda Fricker, *Epistemic Injustice: Power and the Ethics of Knowing* (Oxford: Oxford University Press, 2007).

Sally Haslanger, *Resisting Reality: Social Construction and Social Critique* (Oxford: Oxford University Press, 2012).

Rae Langton, *Sexual Solipsism: Philosophical Essays on Pornography and Objectification* (Oxford: Oxford University Press, 2009).

CHAPTER 21: RECOGNITION

Nancy Fraser, *Adding Insult to Injury: Nancy Fraser Debates Her Critics*, ed. Kevin Olson (London: Verso, 2008).

Nancy Fraser, *Fortunes of Feminism: From State-Managed Capitalism to Neoliberal Crisis* (London: Verso, 2013).

Nancy Fraser and Axel Honneth, *Redistribution or Recognition? A Political–Philosophical Exchange*, trans. Joel Golb, James Ingram, and Christiane Wilke (London: Verso, 2003).

CHAPTER 22: DIRTY HANDS IN POLITICS

C. A. J. Coady, *Messy Morality: The Challenge of Politics* (Oxford: Oxford University Press, 2008), esp. Chapter 4.

Igor Primoratz (ed.), *Politics and Morality* (Houndmills: Palgrave Macmillan, 2007).

Paul Rynard and David Shugarman (eds), *Cruelty and Deception: The Controversy over Dirty Hands in Politics* (Broadview Press, 2000).

Michael Walzer, 'Political Action: the Problem of Dirty Hands', in Marshall Cohen, Thomas Nagel, and Thomas Scanlon (eds), *War and Moral Responsibility* (Princeton, N.J.: Princeton University Press, 1974), pp. 62–82.

Michael Walzer, 'Emergency Ethics', in *Arguing about War* (New Haven, Conn.: Yale University Press, 2004), pp. 33–50.

Metaphysics, Meaning, and Reason

CHAPTER 23: WHAT IS METAPHYSICS?
A. J. Ayer, *Language, Truth and Logic* (2nd edn, New York: Dover Publications, 2002).

David Hume, *A Treatise of Human Nature* (Oxford: Oxford University Press, 2011 [1739]).

Saul A. Kripke, *Naming and Necessity* (Oxford: Wiley-Blackwell, 1991).

CHAPTER 24: THE ENIGMA OF REASON
Jonathan Evans and Keith Frankish (eds), *In Two Minds: Dual Processes and Beyond* (Oxford: Oxford University Press, 2009).

Hugo Mercier and Dan Sperber, *The Enigma of Reason* (forthcoming).

Deirdre Wilson and Dan Sperber, *Meaning and Relevance* (Cambridge: Cambridge University Press, 2012).

CHAPTER 25: MEANING AND INTERPRETATION
Paul Grice, *Studies in the Way of Words* (Cambridge, Mass.: Harvard University Press, 1989).

Stephen Neale, *Matters of Interpretation: Pragmatics, Archaeology, and Law. The 2010 Chandaria Laureate Lecture* (Oxford: Oxford University Press, forthcoming).

Antonin Scalia, *A Matter of Interpretation* (Princeton, N.J.: Princeton University Press, 1997).

Deirdre Wilson and Dan Sperber, *Meaning and Relevance* (Cambridge: Cambridge University Press, 2012).

CHAPTER 26: MEANING IN LIFE

E. D. Klemke and Steven M. Cahn (eds), *The Meaning of Life: A Reader* (Oxford: Oxford University Press, 2008).

Robert Nozick, *The Examined Life: Philosophical Meditations* (New York: Simon and Schuster, 1989).

Susan Wolf, *Meaning in Life and Why It Matters* (Princeton, N.J.: Princeton University Press, 2010).

CHAPTER 27: THE AFTERLIFE

P. D. James, *The Children of Men* (London: Faber and Faber, 1992).

Samuel Scheffler, *Death and the Afterlife*, ed. Niko Kolodny (Oxford: Oxford University Press, 2013).